INDONESIA

A Global Studies Handbook

GLOBAL STUDIES: ASIA

INDONESIA

A Global Studies Handbook

Florence Lamoureux

A B C ⬯ C L I O

Santa Barbara, California • Denver, Colorado • Oxford, England

Library of Congress Cataloging-in-Publication Data

Lamoureux, Florence.
  Indonesia : a global studies handbook / Florence Lamoureux.
    p. cm. — (Global studies, Asia)
  Includes bibliographical references and index.
  ISBN 1-57607-913-9 (hardcover : alk. paper)
  ISBN 1-57607-914-7 (e-book)
  1. Indonesia—Handbooks, manuals, etc. I. Title. II. Series.

DS615.L36 2003
959.8—dc22

                                        2003017652

06 05 04 03   10 9 8 7 6 5 4 3 2 1

This book is also available on the World Wide Web as an e-book.
Visit abc-clio.com for details.

ABC-CLIO, Inc.
130 Cremona Drive, P.O. Box 1911
Santa Barbara, California 93116-1911

This book is printed on acid-free paper.
Manufactured in the United States of America

Contents

Series Editor's Foreword

It is imperative that as many Americans as possible develop a basic understanding of Asia. In an increasingly interconnected world, the fact that Asia contains almost 60 percent of all the planet's population is argument enough for increased knowledge of the continent on our parts. There are at least four other reasons, in addition to demography, that it is critical Americans become more familiar with Asia.

Americans of all ages, creeds, and colors are extensively involved economically with Asian countries. U.S.-Pacific two-way trade surpassed our trade with Europe in the 1970s. Japan, with the world's second-largest economy, is also the second-largest foreign investor in the United States.

American companies constitute the leading foreign investors in Japan.

The recent Asian economic crisis notwithstanding, since World War II East Asia has experienced the fastest rate of economic growth of all the world's regions. Recently, newly industrialized Southeast Asian countries such as Indonesia, Malaysia, and Thailand have joined the so-called Four Tigers—Hong Kong, the Republic of Korea, Singapore, and Taiwan—as leading areas for economic growth. In the past decade China has begun to realize its potential to be a world-influencing economic actor. Many Americans now depend upon Asians for their economic livelihoods and all of us consume products made in or by Asian companies.

It is impossible to be an informed American citizen without knowledge of Asia, a continent that directly impacts our national security.

America's war on terrorism is, as this foreword is composed, being conducted in an Asian country—Afghanistan. (What many Americans think of as the "Mideast" is, in actuality, Southwest Asia.) Both India and Pakistan now have nuclear weapons. The eventual reunification of the Korean Peninsula is fraught with the possibility of great promise or equally great peril. The question of U.S.-China relations is considered one of the world's major global geopolitical issues. Americans everywhere are affected by Asian political and military developments.

Asia and Asians have also become an important part of American culture.

Asian restaurants dot the American urban landscape. Buddhism is rapidly growing in the United States. Asian movies are becoming increasingly popular in the United States. Asian-Americans, while still a small percentage of the overall U.S. population, are one of the fastest-growing ethnic groups in the United States. Many Asian-Americans exert considerable economic and political influence in this country. Asian sports, pop music, and cinema stars are becoming household names in America. Even Chinese language characters are becoming visible in the United States on everything from baseball caps to t-shirts to license plates. Followers of the ongoing debate on American educational reform will constantly encounter references to Asian student achievement.

Americans should also better understand Asia for its own sake. Anyone who is considered an educated person needs a basic understanding of Asia. The continent has a long, complex, and rich history. Asia is the birthplace of all the world's major religions including Christianity and Judaism.

Asian civilizations are some of the world's oldest. Asian arts and literature rank as some of humankind's most impressive achievements.

Our objectives in developing the Global Studies: Asia series are to assist a wide variety of citizens to gain a basic understanding of Asian countries and to enable readers to be better positioned for more in-depth work. We envision the series being appropriate for libraries, educators, high school, introductory college and university students, businesspeople, would-be tourists, and anyone who is curious about an Asian country or countries. Although there is some variation in the handbooks—the diversity of the countries requires slight variations in treatment—each volume includes narrative chapters on history and geography, economics, institutions, and society and contemporary issues. Readers should obtain a sound general understanding of the particular Asian country about which they read.

Each handbook also contains an extensive reference section. Because our guess is that many of the readers of this series will actually be traveling to Asia or interacting with Asians in this country, introductions to language, food, and etiquette are included. The reference section of each handbook also contains extensive information—including Web sites when relevant—about business and economic, cultural, educational, exchange, government, and tourist organizations. The reference sections also include capsule descriptions of famous people, places, and events and a comprehensive annotated bibliography for further study.

—*Lucien Ellington*
Series Editor

Preface

The *Indonesia Handbook* is organized into two parts: Part 1, the Narrative Section, presented as Chapters 1–4, and Part 2, Reference Materials. The chapters cover history, geography, economics, politics, religion, education, the arts, and culture. Each ends with a References section listing resources consulted for that chapter. Part 2 has several components: Key Events in History; Significant People, Places, and Events; Indonesian Language, Food, and Etiquette; Indonesia-Related Organizations; and an Annotated Bibliography. The Reference Section is meant to provide the reader with efficient access to information on specific topics, whereas the Narrative Section offers more in-depth information.

This book provides the reader with pertinent information on the world's fourth most populous nation and the one with the largest Muslim population. The history section begins with information on precolonial times and continues through the colonial period and independence. When Indonesia declared its independence in 1945, its three and a half centuries of colonial rule had a cataclysmic effect on the country's efforts to govern itself. This book gives an overview of those centuries and provides information that will enable the reader to follow Indonesia's progression from the golden age of Hindu kings to Islamic sultans to Dutch governors-general and finally to its present status as a precarious democracy. It covers the Japanese occupation of Indonesia during World War II and explains how that period was a major factor in the country's independence movement. The return of Dutch rule in its former colony in 1945 sparked a revolution and strengthened the focus on independence among Indonesians across the archipelago. The war with the Netherlands ended in 1949, at which time the Republic of Indonesia joined the free nations of the world. The book goes on to evaluate the early Indonesian governments, pointing out the issues that led up to the military coup in 1965 and the subsequent military-oriented presidency of General Suharto.

The economic segment of this book provides information on the difficulties facing a new nation deficient in capital and experience but rich in natural resources. It gives examples of the prevalence of corruption in government and the effect it has had on Indonesia's attempts to participate in international commerce and attract overseas investments. After independence, Indonesia suffered all of the difficulties of an emerging nation, but its economic problems were most concerning. The country's first president, Sukarno, saw his presidency fail because of disastrous economic policies; and his successor, Suharto, notorious for his nepotism, was forced from office in 1998 for the same reason. With his government's economic base insufficient to survive the Asian economic crisis of 1997, Suharto lost the popular support necessary for him to stay in office.

Politics played a major role in Indonesia's development as an independent nation. This handbook looks at the evolution of political parties in Indonesia and the rise and fall of the heads of state that were elected as Indonesia's presidents. It describes local governments and their relationships to each other and to the central government. Corruption and religion have been prominent at all levels and have influenced the formation of all of Indonesia's governments.

Indeed, religion has been a deciding factor in many of Indonesia's crises. This book gives an account of the arrival of Islam in Indonesia and then goes on to explain how the initial form of Islam (Sufism) that meshed so well with the then-prevalent Hindu states later clashed with the fundamentalist type of Islam that gained strength in the country in the early twentieth century. Today Indonesian political parties reflect both traditional (mystical) and modernist (fundamentalist) Islam.

Education is imperative to a country's positive growth, and Indonesia's government-funded and Islamic schools are discussed and compared. Also covered are entertainment—traditional and modern—the arts, village and urban life, the environment—disappearing forests and endangered species—employment, and family life including ceremonies and holidays. The *Indonesia Handbook* looks at the secessionist movements in Aceh and Papua and the violence in eastern Indonesia and Kalimantan. It also reviews the history and independence movement in East Timor, explaining how it came to be separate from Indonesia.

Indonesia and the United States share the experience of a colonial past. However, there are many differences between the two countries. Whereas Indonesia's history reveals centuries of rule by rajahs and sultans followed by 350 years of Dutch control, America's early experience as a British colony was relatively brief and less constricting. Democracy was the model upon which the young U.S. government was based, but Indonesians had little experience with democratic methods prior to their independence. These are only a few comparisons of the two countries; the reader will note many others throughout the book.

Today Indonesia is suffering severe economic problems brought about primarily through corrupt government practices. How terrorism will affect the archipelago is still unknown. Indonesia has survived turmoil and suffering throughout its history and will no doubt weather these afflictions as well. In the writing of this book, every effort has been made to tie together the many pertinent aspects of Indonesia's past and present. It is a diverse and complex country that is emerging from a confining past to participate in a modern and fast-paced world, for which it is not especially well prepared.

This book was not a solitary effort, and I would like to acknowledge the assistance of friends and family who were instrumental in its writing. I am especially grateful to two of my colleagues, Rohayati Paseng Barnard and Belinda A. Aquino. Their careful reading of the manuscript and insightful critiques were invaluable. My editor, Lucien Ellington, was tireless in reviewing my revised pages and offering wise council. I am grateful to the ABC-CLIO staff for their confidence and their professional and gracious manner. Thanks must also go to Mark and Anne for their encouragement and patience.

Acronyms

Acronyms are commonly used in Indonesian government, education, and religion. Here is a selection of common Indonesian acronyms as provided in the newspaper the *Jakarta Post*.

ABRI . . . . .Armed Forces of the Republic of Indonesia

APEC . . . . .Asia Pacific Economic Cooperation

ASEAN . . . . . . .Association of Southeast Asian Nations

ASNFL . . . . . . .Aceh Sumatra National Liberation Front

Bappenas . . . . .National Development Planning Board

DIA . . . . .Aceh Special Province

DPA . . . . .Supreme Advisory Council (this body advises the president on matters in various sectors)

DPR . . . . .House of Representatives

GAM . . . . .Free Aceh Movement (Gerakan Aceh Merdeka)

GOI . . . . .Government of Indonesia

Golkar . . . . . . .Golongan Karya (translates as "functional group"), the government-backed ruling political organization

GPK . . . . .government term meaning peace-disturbing movement or security disturbance groups in Aceh

IBRA . . . . .Indonesian Bank Restructuring Agency

ICMI . . . . .Association of Indonesian Muslim Intellectuals

ICW . . . . .Indonesian Corruption Watch

IGGA . . . . . . .Intergovernmental Group of Indonesia (Dutch-based organization)

IMF . . . . .International Monetary Fund

ITB . . . . .Bandung Institute of Technology

KAPET . . . . . .Integrated Economic Development Zone

LIPI . . . . .National Institute of Sciences

Masyumi . . . . .Indonesian Muslim Congregation

MPR . . . . .People's Consultative Assembly

MPRS . . . . . . .Provisional People's Consultative Assembly

NGO . . . . .nongovernmental agency

NU . . . . .Nahdlatul Ulama, a 30-million-strong Muslim organization

OPEC . . . . . . .Organization of Petroleum Exporting Countries

OPM . . . . .Free Papua Movement

PAN . . . . .National Mandate Party

PDI . . . . .Indonesian Democratic Party (Partai Demokrasi Indonesia)

PDI-P . . . . .Indonesian Democratic Party of Struggle

PETA . . . . .Pembela Tanah Air (Defenders of the Fatherland), the militia set up during the Japanese occupation in 1942. PETA was one of several militias that were incorporated, after the proclamation of independence in August 1945, to become the Badan Keamanan Rakyat (BKR, People's Security Corps). The BKR later became the republic's military, now known as the Indonesian Armed Forces (ABRI), which was established on October 5, 1945.

PKB . . . . .National Awakening Party

PKI . . . . .Indonesia Communist Party (now defunct)

PKP . . . . .Justice and Unity Party

PNI . . . . .Indonesian National Unity, established October 1995; also Indonesian National Party

PPP . . . . .United Development Party

PPPKI . . . . . . .Congress of Indonesian National Political Consensus

PRRI . . . . .Revolutionary Government of the Republic of Indonesia

Repelita, Pelita .Repelita stands for Rencana Pembangungan Lima
Repelita   Tahun (Five-Year Development Plan); Pelita stands for Pembangunan Lima Tahun (Five-Year Development Program). Repelita is the plan; Pelita is the finished program.

RMS . . . . .Republic of South Maluku

SMP . . . . .senior high school

Supersemar . . .An abbreviation of the Indonesian (presidential) Executive Order signed on March 11, 1966, by President Sukarno when the political turmoil in the country reached its peak following the abortive coup attempt the previous September

TIM . . . . .Taman Ismail Marzuki arts center

UGM . . . . .Gadjah Mada University in Yogyakarta

UI . . . . .University of Indonesia in Jakarta

UTD . . . . .Timor Democratic Union

USDEK . . . . . . .acronym for the 1945 Constitution, Indonesian Socialism, Guided Democracy, Guided Economy, and Indonesian Identity; used by Sukarno as a slogan

VOC . . . . .Dutch East India Company

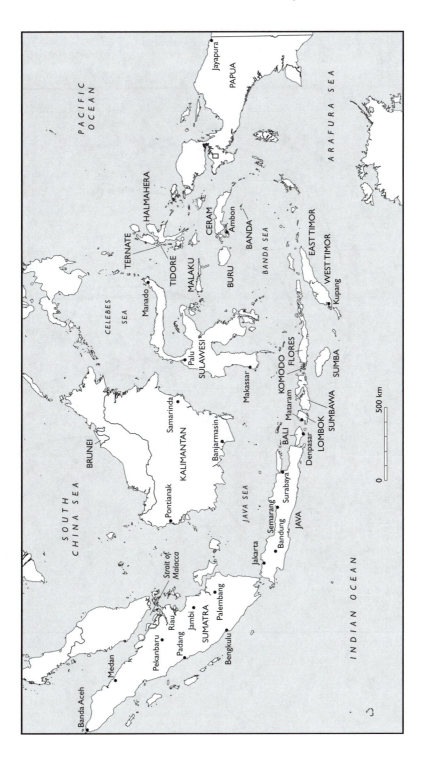

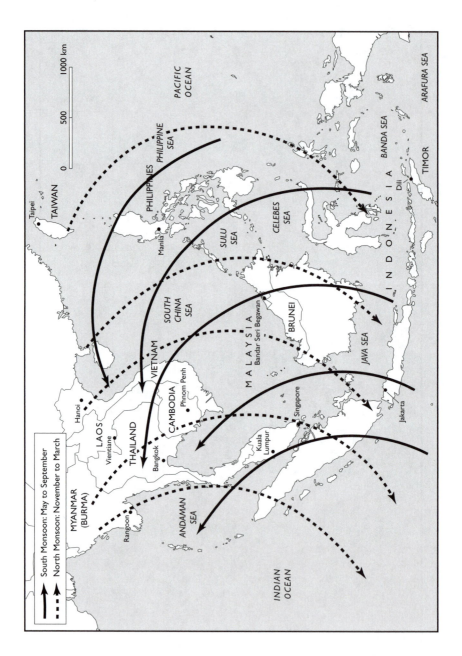

PART ONE
NARRATIVE SECTION

CHAPTER ONE

Indonesia's Geography and History

PHYSICAL GEOGRAPHY

Southeast Asia is a broad term referring to the countries south of China and east of India. The islands of Indonesia, along with the Philippines, Malaysia, Singapore, and Brunei, comprise Island Southeast Asia. Burma (now Myanmar), Thailand, Cambodia, Laos, and Vietnam are referred to as Mainland Southeast Asia. It should be noted that Malaysia is located both in Mainland and Island Southeast Asia: The Malay Peninsula is on the mainland, and the provinces of Sabah and Sarawak along with Brunei are on the island of Borneo. When East Timor gained separate nation status, it became the eleventh Southeast Asian country. The official name of this new nation is República Democrática de Timor-Leste, but because it is commonly referred to as East Timor, this book will use that name.

Although only about 6,000 are inhabited, Indonesia is made up of over 17,000 islands, making it the largest archipelago in the world. The landmass is approximately 760,000 square miles, about three times the size of Texas. If the water surrounding the islands is included, the country extends across slightly more than 3 million square miles (in comparison, the Unites States fills a total area of 3.7 million square miles). The combined coastline of all the Indonesian islands is approximately 33,900 miles. The Indonesian islands are located above and below the equator; some are situated directly on it. The island of Sumatra is the world's sixth largest island, Sulawesi is the eleventh, and Java is the thirteenth. Papua makes up about half of New Guinea, the second largest island in the world, and Kalimantan covers about two thirds of Borneo, the world's third largest island. Indonesia has land boundaries with other nations only on New Guinea (with Papua New Guinea), Borneo (with Malaysia and Brunei), and East Timor (with West Timor).

The islands of Indonesia are divided into four regions. The Greater Sunda Islands are Sumatra, Java, Bali, Kalimantan, and Sulawesi. Lombok, Sumbawa, Sumba, Flores, Komodo, and Timor are the Lesser Sunda Islands. Halmahera, Ternate, Tidore, Seram, and Ambon comprise Maluku. Numerous smaller islands are included in each of these regions. The last division has only West Papua in it. The country extends from the Indian Ocean into the South China Sea and on to the Pacific Ocean. Many islands border on or are surrounded by smaller bodies of water, such as the Strait of Malacca, the Java Sea, Banda Sea, Celebes Sea, and the Timor Sea.

Wallace's Line

Alfred Russell Wallace, a naturalist in the late nineteenth and early twentieth centuries, studied the flora and fauna within the Indonesian archipelago and proposed the theory that plants and animals in the island chain differ dramatically depending on which side of an imaginary line they are located. Wallace observed that some of Indonesia's plants and animals (tigers, elephants, and tropical rain forests) had distinctly Asian characteristics while others were closely related to Australian wildlife (marsupials, lizards, and dry land vegetation). Wallace's boundary runs between Bali and Lombok and continues northward between Sulawesi and Borneo. His theory supports the fact that plants and animals in the islands west of Lombok and Sulawesi are more like those found in Asia while the plants and animals east of Bali and Borneo are more similar to those in Australia. The Lombok Strait, running between Bali and Lombok, is the deepest in Indonesian waters. This narrow rift is of such great depth that it supports Wallace's theory that early animals could not have crossed by land from Lombok to Bali or from Borneo to Sulawesi, and plants could not have been transported for the same reason. Therefore, it is probable that Lombok at one time was attached to the same landmass as Australia and that Bali was attached to Asia. This theory is also supported by the physical characteristics of the people in these regions. The inhabitants of the islands west of Lombok and Sulawesi more closely resemble the Malay peoples of Mainland Southeast Asia. Those living east of Bali and Borneo have physical characteristics more like the aboriginal peoples of Australia. Intermarriage over the centuries has blurred any precise line between the Malay and aboriginal areas, especially in the islands bordering the Lombok Strait.

Volcanoes

Indonesia has between 80 and 125 active volcanoes and perhaps 300 inactive ones. Volcanoes can remain dormant for many years, but considering them as such can prove dangerous. Like monsoon rains, volcanoes can bring anguish as well as prosperity to the Indonesian farmer. Although ash from erupting volcanoes provides the richness in Javanese soil, lava has swept away rice fields and entire villages.

For centuries the great majority of Indonesian families have survived by tilling the land, but like farmers everywhere else in the world, they have often been at the mercy of nature. Not only volcanoes and heavy rains but also earthquakes are a constant worry.

The theory of plate tectonics explains that the earth's crust is made up of several huge plates that move independently. Continental crusts refer to plates under landmasses; oceanic crusts lie under the floors of the oceans. These plates rest on a deep, hot, flowing asthenosphere that moves. This movement can separate neighboring plates, move them in a parallel direction, or shift them in such a way that they crash into one another. This last action causes earthquakes. The Indonesian islands are located on three different plates: the Indian Australian Plate, the Eurasian Plate, and the Pacific Plate. This situation provides significant opportunity for plates within the same country to collide and affords a reasonable explanation for the large number of earthquakes in Indonesia.

Indonesia's most renowned volcano is Krakatoa, located in the Sunda Strait between Sumatra and Java. The most recent eruption of Krakatoa, in August 1883, thrust so much ash and debris into the earth's atmosphere that weather and crop growth were severely affected worldwide for years after the lava flow subsided. It is estimated that more than 36,000 people perished in that eruption. In 1925 a smaller volcanic mass appeared near Krakatoa. Like all volcanic land it continues to expand through ongoing eruptions. This new land has been labeled Anak Krakatoa (Krakatoa's child).

Another volcano, less well known than Krakatoa, is Mt. Merapi, located in Central Java. An active volcano probably since the tenth century, Merapi erupts regularly, causing villagers in the area to abandon their homes with goods and livestock in tow. The worst recorded eruption of Mt. Merapi was in 1930 when approximately 1,300 villagers were killed. The positive side of these devastating eruptions is the enrichment of the soil by volcanic ash, a major reason why Java, with its many active volcanoes, can support more people than any other Indonesian island.

Climate and Agriculture

The Indonesian islands are located in the subtropical zone, where the weather is hot and humid year round. Indonesia's climate is prima-

Rice terraces on Bali (Courtesy of Florence Lamoureux)

rily controlled by monsoon winds, and the amount of rainfall depends on these seasonal airstreams. From November to March, Indonesia is dominated by the north monsoon, blowing down from China. From May to September the country is dominated by the south monsoon, which blows south to north from the Indian Ocean and Australia. Because the chain of islands covers such a great distance, the periods of drought and heavy rainfall are not uniform throughout the country. Indeed, the further east one travels in Indonesia the more pronounced the dry season. For example, the dry season in Sumatra lasts from one to three months; in West Timor it lasts from nine to eleven months.

The most fertile and hence the most densely populated island in the country is Java, with about 100 million people, or over 45 percent of the population. Although the soil on all of the Indonesian islands is volcanic, on Java the several active volcanoes provide a continual source of nutrient-rich ash that restores the soil's fertility. The rich soil and the extensive rainfall combine with the warm climate to create an almost perfect greenhouse effect. The most common crop by far is rice, the mainstay of the Indonesian people's diet; but vegetables—especially in West Java—grow in abundance as well.

Fruit trees—bananas, mango, durian, rambutan, mangosteen, and all types of citrus fruits—are in evidence across the landscape. Apples, strawberries, and other seasonal fruits have been introduced from the West and are now grown at higher elevations. The main source of protein in the Indonesian diet is fish—not surprising, considering the proximity of the ocean. The main starch is rice, not only the mainstay of the Indonesian diet but also an integral part of the culture, with village councils being organized around its planting, irrigation, and harvesting. The Indonesian language has many words for rice: *padi*—the rice plant; *gabah*—threshed rice (unhusked rice); *beras*—milled, hulled grains (white rice); and *nasi*—cooked rice, are just a few.

Until the 1980s, despite the high productivity of wetland rice cultivation (rice grown in flooded fields) on Java, Indonesia was not able to produce enough rice to feed itself. At that time rice plants were three to six feet tall with a yield of one or two crops per year, and they could not be threshed in the fields immediately after cutting. By contrast the "Miracle Rice" developed at the Rockefeller Foundation International Rice Research Institute (IRRI) in the Philippines grew only two to three feet high, could be harvested in the field, and yielded three crops per year. When first introduced, the new rice was not always welcomed. It lacked the fragrance and taste of the rice Indonesians had eaten for centuries, and the pesticides and fertilizers necessary to produce it were expensive. Eventually adjustments were made, and now farmers have developed varieties that have some of the characteristics of the traditional varieties and still produce high yields. Today on Java one square mile of rice can feed around 5,000 people.

HUMAN GEOGRAPHY

In July 2001 Indonesia's population was estimated to be approximately 225 million, with an annual growth rate of 1.6 percent. The population breakdown by age at that time was roughly: 0–14 years old—30 percent; 15–65 years old—65 percent; and over 65—4.5 percent. Life expectancy for females is 70.4 years and for males 65.6. The infant mortality rate is 42.2 deaths per 1,000 live births.

Indonesia's motto is Unity in Diversity, which is nowhere better reflected than in its population, composed of many ethnic groups. The largest of these are the Javanese, Acehnese, Minangkabau, Batak, Balinese, Sundanese, Dani, Dayak, Punun, and Bugis. Religion is of primary importance in the culture of each ethnic group. The Javanese,

Muslims but less devout than people in many other parts of Indonesia, are the dominant group in Indonesia. They are found primarily on Java and as stated previously make up about 45 percent of the country's population. The Sundanese live in West Java and for the most part are devout Muslims. The Acehnese, located in northwest Sumatra, are fervent Muslims and are currently seeking to distance themselves from the Indonesian central government. The Minangkabau are a Muslim matriarchal society in mid-Sumatra, and the Batak, whose religion was based on animism with Hindu elements until they became Christians, are located between the Acehnese and the Minangkabau. The Balinese adhere to Hinduism and live primarily on Bali. The Dani, who also seek independence from Indonesia, make up the more or less 250 tribes in Papua, and though they were until the twentieth century primarily spirit/nature worshipers, they are now primarily Christians. The Dayak, who were also once spirit/nature worshipers, are now Christians. They live in about 200 tribes in Kalimantan (Indonesian Borneo). The Punan, with a similar religious history, are spread across Kalimantan, surviving as nomadic hunters and gatherers. The Bugis, who practice Islam, can be found mostly in south Sulawesi, but they roam the length and breadth of Island Southeast Asia. They are shipbuilders and warriors and once were best known as pirates. Indonesians are 88 percent Muslim, 8 percent Christian (5 percent Protestant, 3 percent Catholic), 2 percent Hindu, 1 percent Buddhist, and 1 percent other. These figures are somewhat misleading, for some people who identify themselves as Muslim practice a religion that combines, for example, the tenets of Islam and Hinduism or Islam and Buddhism.

Over 250 different languages and dialects belonging to the Austronesian language family are spoken throughout Indonesia; some sources put the number as high as 600. It is difficult to determine an exact number as some islands have numerous dialects, and it is not unknown for people from one village to be unable to communicate with neighboring villagers if they are separated by mountains or significant bodies of water. In their homes and within small villages, most Indonesians speak local dialects, but in the larger markets and in schools, businesses, and government offices everyone speaks Indonesian. Before independence Indonesian was referred to by outsiders as coastal Malay. It was the language of commerce and had existed in the region for centuries. Upon its independence Indonesia's government needed to name a national language. Although the largest number of Indonesians spoke Javanese, to select that as a national language would have appeared to favor the Javanese people. Because they were already considered to have more than their share of political clout due to their sheer numbers, this would have created a strain on the already burdened new country. For this reason, Indonesian was named the national language. Although it was essentially no one's first language, just about everyone in the country could speak it.

Indonesia's government is based on a set of five principles called *Pancasila*. One of these proclaims that each Indonesian should worship only one god. Hinduism and Buddhism are polytheistic religions and thus in a sense are contrary to Indonesia's founding philosophy. Despite this, the Indonesian government considers that the followers of these religions act in accordance with *Pancasila*.

HISTORY

Prehistory

The earliest record of humans in the Indonesian archipelago is Solo Man, or *Homo erectus*. Remains of such a man were found in Central Java in 1891 and are estimated to be 150,000 years old. Forty-five hundred to five thousand years ago, centuries after Solo Man first appeared in Indonesia, archaeologists found indications of the deliberate planting of crops and domestication of animals. These were probably Austronesian language speakers, descendants of southern coastal Chinese people. They most likely intermarried with the indigenous people in Indonesia, their culture then becoming the dominant way of life. They in turn would have intermarried with traders from foreign lands, and it is their descendants who are the ancestors of today's Malaysians and Indonesians.

India's Influence and the Srivijaya Empire

The earliest recorded empire in the region defined today as Malaysia and Indonesia was Srivijaya—a Buddhist maritime kingdom that held power in an area encompassing the Strait of Malacca and both coasts of the Malay Peninsula, the east coast of Sumatra, and western Java. From the seventh to the fourteenth century Srivijaya controlled this major trade route frequented by Asian and Middle Eastern merchants. Their mutually beneficial relationship with the pirates who frequented those sea-lanes further empowered Srivijaya and contributed to the empire's longevity. China was predominantly Buddhist at that time, and that common bond with Srivijaya, as well as a keen interest in trade, made China a major trading partner of this state. Tang Dynasty records as early as 670 chronicle China's trade with Srivijaya. In the late seventh century the Chinese pilgrim I-tsing visited Srivijaya and wrote that there were over 1,000 Buddhist monks there. Later records show that Srivijayan rulers held a monopoly on the spice trade beginning in the tenth century.

Both Hinduism and Buddhism originated in India, and these religions and myriad other aspects of Indian culture had a significant influence on Indonesia. The influencing of Indonesia's local religion, language, art, and architecture by India's culture was well established in many regions of Southeast Asia seven to eight centuries before the arrival of Europeans in the fifteenth century. Adaptation of Indian art, religions, and political systems was apparently intentional on the parts of both India and the areas of Indonesia where Indian culture was accepted. That it was not brought about through warfare, as foreign influence often is, but rather by selective assimilation, is apparent for a number of reasons. Among them are that Indian records of the times indicate no conflict with Indonesia; there is no significant Malay-Indian racial mixture in Java and Bali, where Indian influence was the strongest; and the Indonesian language has many words borrowed from Sanskrit—the language of scholars, not warriors. Although both Hinduism and Buddhism were practiced in Indonesia at roughly the same time, especially on Java, Bali, and Sumatra, in the case of Hinduism not all aspects of the religion permeated Indonesian culture. For example, there was no strict caste system in Indonesia. Bali is the only island in Indonesia that still practices Hinduism, and although there is historical evidence that rulers, religious leaders, and wealthy businessmen held hereditary positions, no substantial data show that there was ever an untouchable caste. Today Bali still maintains characteristics prevalent centuries ago, when the Hindu culture was dominant on Java and throughout sections of the archipelago.

The earliest Indian influences in Indonesia, both Hindu and Buddhist, were not necessarily found along the coastal areas, where merchants and sailors often had a strong impact on local cultures, but at royal residences inland, especially on Java. As a rule, the commercial contacts found in port cities don't significantly transmit the cultures of ruling classes. Indeed, there is evidence not only that Indians came to Indonesia but that Indonesians traveled to India and brought back selected aspects of the culture, which were integrated into their way of life. Even later, with the advent of Islam from the

Middle East, adherence to the tenets of that religion was modified to blend with the indigenous culture, which remains pervasive throughout Indonesia's history.

In addition to the Chinese records, scholars have obtained information about Srivijaya from stone inscriptions. We know that this empire concentrated its efforts on trade but unfortunately, in contrast to later empires, left few monuments or archaeological remains from which anthropologists have been able to draw conclusions about the peoples' daily lives.

The Sailendra Empire and Borobudur

Other great empires were in place at the time of Srivijaya. Early in the eighth century the Sailendras ruled in Central Java. They, too, were a Buddhist society and are best known for the magnificent Borobudur monument that they erected between the end of the eighth and the middle of the ninth centuries. It is estimated that the construction of Borobudur took up to 75 years. It is a square-based, nine-tiered monument built in a Mandela pattern, with statues located at specific locations around concentric circles and with a unique drainage system. Borobudur was most likely constructed by

Borobudur, eighth–ninth century Hindu monument (Courtesy of Florence Lamoureux)

workers paying their taxes to the king in the form of labor. It has 504 statues of the Buddha and 2,700 stone panels of carved relief depicting stories of the Buddha and his followers. When the Sailendras left Central Java, Borobudur was abandoned and left to the destructive forces of earthquakes and the elements. Although attempts were made to restore the monument, it was not until 1974 that the United Nations began a massive restoration program. Borobudur opened to the public in 1983 and, along with Prambanan, a Hindu complex, is one of Java's leading tourist attractions.

Sanjaya Kingdom and Prambanan

During roughly the same time that the Sailendras were in Central Java a Hindu kingdom was in the same region. The Sanjaya rulers established a Hindu empire that emerged in Central Java in the middle of the eighth century, and as it grew in strength, conflict erupted between the Buddhist Sailendras and the Hindu Sanjayas. Buddhism was at its apex at the beginning of the ninth century whereas Hinduism appeared to be declining. In 825 Hindu reaction against Buddhism, as evidenced in the Sailendra building of Borobudur, initiated a new interest in Hinduism, resulting in the erecting of a number of temples, the most notable being the complex at Prambanan.

Prambanan, ninth–century Hindu monument (Courtesy of Florence Lamoureux)

The rulers of the Sanjaya kingdom completed the building of Prambanan in 856. This extraordinary Hindu temple complex is located only a few miles from Borobudur. Prambanan is made up of three large temples and two smaller ones. The main temple is dedicated to Shiva, the other two to Brahma and Vishnu. Like Borobudur, Prambanan has extensive stone relief panels; however, here they depict stories of the Hindu deities. During the Napoleonic Wars, when England was in control of Java, a captain of Sir Stamford Raffles who was overseeing the removal of debris from Prambanan made this comment about the Hindu Temples: "In the whole course of my life I have never met with such stupendous and finished specimens of human labor and of the science and taste of ages long since forgot, crowded together in so small a compass, as in this little spot [Prambanan], which to use a military phrase, I deem to have been the headquarters of Hinduism in Java."

Prambanan has also been restored, but not as completely as Borobudur, and is frequently visited by Indonesians and foreign travelers alike. Throughout Central Java one sees many less majestic temple complexes, both Hindu and Buddhist. A great number have fallen into disrepair due to weathering and neglect. Some have been purposefully dismantled and the stones used for state and private construction projects.

Late in the 800s the Sanjaya kingdom dominated East Java, and the Buddhist Sailendras fled to Sumatra, where the Srivijaya Empire was dominant. At its height the Sanjaya Empire spread even further to the northeast, to Sumatra and the Malay Peninsula. The Sanjaya Empire declined in the tenth century.

Kediri and Singasari Empires

A prominent Javanese king of the Sanjaya line was Airlangga (991–1046), a Balinese who married a Javanese princess and became ruler of a Javanese empire. Airlangga was a patron of the arts, and during his reign *gamelan,* the Indonesian percussion orchestra; *wayang,* the elegant puppets that are used to tell stories of the Indian epics the *Mahabarata* and the *Ramayana;* and literature flourished. Agricultural methods also improved. Airlangga was equally tolerant of Hinduism and Buddhism, and both religions prospered during his reign. He was indeed a superior statesman, and today one of Java's most prestigious universities is Airlangga University in Surabaya. Prior to his death Airlangga divided his kingdom between his sons, who established the Kediri and Janggala empires, with Kediri, a Hindu kingdom, becoming the better known.

In East Java in 1222 the Buddhist Singasari Empire emerged under the ruler Ken Angrok. Although it vied with Kediri for control of Java, by 1289 Singasari became such a powerful state that the emperor Kublai Khan demanded it pay China tribute. The Singasari king, Kertanagara, not only refused but cut the faces of the Chinese emissaries to his country and sent them home disfigured. As a result, the angry Kublai Khan ordered an invasion of Java. However, before Khan's forces arrived, Kertanagara was assassinated by a rival who then took over the throne. Kertanagara's son-in-law, anxious to avenge his father-in-law's death, joined Khan's forces, and together they overthrew the usurper. The young prince then turned his loyal forces against Kublai Khan's army and was successful in driving the Mongol army out of Java. Thus Kertanagara's line regained the throne.

Golden Age: The Majapahit Empire

In 1350 the Majapahit ruler Hayam Wuruk came into power. Although this empire claimed to be Buddhist, rulers and subjects alike also worshiped Siva and Vishnu. Together with his brilliant prime minister, Gadjah Mada, the king had a profound influence on the governing of the archipelago and its culture. At its peak, Majapahit merchants traded with Burma, Siam, Cambodia, and China. The *Nagarakertagama* texts, Javanese inscriptions written during Hayam Wuruk's reign, describe elegant art, literature, and religious practices in the Majapahit court. Although not authenticated, the *Nagarakertagama* claims the empire ranged from Sumatra to Papua New Guinea. We do know that the Majapahit empire exchanged envoys with a number of Asian countries. The Majapahits probably prospered to such a great degree because of prime agricultural land for rice farming and the development of a sophisticated irrigation system. It was a golden age for Indonesia in both the political and artistic arenas and was Indonesia's greatest pre-Islamic kingdom. The Majapahit empire ruled East Java during the fourteenth and fifteenth centuries, until it fell to the Islamic state of Demak in 1478.

Muslim Traders and the Mataram Empire

Islam grew in popularity in Indonesia in the thirteenth century when the Mongols restricted caravan trade through Central Asia, thus causing the sea-lanes through the Indian Ocean to become major trade routes. This busy seaway soon became the thoroughfare for Muslim traders to access Indonesian products. As commerce between the Middle East and the Indonesian archipelago burgeoned, so did Muslim social and political influence along those trade routes. Seaports that were predominantly Islamic appeared on the Indonesian and Malay coasts and especially along the busy commercial Strait of Malacca, where Muslim entrepreneurs quite rapidly established trading centers and gained power. Sultans, rather than kings, consequently emerged in ruling positions. (It should not be inferred that Islam came to Indonesia only with Arab traders. Sufi Islamic scholars were clearly among the early Muslim arrivals in the region, bringing this form of mystical Islam with them. A parallel situation may be found in the coming of Indian culture—and attendant Hinduism and Buddhism—to Indonesia in earlier times.)

By 1478 Islam had been in Indonesia for some time. Indeed, the earliest documentation of Islam in the island chain is a tombstone in East Java dated 1082. Majapahit records show that by the late thirteenth century the religion was established in North Sumatra and that Demak, a city in East Java, was predominantly Muslim. Arab traders, geographers, and clerics had been a presence in the archipelago for centuries, and these men were precursors of the Mataram. The rise of Demak and the final collapse of Hindu-Buddhist states in interior Java occurred around 1527.

In the late 1500s a Mataram ruler, Senapati, extended the empire across Central Java, and records show that his son confronted early Dutch traders. However, the greatest of the Mataram rulers was Sultan Agung (r. 1613–1646), who in the course of thirty years spread his rule across Central and East Java to the island of Madura. His plans to capture West Java were thwarted by the Dutch under governor-general Jan Pieterszoon Coen, and the powerful Mataram ruler experienced a major defeat in Batavia (now Jakarta) in 1629. Sultan Agung ruled at the time when the colonial presence in Indonesia was on the rise. In addition to this, two other factors came into play in the decline of the Mataram empire: First, Sultan Agung's wars across Java were extremely destructive, leaving cities and agricultural lands devastated; and second, the sultan had little interest in commerce, and though he controlled coastal cities he never took advantage of maritime trade as a way to finance his wars and support his empire.

Prior to the arrival of Europeans, the growth of Islam in the region was greatly enhanced by compliant access to the Strait of Malacca. As European traders entered this major commercial waterway, that access was challenged. As mentioned previously, the Mataram empire coincided with the arrival of the Dutch in Indonesia and the advent of the colonial period. Some scholars ascribe this Dutch interruption of Indonesian rule as a factor that negatively impacted the growth of Islam in Indonesia. They attribute the moderate expansion of the religion throughout the Dutch colonial era (fifteenth century through the first half of the twentieth century) to the fact that Islam had insufficient time to become fully entrenched in Indonesian society by the time the Dutch dominated the country. A reemergence of Islam in Indonesia took place in the late nineteenth and early twentieth centuries, when it became a primary factor in the growth of the nationalist movement.

The European Arrival

In the fifteenth century the European exploration of Asia was just beginning. Even earlier though, as the Mongolian emperor Kublai Khan was expanding his rule, the Venetian Marco Polo was exploring Asia. Polo spent twenty-four years traveling in Asia, from 1271 to 1295, and the stories he told upon his return to Italy whetted the appetites of Europeans for the riches of the "Far East." Two hundred years earlier, in 1095, Pope Urban II had challenged his Crusaders to remember the noble accomplishments of their predecessors and capture the holy places in Palestine for the church. There is little doubt that upon their return home these European soldiers, who traveled into North Africa on their religious quests, did much to spread word of the exotic products of the Orient that were among the goods brought to Africa by Arabic traders.

Trade Routes

In the mid-1400s Constantinople (now Istanbul), a city frequented by the Christian Crusaders, had been under Byzantine rule for almost 1,000 years. The Orthodox Turks of the city had grown rich on the trade in black pepper, nutmeg and cloves, silks, perfumes, and other unusual products brought from Asia. Trade items had been transported over the Silk Road and the Levant trade routes to this city and into Europe for centuries. In 1453 the Ottoman ruler Mehmet II laid siege to Constantinople and closed that gateway city to European trade. His capture of this port, so vital to Europe's connections with Asia, resulted in the closure of the main overland course through which goods from Asia entered the European market. This move altered the course of history. With the loss of that avenue of trade, it became essential to Europeans that another route to Asia be established, a sea route if possible. In 1492 Christopher Columbus's journey gave the needed boost to seafaring merchants who were seeking an easier and less expensive route to the overland caravan roads, and soon European ships were venturing into unknown waters in search of spices, silks, and other products of the Orient.

The first Europeans to successfully sail into Asian waters were the Portuguese. In 1498 Vasco da Gamma's journey around the southern tip of Africa and on to India proved to European merchants that Asia could be accessed by sea, thus eliminating the arduous land routes with their high tariffs and political barriers. Lisbon soon became one of Europe's busiest ports as Portugal dominated the Indian Ocean and remained the primary European trader in the region over the next 100 years.

When Europeans began to travel to the East Indies by sea in the late fifteenth century, commerce within Asia had been ongoing for centuries. Chinese junks had bartered goods throughout Asia before history was officially recorded in Indonesia. Muslim sailors, coming from the Middle East and trading in the Indian Ocean and South China Sea, had long used a combination of land and sea routes to reach the Spice Islands in eastern Indonesia. As a rule their ships made use of the strong monsoon winds to travel in Asia, although some of the smaller ships and boats that could travel closer to shore were able to manipulate their sails well enough without the benefit of these strong winds. The prevailing winds carried these traders to Indonesia from September through February and back to the Middle East from March through August.

Not surprisingly, Arab traders displayed considerable hostility to the arrival of the Europeans. They had long maintained a veritable monopoly on the spice trade, and with the Europeans taking to the oceans, they stood to lose a great deal.

The Portuguese

Although the Portuguese established their first base port in Goa on India's east coast, they soon realized the advantages of locating closer to the Spice Islands in Indonesia. The site they chose for their new factory was Malacca, the port that controlled the Strait of Malacca. (*Factory* is a term the Europeans used to refer to a trading station or port where goods could be stored for exporting back to Europe or importing into Asian countries.) Malacca was an ideal location, as all sea trade to the Spice Islands went through the Strait of Malacca.

The Portuguese had serious problems in Malacca. They were forced to rely on the Malay and Chinese people who lived there for food and ship supplies. Their disregard for long-accepted procedures and their self-serving decisions antagonized the local residents. Malacca had been a well-organized and safe port under the Malays, but when the Portuguese captured it they ignored the strictly enforced rules and regulations that the Malays had established. The Portuguese set new and very high taxes on ships coming to trade in the strategic port, and they failed to continue to guarantee the protection of the merchants who came to the port to barter goods. As a result, trade through the Strait of Malacca declined, and what had held the prospect of a successful Portuguese venture turned bitter. The islands where Portugal had a more lasting influence were the Spice Islands, or Maluku, sometimes referred to as the Moluccas (not to be confused with Malacca) in Indonesia.

Portugal's first port of call in the Spice Islands was the largest of the Banda Naira Islands, Lontar, where their ships' captains purchased nutmeg, mace, and cloves. At that time the sultans of Ternate and Tidore, two spice-producing islands in Maluku, were on poor terms with one another. Each approached the Portuguese asking for military support to wage war against the other; the Portuguese commander decided to support the sultan of Ternate. With that decision, the Portuguese sailors commenced to build a fort there.

Over the next two decades the Portuguese fought to maintain their control of Ternate, but the governors they sent out from Goa always seemed to be incapable of winning over the indigenous people, who resented their presence and attempts at religious conversion.

Religion did play a major role in sixteenth-century Maluku, but it was not the men on the ships or their officers who substantially furthered its cause. Credit for that must go to the Jesuit priest Fr. Francis Xavier, a Spaniard who was proselytizing in Maluku during the time the Portuguese were there. The Portuguese supported Xavier, a tireless and extremely successful missionary who converted between 50,000 and 60,000 Maluku natives to Christianity. He laid down the foundation for a permanent mission there, and many of these islands are still predominantly Christian. The substantial acceptance of Catholicism in Maluku and the Lesser Sunda Islands was not experienced to the same degree anywhere else in Indonesia.

The Portuguese left behind other signs of their culture. Such Portuguese names as de Costa, Dias, and Mendosa are still common in Maluku, and words such as *pesta* (party), *sepatu* (shoe), *nanas* (pineapple), and *sabun* (soap) are among many common Indonesian words derived directly from the Portuguese.

Over the years the Portuguese named a number of governors to rule Ternate. Each held the position only a few years before confrontations with the indigenous people made them ineffective and resulted in the ending of their terms. These conflicts sometimes were triggered by religious differences with the local Muslims and sometimes by corruption within their own administrations. Whatever the reasons, it was not until July 1575 that the people of Ternate were finally able to force the Portuguese permanently off of their island.

With the loss of its Ternate station Portugal began to turn its interest elsewhere. In 1557 Portugal established a colony at Macao, a few miles from Hong Kong, where it set up regular trade with China. This would become Portugal's main colony in Asia. Although still a presence on the island of Ambon in Maluku and Timor, Portuguese influence in the Spice Islands was gradually fading.

The Spanish

Another presence in the Spice Islands during this period was the Spanish. Although they never made the inroads into Maluku that the Portuguese did, early in the sixteenth century the Spanish spearheaded a serious effort to gain a share of the spice trade. They first came ashore in Tidore in 1521 when the crew of Magellan's ships that had been around the southern coast of South America brought their vessels to the Spice Islands. With fifty pair of scissors and ten lengths of cotton cloth, the Spanish captain purchased 600 pounds of cloves. Much to the consternation of the Portuguese, the Spanish set out to establish a base on Tidore, an island in close proximity to Ternate and much the same size.

For over half a century Spain and Portugal fought continuously, gaining and losing control of Ternate and Tidore as each tried to dominate the spice trade. Early in the 1600s, for a short while, the Spanish did dominate northern Maluku and ran their operation out of a fort on Ternate. However, Spain's holdings in South America and the Philippines were its main focus of interest, and the last of the Spanish captains finally departed the Spice Islands in 1663.

The Dutch

Late in the sixteenth century a new presence made itself known in the Spice Islands—the Dutch. They differed from the Portuguese in that they were exceptionally well organized and had ample financing as well as a good supply of weapons and ships. Armed with these essentials, the Dutch almost achieved control of the spice trade in Indonesia, a goal Portugal had been unable to attain. The single most important difference between the two countries was the permanent foothold the Netherlands (Holland) later established on Java—a factor that ultimately led to Dutch colonial rule over Indonesia for 350 years.

The Netherlands emerged as a power in Europe when they declared their independence from Spain in 1581. Prior to that, during the approximately 57 years before the signing of the Treaty of Westphalia actually granted Holland its independence from Spain, the Dutch more or less ignored Spanish attempts to dominate them. The Dutch were busy in those years as they made plans to expand their economic base and concentrated on exploration.

For years the Dutch had played the role of middleman in selling the spices Portugal brought into northern Europe. But in 1580 Spain and Portugal closed the port of Lisbon to the Dutch. This resulted in a decrease in the quantity of spices brought into Amsterdam to be resold on the European market. This action on the part of Spain and Portugal caused the Netherlands to consider the prospect of going directly to the source of the spices and purchasing cloves and nutmeg there. Spices commanded exorbitant prices on the European market, in part because the strong aromas and flavors of cloves and nutmeg would mask the smell and taste of less than fresh meat (keep in mind that refrigeration did not exist). In addition, they were thought to have medicinal value as well. In his writings, Dutch traveler Jan van Linschoten described the many uses of nutmeg: "Comforts the brain, sharpens the memory, warms and strengthens the maw, drives wind out of the body, makes the breath sweet, drives down urine, and is good against all cold diseases in the brain and the maw."

Although Spain and Portugal were certainly not interested in helping Holland, neither did they see the small nation as a serious threat, and at first they generally ignored it. The Portuguese had always tried to keep their navigational knowledge of Asia secret, but for a number of decades they had employed Dutch sailors on their ships and Dutch civil servants in their trading centers at Goa and Malacca. The most famous of these men, Jan van Linschoten, had worked in Goa as an aide to the archbishop. He had traveled extensively on Portuguese ships in the Asian seas and had kept meticulous notes of his observations. In 1596 van Linschoten's book, *Itinerary to the East or Portuguese Indies,* was published. It contained detailed maps and pertinent information on Portuguese discoveries in Asia. In 1595 the first Dutch expedition was dispatched to the Indies (the Dutch term for Indonesia) under the command of Captain Cornelius de Houteman. Four ships made the long and arduous trip to Banten, a black-pepper growing center in West Java. De Houteman encountered a great deal of misfortune along the way. He became involved in sea battles with both Portuguese and Indonesians, and when he sailed into East Java twelve of his men were killed in an attack by the Javanese. A little further on, off the coast of the island of Madura, his sailors killed a local ruler who was rowing out to welcome them. The trip was not a smooth one, and the Dutch encounters with the Indonesians were hostile all along the way. Despite de Houteman's many problems, a year after this fleet had departed, three ships returned to the Netherlands; and although they showed no profit, this journey indicated to the Dutch that with improved organization there was money to be made in the Indies spice trade.

Word of de Houteman's voyage spread rapidly, and within a year twenty-two ships from five competing Dutch companies set sail for the East Indies. In 1599 the first Dutch ship to reach the Banda Islands in Maluku was well received; it returned to Holland with enough spices to show a 400 percent profit. Most of the other Dutch fleets that set sail that year also showed a profit.

The competition among these shipping companies caused the cost of spices in Maluku to escalate, and the increasing supply of cloves and nutmeg coming into Europe was forcing profit on these goods to decrease. To solve the problem, the competing Dutch trading companies agreed to merge and regulate trade in the Spice Islands. As a result they formed the Dutch East India Company (Vereenigde Oostindische Compagnie). The Dutch acronym VOC became their recognized symbol and is still in evidence throughout Maluku, especially on the island of Banda. The VOC had seventeen directors who were referred to as the Seventeen Gentlemen; their headquarters was located in Amsterdam.

The Dutch government charter gave the VOC substantial powers. It could hire personnel on an oath of allegiance, wage war, and draw up and sign treaties throughout Asia. Those who took the oath often were not the most respectable. Honorable men who wanted to

VOC symbol for Dutch East India Company (Vereenigde Oostindische Compagnie) on church floor in Maluku (Courtesy of Florence Lamoureux)

undertake dangerous ventures in Asia in the seventeenth century were few and far between. Life aboard a small sailing ship was brutal. In the ship's log of Magellan's journey around the world the historian Pigafetta wrote about conditions as the ships rounded Cape Horn at the tip of South America in 1519: "They ate biscuit and when there were no more of that, they ate the crumbs which were full of maggots and smelled of mouse urine. When even the crumbs gave out, our men captured the ship's vermin and auctioned them off as food."

Although the VOC showed a profit, initially it had little success compared to the Spanish and the Portuguese traders who had been in Maluku for several decades. At this time the Portuguese were still in Ambon but were barely able to win a battle against the Ambonese who wanted them out of Maluku. The arrival of the Dutch on that island provided the Ambonese with an alternative to the Portuguese, and in 1600 the Dutch joined with local forces in an anti-Portuguese alliance. In return for military support, the Ambonese gave the Dutch exclusive rights to purchase spices on the island of Hitu. This was a common tactic that the local people employed: enlisting the aid of one European power to oust another European power. This scenario inevitably ended with the Indonesian-ruled island being controlled by the new, and often more oppressive, foreign force.

Two years later, in 1602, a large Portuguese force arrived in Ambon from Malacca and briefly reestablished Portuguese dominance in Maluku. Portuguese control of Ambon was short lived, however, as three years later the VOC fleet renewed its alliance with Hitu and in the face of obvious defeat the Portuguese surrendered and the Dutch took over the Portuguese fort.

The Dutch more or less limited their commercial activities to Ambon during this period since in 1606 the Spanish were the prevailing authority on the Banda Sea. It was clear to the VOC that more extreme measures must be taken if they were to achieve their goal and prevent other Europeans from trading in the Spice Islands. The Dutch, like their European predecessors, wanted to have a monopoly in the spice trade in Maluku.

At first the Seventeen Gentlemen ran the VOC from Amsterdam, but the distance between Holland and Indonesia required three years for an exchange of messages. To remedy this dilemma, in 1610 the VOC created the post of governor-general. Although the Seventeen Gentlemen appointed and controlled the governor-general, from that time onward Dutch activities in Asia were determined by the person who held that position. The first three men to serve as governor-general operated out of the VOC headquarters that had been established in Ambon. It soon became apparent, however, that this center of the spice trade was too far from the main trade routes of Asia and other growing Dutch enterprises in Japan and Africa. The Dutch began to search for a more suitable site, preferably one closer to the Strait of Malacca. A permanent VOC trading post had been established in 1603 at Banten on the island of Java, but the Dutch thought it would not be an appropriate location for their central administration. There were too many Chinese and English traders there, and also there was a strong local ruler with whom they would need to contend.

The British

By this time the British were joining the competition for the spice trade. In 1600, Queen Elizabeth I granted a charter to the British East India Company and named Sir James Lancaster its commander. Lancaster was a hero of the British defeat of the Spanish Armada in 1588. On his first voyage to the Indies in 1602, Lancaster set up a trading post in Banten—a year before the Dutch built theirs. British activity in Indonesia centered on that area for over eighty years.

The expectation that Portugal and Spain were well established in Asia was probably a major factor in the delay of the Netherlands and England to expand their mercantile operations in Asia. There is little doubt that both countries had knowledge of Portuguese and Spanish commercial activity in the Indian Ocean and South China Sea. They would have been aware of the 1494 Treaty of Tordesillas, signed by Spain and Portugal and sanctioned by Pope Julius II in 1506, that divided the New World between Spain and Portugal. Prior to Columbus's journey the pope declared that all points south of the Canary Islands would go to Portugal, and those north to Spain. In 1493, a year after Columbus's first voyage, he amended his previous edict and proclaimed that all lands east of 38 degrees west longitude were to go to Portugal and all else to Spain. The Tordesillas Line reset the demarcation this time at 46 degrees 37 minutes west longitude. At first this line caused no end of trouble in the Indies, but after a while, as other countries traveled to Asia, it was simply ignored.

A few years after the establishment of the British East India Company, the British sailed to Maluku and visited Ternate, Tidore, Ambon, and Banda, but VOC hostility gave the Englishmen reason to approach the spice trade with caution. In 1616 the British began building a fort on a tiny island in the Spice Islands that was without fresh water or building material and apparently had little appreciable merit. This move irritated the Dutch, who were trying to enforce monopoly regulations on all of the islands that grew cloves and nutmeg and did not appreciate the British presence in Maluku, no matter how inhospitable the land they occupied. By 1618 the Dutch were making regular inspections of the spice-growing islands, which they called duty rounds, to see that no spice farmers were growing nutmeg or clove trees in areas the Dutch had identified as off limits. The British continued their interest in Maluku and set up trading posts on Java, Sumatra, and Borneo as well. The Dutch observed this expansion, and the tension between the two European powers grew. Having other more extensive colonial obligations throughout the world—North America, Africa, and Asia—the British soon lost any serious interest in the Spice Islands and shifted their interest in Indonesia to Banten. They were never the serious threat to the Dutch spice trade that the Portuguese and Spanish were.

Dutch Spice Monopoly and Colonialism

If his three predecessors had harbored any hesitancy about use of force to achieve their goals, governor-general Jan Pieterszoon Coen did not. Before his appointment to the Dutch leadership post, Coen had announced to the Seventeen Gentlemen that they could not have trade without war nor war without trade. Under Coen, the Dutch made steady progress in their attempt to set up a spice trade monopoly in the Spice Islands. One of the reasons for their success was that the local populations were in no position to challenge Dutch naval supremacy.

Maluku spice growers who had traded on the open market for centuries hated the Dutch monopoly rule and circumvented the VOC by smuggling nutmeg and cloves to non-Dutch buyers. In the 1620s smuggling activities on Banda incensed Coen to the point that he retaliated by launching an attack on the people of Banda—an island that had especially productive nutmeg orchards. To appease the Dutch, the Bandanese promised to recognize Dutch sovereignty but ignored the rest of the Dutch conditions. The Dutch wanted more than a promise, and when some of the Bandanese escaped from a building where they were being held prisoner for violating Dutch laws, the VOC used that incident as an opportunity to react. Once recaptured, several of the village headmen admitted that they had broken the spice monopoly. Coen sent men to round up the people and burn and raze villages on all of the Banda islands. As a result, most of the population of Banda was either killed or deported. The Dutch then brought farmers from Holland to Maluku to oversee the spice orchards.

Just before Jan Pieterszoon Coen ordered the devastating attack on Banda, the VOC had been concentrating on finding a central location to establish its Asian headquarters. On the island of Java, the Dutch already had a trading post in Jakarta (which they would rename Batavia), and Coen preferred it to Banten as the site of permanent headquarters.

Jakarta was ruled by Prince Wijayakrama, a vassal of Banten, and there were tensions between his kingdom and that of the Mataram leader, Sultan Agung, who was based in East Java. At that time both the Dutch and the British were interested in establishing headquarters in Jakarta. Matters came to a head in 1618 when Indonesian forces from Banten attacked the VOC trading post in Jakarta with the aid of a superior British naval force. Not to be deterred by this, Coen ordered a group of his men to hold the fort in Jakarta while he sailed off to Maluku for reinforcements. While he was gone the British forces held the VOC fort in Jakarta under siege. When the Dutch troops inside the Jakarta fort were about to surrender, the sultan of Banten came to their aid, turning away the British and remaining in Jakarta until they were called away to fight in a local war. While waiting for Coen to return, the Dutch soldiers in the fort changed the name of their location from Jakarta to Batavia, the name of an ancient German tribe of the Netherlands. In May 1619 Coen returned from Maluku with seventeen ships. His forces stormed the town, driving out the remaining Banten forces. Thus the VOC trading post in Batavia became the VOC headquarters and the center of the vast Dutch East India Trading Company.

The Dutch could now settle down and develop a military and administrative center. They could store and exchange goods from throughout the archipelago, with access to the trade routes of Maluku, the Far East, and the West. The Dutch engaged in sporadic confrontations on Java with the armies of Sultan Agung, the powerful head of the Mataram empire, but they maintained Batavia as their headquarters throughout the colonial period. Animosity between Coen and Sultan Agung escalated, and in 1929 the Dutch defeated the sultan's forces in West Java.

Meanwhile, back in Maluku, Banda Naira had become a primary spice growing area for the Dutch, who built two forts there—Fort Beluga and Fort Nassau. With the local spice growers gone from these islands the Dutch implemented a plan to bring Dutch colonials to Maluku. They would oversee the spice production and use slave labor to handle the planting, routine care of the trees, and harvesting of the fruit. These Dutch spice farmers were called *perkeniers,* and the plots of land, or gardens, that the Dutch assigned to them were called *perkens.* In the beginning this system was reasonably successful, although fraught with troubles—lack of the agricultural knowledge necessary to produce the tropical fruit, and dissatisfaction with life on Banda, where the amenities of the Netherlands were few and far between. Today in Banda one can still see the shells of the once elegant *perkenier* mansions, built in an effort to recreate the luxurious Amsterdam social life the colonists wanted to emulate. Limited by location and circumstances, the *perkeniers* never achieved this goal.

Although not seriously concentrating their efforts on the spice trade, the English remained an annoyance to the Dutch in Maluku until 1667, when the Treaty of Breda was signed between the Netherlands and England. This pact resolved many long-standing Dutch-English disputes. One interesting item approved in the treaty was the exchange of a small British controlled island, Run, in eastern Indonesia for Dutch-held territory in North America. That Dutch territory included the island of Manhattan.

The *perkeniers* continued to grow spices, but the spice trade eventually became unprofitable, a state of affairs brought about by the law of supply and demand. No matter how many restrictions the Dutch imposed on the growers, nor how closely they guarded the spice trees, young seedlings were smuggled out of the Dutch-controlled islands by the British and other Europeans anxious to share in the lucrative trade. Once this was done, and spices were available from a number of countries, the spice markets in Europe were greatly oversupplied, and prices plummeted.

As this was happening in the Spice Islands, the population of Batavia was expanding. Administrators and merchants from the Netherlands joined Indonesians and Chinese who came to take advantage of the vigorous commercial activity. Food had to be imported, as did timber for houses and building ships.

Decline of the Dutch East India Company

All of these matters entailed heavy expenses and, coupled with the VOC's increasing involvement in the internal affairs of the Javanese rulers, led to the steady weakening of the company. The VOC was a mercantile company, and one of its biggest mistakes was becoming mired in local wars and expensive administrative procedures. To collect the agricultural products—coffee, tea, tobacco, and sugar—they needed for export, the Dutch made their demands on the Javanese nobility, who in turn passed the VOC's production demands on to the villagers. The village farmers had always been in the position of paying taxes to the nobility, and now they had to endure the added burden placed on them by the Dutch.

Eventually the VOC became bogged down with corruption and debt, and the Dutch government was unable to bail it out. While trying to maintain Dutch commercial enterprises around the world, Holland had long been facing tremendous expenses at home. As early as 1652 Holland was at war in Europe, and Dutch resources were increasingly consumed by the wars with England and France that continued until 1678. Holland also had expenses with its many other holdings. In 1621 the Dutch government had chartered the Dutch West India Company. This commercial organization forbade Dutch citizens to conduct any trade between the Tropic of Cancer and the Cape of Good Hope on the African coast and on the west coast of America between Newfoundland and the Strait of Magellan without company approval. The Dutch West India Company did not have the success of the East India Company, and it finally lost its charter in 1791.

Rule by the Dutch Government

On January 1, 1800, the VOC was formally dissolved and all of its possessions became the property of the Dutch government. This was a difficult time for the Dutch. In 1795 the Dutch *stadholder* (leader; the title of king was not used at this time) had fled to England as French general Napoleon Bonaparte's forces spread across Holland. From 1808 to 1811 Java was ruled by the reformist Dutch governor-general Herman Daendels, who initiated several measures that favored the farmers on Java. The Dutch *stadholder* had asked England to take over Indonesia until Holland was free of the French, and in August 1811 British forces arrived in Batavia. By the end of the month the English had accepted the surrender of Java's French-appointed governor-general, Jan Willem Janssens, who had replaced Daendels. Sir Thomas Stamford Raffles, who went on to establish Great Britain's colony in Singapore, was then named the British lieutenant governor of Java, a position he held until 1816. He too planned significant reforms to relieve the burden of the beleaguered Javanese farmers, but few of his ideas were actually implemented. In 1816, after Napoleon's defeat, Indonesia was returned to the Dutch.

From time to time the Indonesians rebelled against the Dutch. Most impressive of these rebellions was the one led by Prince Diponogoro of Yogyakarta in 1825. The prince made a strong military effort to turn back the colonial tide that had been gaining momentum on Java since the beginning of the nineteenth century, but the colonial involvement there was already too entrenched. Some members of the Javanese aristocracy supported the Dutch in this conflict, which strengthened Dutch determination to work exclusively with the Javanese ruling class and have them in turn work with the village people. The Javanese elite were in a no-win situation. They recognized the strength of the Dutch and were well aware that failure to carry out the colonial policies would mean the end of their power and positions as local rulers. The peasants saw the Javanese rulers as capitulating to the foreigners and resented them for their lack of concern for their own people. Members of the Javanese noble class often were bitter about their subservient role under Dutch rule, but they accepted the Europeans as a stronger power and one they were incapable of eliminating. To maintain their positions and territorial holdings, members of this elite class continued to cooperate with their Dutch rulers at the expense of the peasants. The *priyayi* class, the Javanese nobility, had served as overseers of kings' rulings before the Dutch took over Java. When Indonesia became a Dutch colony, the *priyayi* assumed the same role for them.

The Dutch government continued to demand agricultural goods from Indonesia that could be sold on the world market, but it revised its collection process. The new "cultivation system" was put into effect in 1830. It required that the taxes assessed regional rulers be paid in agricultural products, which the Indonesian official in turn demanded from the peasant farmers. The amount of goods and crops Indonesian farmers were required to provide to their local ruler increased markedly as the demands the Dutch administrators made on the regional rulers escalated. Separate lands were set aside to grow the crops necessary to meet the high taxes. The additional hours that farmers were forced to work these lands left insufficient time to plant and harvest their own crops. This assessment system, with its lands designated for crops to be grown to meet Dutch levied taxes, lasted until approximately 1870 and was the precursor of the later plantation system.

Takeover of Bali

By the middle of the nineteenth century the Dutch controlled most of Indonesia, but there were still some areas not under Indonesian control. One of these was the island of Bali. The Dutch had not yet identified Bali as agriculturally profitable, as was Java with its rich sugar, tea, and coffee growing regions. They had therefore paid little attention to this small island off the coast of Java. Much of the Dutch energy had been focused on international trade and the profits they could realize from food crops. In nineteenth-century Bali the people still held their rajas in the same high esteem that they had since early Hindu influence first gained prominence on the island. Life under this traditional Balinese-Hindu culture began to change when the Dutch launched their first military expedition against Bali in 1849. By the end of that year the Dutch had taken control of most of northern Bali, and over the next several decades, they concentrated on turning that part of the island into yet another profitable colonial enterprise.

The Dutch takeover of the rest of Bali started on May 27, 1904. A Chinese-owned ship, the *Sri Kumala,* out of Banjarmasin, a city in southeastern Borneo (now Kalimantan Selatan), was shipwrecked on the reef off Sanur Beach, on the southeast coast of Bali. The Balinese boarded the ship and exercised their rights of salvage, a right denied to indigenous people by the Dutch government. Angered by his substantial loss, the ship's owner went to the Dutch and demanded exorbitant restitution for his lost goods. The Dutch scaled down the owner's demands and presented his bill for the "stolen" goods to the raja of the district of Badung, who refused to pay. This resulted in the deployment of Dutch forces on the south shore of Bali. The troops then marched toward the raja's palace in Denpasar. As they drew closer, the soldiers could see a silent procession leaving the palace gates. It was led by the raja, followed by officials of his court, armed guards, priests, his wives and children, and retainers. The surprised Dutch forces began to fire but not before the Balinese used their swords to commit suicide. The palace was destroyed, and the royal family and many members of the court died. The ritual suicide committed by the court is referred to by the Balinese term *puputan,* meaning end or finalizing. In 1908 another Dutch military action prompted a *puputan* in which the Raja of Klungkung died with his court. The death of this raja—the Dewa Agung—and his court marked not only the end of Balinese resistance to the Dutch but the end of the era of rule by Hindu kingdoms in Southeast Asia.

Word of the ceremonial suicides in Bali spread rapidly and initiated protests against the colonial government from around the world, where the Dutch reprisals were viewed as disproportionate to Balinese offenses. *A Tale from Bali,* a popular novel by Vicki Baum published in 1937, tells this story and did much to bolster the sympathy of liberal Europeans for Indonesian independence.

Growth of Nationalism

In 1860 the book *Max Havelaar* was published. Douwes Dekker, the author of this exposé of the colonial government's alliance with Javanese royalty, was a former colonial administrator, and his book succeeded in bringing the intolerable labor conditions for peasant farmers on Java to the attention of the international community. Chastened by the world's reaction, the Dutch government in Indonesia introduced reforms throughout the Dutch East Indies. In 1901 Holland's Queen Wilhelmina announced the "Ethical Policy." This new colonial rule policy was encouraged by a group of men who were troubled by reports of the declining welfare of the Javanese people. These Hollanders were determined to create a new class of modern, well-educated indigenous people. To achieve these ends they developed a substantial Dutch language school system and launched a series of welfare programs.

Of the children who were educated in the newly established Dutch language schools, a handful went on to attend universities in the Netherlands. Meanwhile, the European school system, which prior to the Ethical Policy reform had been intended only for the children of Dutch colonial administrators and businessmen, was modified to include indigenous children. For the first time education was becoming available to most of the Indonesian people.

Many who studied abroad were children of the *priyayi,* Javanese elite. However, Indonesians who were permitted to travel abroad and who received Dutch university degrees were not always from Java's noble class. When these nonelite university educated Indonesians returned home, their presence often caused problems in the class-conscious Javanese culture. Their lack of respect for members of the *priyayi,* many of whom often had only a superficial if any education, was heretofore unheard of. In the political climate of the early 1900s Indies they were still considered inferior in the hierarchy of *priyayi* and colonial administrators. The result of this treatment of the newly educated sector of the population as second-class citizens was the emergence of a flurry of nationalist organizations. For the most part they were organizations with special interests, but they had a common theme—a desire for independence—and because of the intensity and popularity of their cause they flourished over the next few years.

For example, the group Budi Utomo was founded by a group of *priyayi* who wanted to create a modern Javanese cultural foundation through which they could encourage an attitude of self-respect and from which they could somehow claim a greater say in national affairs. Initiated by the elite, Budi Utomo never made the inroads into the peasant community that later groups did.

Sarekat Islam, founded by a Surakarta batik merchant, was a successful folk movement that encompassed Muslims and to some extent Chinese and Dutch merchants, discontented intellectuals, and a host of others who wanted to express their dissatisfaction with the status quo. At some point in its development, Sarekat Islam became more restrictive, excluding not only *priyayi* but Chinese and Dutch merchants as well. Complementing these organizations was a plethora of printed material supporting nationalism and nationalist causes. Many of the writers, such as Pramoedya Antara Toer and Mochtar Lubis, later became part of the Generation '45, a name given a group of prominent authors of the revolutionary period. Their novels, poetry, essays, and newspaper editorials kept the cause of nationalism constantly before the Indonesian people. In 1918 in an effort to give Indonesians a forum to voice their opinions, the Dutch admitted them to the colonial decision-making body, the Volksraad (People's Council), as nonvoting members. By 1929 Indonesians actually held a majority of the seats in the Volksraad, but they were still without any significant power. The greatest advantage of their participation in this body was the opportunity it gave Indonesian nationalists to express their desire for independence. In pre–World War II Indonesia, independence did not have the urgency among the people that it had after the war. The colonial government, not sensing the threat of an immediate independence movement, allowed Indonesians to have their say—however restricted—in the affairs of their country. However, apprehension on the part of the Dutch government over the power of the growing independence groups did eventually result in the scaling down of the government's Ethical Policy.

Reform Islam

Another change was taking place on Java. This was the increasing interest in reform Islam. The *priyayi* considered themselves to be Muslims, but they were not devout and for the most part had absorbed Islam, along with much that was Hindu, Buddhist, or faith in mysticism, into a larger complex belief—a Javanese folk religion. The term for these believers of folk Islam is *abangan.* In contrast, *santri* are strict Muslims. The *santris'* devout adherence to the tenets of Islam provided them with another vehicle for opposition to Christian-based Dutch rule. Educated Muslims in Indonesia were spearheading a revitalization of Islam and wanted to see significant reform in the practice of their religion. The Dutch had discouraged the practice of fundamentalist Islam until the 1900s, but once the government became more tolerant of the practice of "modernism" (a belief in the stricter tenets of the religion), this pure form of Islam spread rapidly in the colony—especially on Sumatra and Java. The new modernist believers were well educated in the Koran (*Qur'an*), the holy book of Islam, and many of them had made the pilgrimage to Mecca. Some had traveled and studied comprehensively in the Middle East. When they returned home they took the title of *haji* and often accepted positions as teachers in Indonesia's new Islamic schools. The first modernist school opened in 1909 in Sumatra, and subsequent schools appeared in West Java, a much more devoutly Islamic region than Central and East Java. Meanwhile the Javanese aristocracy, who were *abangan,* continued to practice their version of Islam that encompassed *adat* (traditional law) as well as elements of Hinduism and mysticism. The most successful of the modernist groups, Muhammadiyah, was founded by Kyai Haji Ahmad Dahlan. It first came to light in Central Java in 1912 as an educational organization emphasizing strict Islamic doctrines and focusing on invalidating Christian and local mystical beliefs. Along with Budi Utomo, it eventually changed its focus toward seeking political reform. Also during this time, in 1911, a leftist organization called the Indies Socialist Democratic Association (ISDV) was formed. It later became the Communist Party in Indonesia.

The Indonesian Nationalist Party

As nationalist organizations continued to emerge across Java, the Indonesian Nationalist Party (Partai Nasionalis Indonesia, PNI) appeared in 1927, headed by a young engineer named Sukarno. This party declared an end to "waiting for an airplane from Moscow or a caliph from Istanbul" (Steinberg et al. 1976, 296).

In 1928 a congress of youth organizations came forth with the phrase "One nation—Indonesia; one people—Indonesian; one language—Indonesian." The congress also adopted the red-over-white national flag as its own and sang the Indonesian national anthem, "Indonesia Raya."

Hundreds of new organizations with the word *Indonesia* in their titles appeared. Virtually all modern educated men and women came to think of themselves as Indonesians. The use of the terms *Indonesia* and *Indonesian* had a profound effect on the many nationalist movements.

In the final analysis it was the Indonesian Nationalist Party that emerged the most powerful among the nationalist organizations and Sukarno, through his charismatic personality, who brought Indonesian nationalism into the Dutch East Indies and ensured its success. As the PNI attracted more members, the Dutch perceived Sukarno as a risk, and in 1929 he was arrested for being a threat to public order and was sentenced to four years in prison. The Dutch colonial government at that time was especially conservative. The governor-general in 1929

Portrait of Sukarno at sidewalk shop in Yogyakarta (Courtesy of Florence Lamoureux)

was Bonifacius de Jonge, director of the profitable Royal Dutch Shell Company. The recent invention of the automobile had made Indonesia's rubber and oil resources valuable commodities on the international market, and Holland did not want to jeopardize its political control over the colony that produced these resources. The PNI languished without the leadership of the exuberant Sukarno, and though he was released from jail in 1931, he was rearrested in 1933 and this time exiled first to Irian Jaya and then to Sumatra. In 1934 two other prominent nationalists were also taken into custody. Mohammad Hatta, who later became Indonesia's first vice president, and Sutan Sjahrir, the country's first prime minister, were arrested and exiled to Banda.

A National Language

Of major significance to the independence movement was the decision to adopt a national language. In 1928 a congress of youth organizations came up with the slogan "one nation—Indonesia; one people—Indonesian; one language—Indonesian." The nationalists never expected people to stop speaking their village dialects or local languages, be it Javanese or one of the hundreds of other languages spoken throughout the archipelago. What they wanted was a common denominator to unite all of the people in the country. Coastal (or bazaar) Malay language is very similar to Indonesian, and it had been the *lingua franca* of commerce in the archipelago for centuries. Long a coastal trading language of the Arab merchants and sailors, it had the distinction of being spoken by almost all of the indigenous peoples and yet being the first language of no one. By adopting this form of Malay as a national language—which came to be called, simply, "Indonesian"—a strong cultural tie would be provided among all of the peoples of Indonesia. Indonesian is a democratic language and does not require special words for people of higher or lower social rank, as does Javanese. Lack of the elaborate status levels of Javanese made Indonesian a much more readily accepted language for a democratic government. Selecting Javanese, the native language of more than half of the Indonesians, would have alienated non-Javanese throughout the archipelago and created friction in the fragile independence movement.

Stymieing Independence during the 1930s

Throughout the 1930s, the concept of independence was still actively supported by a very small percentage of the population—those who had the advantage of a modern education and supported independence and freedom to make one's own decisions.

Independence movements continued to grow in Indonesia but without any substantial Dutch support and often in spite of the government's attempts to crush them. Anxious about the growing interest in independence, the Dutch had exiled three of the most vocal nationalist leaders—Sukarno, Hatta, and Sjahrir. The Dutch were especially diligent in their attempt to halt the myriad critical publications that many of the nationalist groups dispersed throughout Java. Several of the novels of modern Indonesian writer Pramodeya Ananta Toer focus on this period and provide excellent insight into these movements' activities and their consequent harassment by the colonial government. The catalyst that finally created an environment that would clear the way for Indonesian independence was the arrival of Japanese occupation forces in Indonesia in March 1942 at the onset of World War II.

Japanese Occupation in World War II

The Indonesians first viewed the victory of the Japanese over the Dutch positively. The Japanese had defeated the Russians in the Russian-Japanese war of 1905, and many people throughout Asia were glad to see a powerful European nation humbled by an Asian one. The Japanese occupation forces organized several military and political groups in Indonesia. In 1943, two of the most successful were Heiho and Putera (Pusat Tenaga Rakyat Center for the Power of the People). Heiho was an Indonesian unit of the Japanese army, and Putera—headed by two nationalists, Sukarno and Hatta, and two education specialists, Ki Hadjar Diwantara, founder of the Taman Siswa schools, and Kyai Haji Mas Mansur, founder of the Muhammadiyah schools—was to be an active political organization. The Japanese recognized the commitment of these Indonesian nationalists to their cause and never sufficiently empowered Putera to a point that they could accomplish serious meaningful reform.

The initial positive reaction to the arrival of the Japanese army of occupation soon changed. For although their military establishment in Indonesia assured the people that they would be granted their independence as soon as possible, the Japanese had more important matters that required their attention. They were badly in need of resources—both human and natural. The oil, rubber, tin, and other raw materials needed to fight a war were to be found in abundance in Southeast Asia, but the Japanese could not spare the manpower to mine and produce the needed goods. Therefore, Indonesians were soon enlisted to do this, often being taken from their villages to work in mines and on plantations. In 1943 the Japanese ordered the recruitment of "economic soldiers," or *romusha*. These were men drafted from their villages and put to work as laborers wherever the Japanese needed them. Some went as far away as Thailand and Burma. Their families were often left in dire circumstances. Food was soon in short supply, and the army had to be fed first. At the same time the *romusha* practice was initiated, the Japanese introduced new regulations for the compulsory sale of rice by Indonesian farmers to the military government at low prices. This combination of *romusha* recruitment and the requisitioning of rice for their army made clear to the Indonesians that the Japanese occupation was not a golden opportunity for the country to prepare itself for independence. Instead, it became an opportunity for the Japanese to take advantage of Indonesian resources, as the Dutch had been doing for centuries.

Leaders in the Independence Movement

During the war years several Indonesians who had been active in prewar nationalist movements continued to play key roles. Sukarno cooperated with the Japanese, making frequent radio broadcasts for the military government. He later justified this cooperation as a means of keeping the Indonesian independence movement in the forefront of people's minds, even in the midst of misery. Sukarno not only kept the independence movement alive, but his name became familiar to all who heard those broadcasts. By the end of the war Sukarno was more closely associated with the movement for Indonesian independence than any other leader throughout the country. Mohammad Hatta, a Sumatran slated for the vice presidency, also cooperated with the Japanese in hopes of making as much headway as possible in setting up an independent Indonesia before the war ended and the Dutch returned. Sutan Sjahrir, whom the Dutch had exiled to Banda with Hatta and who was to be prime minister after independence, did not cooperate with the Japanese occupation forces. Instead, he went underground and openly opposed the Japanese occupation, believing that assistance given to the Japanese would negatively impact any reasonable postwar arrangement between the Dutch and the Indonesians. Sjahrir had studied law in Holland, and although he longed to see his country free, he felt that Indonesian democratic rule could only be

achieved through cooperation with the Dutch. In the days prior to
World War II, Sjharir had given the Netherlands this warning: "Indonesia and Holland must cooperate to save Indonesia; therefore Holland
will have to work with Indonesia's nationalist leaders—now by choice,
or later by circumstance."

Another active nationalist who worked with Sukarno, Hatta, and
Sjahrir for independence was Adam Malik, a newspaper publisher from
Sumatra who was educated in Dutch schools. In 1946 he established
the People's Party.

From 1941–1945 these men, despite their different wartime positions, approached Indonesian independence with different tactics.
They maintained contact with one another throughout those years,
and each did all he could to promote their country's eventual independence.

Independence

The Japanese surrendered to the allies in Indonesia on August 15,
1945. Sukarno and Hatta declared Indonesian independence two days
later, on August 17, when Sukarno read a proclamation of freedom in
Jakarta. This is still celebrated in Indonesia as Hari Merdeka, Independence Day, although it would be four years before the Dutch finally
accepted the country's independent status and withdrew from Indonesia. Sukarno was named president of the new nation, with Hatta as
vice president.

The independence movement progressed quickly, and by September 19 approximately 200,000 Indonesians converged in what is now
Merdeka Square in Jakarta to demonstrate their support for the new
republic.

A major problem for the Indonesians in Jakarta was running the
many government offices. The Dutch had placed very few Indonesians
in civil service positions, and the Japanese occupation government
had appointed Indonesians to administrative positions only after
Japanese who had been filling Indonesian government jobs were reas-
signed to more militarily strategic posts toward the end of World War
II. This small pool of Japanese-trained civil servants was all Sukarno
had to fill administrative positions in his fledgling government in September 1945.

Meanwhile, the rest of the world was clearly not aware of the extent
to which the Indonesian independence movement had progressed. On
August 15 the Japanese had turned the island of Java over to Lord

Mountbatten, commander of the allied forces in Southeast Asia. Mountbatten had neither enough troops nor transportation to organize the rapid reoccupation of the island, and his intention was to return Java to the Dutch government as quickly as possible. The only Dutch in Jakarta at that time, however, were those who had been Japanese prisoners of war. Newly released from the prison camps, they were certainly not organized to an extent that they could challenge the legality of the new republic.

Even though Holland had been devastated by the war in Europe, by September 1945 the Dutch government had sent Lieutenant Governor Hubertus J. van Mook to Indonesia to oversee the reoccupation of their former colony. Dutch troops gathered in eastern Indonesia to prepare for this eventuality. British forces were representing the allies on Java and were expected to merely provide general military cover to the returning Dutch administration. As the strength of the newly formed republic became clear, the British commander informed the Dutch that England was not prepared to fight a colonial war on behalf of the Netherlands. Indeed, Britain had its own colonies in India, Burma, and Malaysia to worry about.

It soon became evident that the Netherlands was not going to easily relinquish control of a colony it had possessed for 350 years, and Dutch troops, aided by Ambonese soldiers, soon arrived in Jakarta to reclaim the city. The Dutch made steady progress in their plan to return to Indonesia. By January 1946, Sukarno feared more problems with British forces and the returning Dutch officials who set up their headquarters in Jakarta. Despite the presence of the Indonesian government there, Sukarno made the decision to move the seat of the new independent Indonesian government to Yogyakarta, in Central Java. The sultan of Yogyakarta, Sultan Hemengkubuwono IX, was sympathetic to the revolution and supported the decision to have his city named as the revolutionary capital. By January 20, 1946, Jakarta was again in Dutch hands.

The Indonesians were anxious to settle the matter and realized that the Dutch were still a powerful force with which to be reckoned. The British refused to withdraw their troops until an agreement was signed, and on November 12, 1946, the Dutch and the Indonesians signed the Linggajati Agreement. This agreement promised a commonwealth relationship. The Dutch government would recognize the republic as *de facto* authority on Java and Sumatra, and both sides would work toward the establishment of the United States of Indonesia. This entity would then join with the Netherlands in a Netherlands-Indies Union.

The Republic of Indonesia would consist of Java, Sumatra, and Kalimantan. The Dutch would retain Suluwesi, the Lesser Sundas (Sumbawa, Sumba, Flores, Komodo, Alor, and West Timor), Maluku, and West New Guinea. However, on July 21, 1947, the Dutch charged the Indonesians with treaty violations and extended their control over Java and parts of Sumatra, justifying their accomplishment by calling it a police action. In June 1947 Sutan Sjahrir left the government to concentrate his efforts on persuading the United Nations to support Indonesia's independence. Indonesia did not join the UN until the 1950s. When Sjahrir resigned, Amir Sjarifuddin replaced him as prime minister. Sjarifuddin was considered to be an extreme liberal and was later active in the Communist Party. As such he brought a new element to the emerging independent government.

Once again the Dutch were the target of tremendous international criticism. The climate of the late 1940s was not one that condoned continuing colonialism. A long and costly war had just been fought over freedom, and there was little sympathy for the Dutch attempt to control a nation that did not want anything to do with its former colonial ruler. As a result of the Dutch effort to take over Java and Sumatra, India and Australia brought the matter before the recently formed United Nations, where the Security Council set up a "good offices committee" to settle the dispute. The result of this was an agreement reached in January 1948 aboard the USS *Renville.* The so-called Renville Treaty called for a cease-fire at the line of the most advanced Dutch positions, "the van Mook Line." The Indonesian signatories to this treaty document had to signify that they had no more ammunition, and in so doing they won American support. It should be noted that at that time, Islamic groups—most notably Masjumi—and the Indonesian Communist Party (Partai Komunis Indonesia, PKI) both opposed the Indonesian government's policy of supporting this treaty. The PKI had been in Indonesia since the 1920s and saw this treaty as a compromise of Indonesia's independence. Thus it was that during the revolution with the Dutch, Indonesian government forces also had to fight Indonesian communist rebels who wanted to take control of the new country's independence movement. Things came to a head in Madiun in East Java, where the communists urged the people there to overthrow the new government. Given the choice of supporting Sukarno or a communist regime, the people backed Sukarno. This gave him the impetus he needed to defeat the communists in Madiun in September 1948. Sjarifuddin, who was with the communist forces there, was later executed for his role in that rebellion. The fact that the government forces defeated the communists in Madiun had a positive impact on Indonesia's relationship with the United States. It indicated to the Americans that the new Indonesian government was anticommunist and that it was capable of defeating communism within its borders. The PKI was severely weakened in the Madiun Affair, but it regrouped and became a major political power in Indonesia in the 1950s.

In December 1948, the Dutch defied the UN cease-fire and, assisted by British forces, attacked Yogyakarta, capturing Sukarno and Hatta. Several government officials escaped and set up the government of the republic on Sumatra. This incident prompted even greater furor from the international community. Bowing to the pressure, the Dutch freed Sukarno and Hatta and called for a Round Table Conference at the Hague to discuss the transfer of authority of most of Indonesia to the new United States of Indonesia. On February 7, 1949, the United States threatened to withdraw Marshall Plan aid to Holland if it did not cease its military activity against Indonesia. On December 27, 1949, Holland transferred sovereignty of all of the Dutch East Indies, except Irian Jaya, to the Republic of the United States of Indonesia. The term *United States* was used by the Dutch to encourage the different regions of the country to maintain their separateness. Regionalism was indeed strong in this sprawling island nation, but the country did develop a single polity, and the Republic of Indonesia superseded the Republic of the United States of Indonesia.

One region that actually supported the Dutch return to Indonesia after World War II was Maluku. Residents, along with men who had been in the Dutch colonial army, in 1949 set up a government separate from Suharto's Republic of Indonesia. They called this new country the Republik Maluku Selatan (Republic of South Maluku). When they lost Dutch support in 1950 they were forced to abandon their secessionist movement. Many who supported this free state of Maluku moved to Holland, where there is a sizable Malukan enclave today.

The revolution against the Dutch was also a revolution against Javanese officials and traditional rulers who had cooperated with the Dutch, and against the Chinese and the Eurasians who had been given special treatment by the Dutch. In short, it covered a wide range of injustices perpetrated on oppressed people.

The politics of the post-independence period was dominated by economic factors. Indonesia, a country of vast untapped natural resources, was an agrarian country. Not having the needed technology to develop its own resources, it was dependent on the export of food products for foreign exchange. To complicate matters the population was growing rapidly. In 1940 Indonesia's population was 70 million; in 1961 it was 97 million. New institutions emerged with power bases—the army, religious and ethnic groups, and political parties. Ethnic distrust became open hostility in some areas. The Madiun Affair in 1948 had arisen mainly out of the differences of party politics. It led to open and savage fighting in Java between *santri,* the strict Muslims, and *abangan,* the village people who often favored the communist land reform policies and who referred to the *santri* as wealthy Arab snobs.

In postrevolutionary Indonesia there was essentially no infrastructure for government, education, transportation, health care, and foreign trade. However, a military force was in place. It was made up primarily of men who had fought against the Dutch and were now prepared to defend Indonesia's independence. The primary government model the Indonesians had was one based on a system that was effective in a geographically small European nation with a homogeneous population—that is, the Netherlands. The contrasts between the two countries are obvious, and solutions to government dilemmas in the Netherlands were not effective in Indonesia.

Sukarno

Over time Indonesia's problems worsened. Faced with falling export revenues and rising demands on the country's resources, the Sukarno government began to practice deficit financing, starting a rapid cycle of inflation.

In the wake of growing dissatisfaction, the Communist Party, which was reactivated in the 1950s and actively supported Sukarno, grew rapidly and gained widespread administrative powers. In an attempt to better control the skyrocketing inflation and a generally worsening economy, Sukarno declared martial law in March 1957.

Later that year, when the United Nations rebuffed Indonesia's claim to Western New Guinea, the Indonesian government seized all Dutch businesses in the country, further damaging the nation's already disastrous economy. On December 5, 1957, the government ordered about 46,000 Dutch citizens out of Indonesia. In February 1958 a rebel government, the Revolutionary Government of the Republic of Indonesia (Pemerintah Revolusioner Republik Indonesia—PRRI) emerged in Sumatra with reported U.S. support. The PRRI supporters were apprehensive over the increasing influence of the PKI in Sukarno's government. The Communist Party's power had been escalating, and the United States was becoming increasingly alarmed over the protection of American citizens and property in the Sumatran oil fields. The United States even offered to send armed forces to Sumatra to protect American interests there. Stanvac, Caltex, and Shell oil companies eventually obtained the Jakarta government's assurance that they would be protected. Rebellions were fomenting in another region over this same issue—Sulawesi, where the Permesta revolutionary movement had become established. These antigovernment uprisings were supported by Islamic organizations such as Masjumi who feared Communist control of the country. The Indonesian government forces, however, were successful in combating the PRRI rebels and in a short time reduced their opposition to what amounted to rural insurgencies. By mid-1958, Indonesian government forces also put down the Permesta rebellion in Sulawesi. A year later, in the summer of 1959, Sukarno declared the constitution void and inaugurated a policy he called "Guided Democracy," which he described as a return to the ways of the precolonial Mataram empire. While the economy faltered, Sukarno built stadiums and statues, but his power was dependent on the manipulation of men who had money and real power. His return to the days of the Mataram empire's Sultan Agung in many ways more resembled Indonesia's days of colonial rule. During the next six years political power in Indonesia was in a shaky balance between the military on the one hand and Sukarno, who had the support of the Communist Party, on the other. It was not a government that debated policy and made laws, and members of the other parties opposed Sukarno's style of government. However they were not in a position to take on either the military or the PKI. At that time the PKI was the third largest Communist Party in the world, following China and the Soviet Union.

Facing astronomical inflation, the government launched two confrontations, ostensibly to draw attention away from the many serious internal problems facing it. The Indonesian army had defeated the PRRI rebel forces in Sumatra and the Permesta uprising in Sulawesi and was free to take on these battles. The first was against the Netherlands for recovery of Western New Guinea (now Papua). On August 15, 1962, the Dutch agreed to turn Western New Guinea over to an interim UN administration on October 1, and it was renamed Irian Jaya. The UN would then turn Irian over to Indonesia on May 1, 1963. Under this agreement, by the end of

1969 there would be an election and the people of Irian could decide whether or not they wanted to remain part of Indonesia. The second confrontation, in June 1963, was against the newly formed Federation of Malaysia contesting its claim to lands on Borneo. To pursue these wars the government imported vast quantities of military equipment from the Soviet Union. It was during the confrontation with Malaysia in Borneo that Sukarno withdrew Indonesia from the United Nations. During this same period a giant sports arena as well as several large national monuments and statues were built in Jakarta. Sukarno seemed to come up with an unending stream of new slogans and highly visible sculpture that depicted phases of the revolution against the Dutch, while the country's economic condition was rapidly spiraling downward. It was during this period that Sukarno told the United States to take its aid and go to hell. Both the PKI and the Indonesian army had grown in strength, and both vied for power under Sukarno. It was evident that one of them would soon become the dominant player in Indonesia's future.

The Communist Party of Indonesia

As mentioned earlier, the Partai Komunis Indonesia (PKI) had existed in Indonesia since the colonial period. It expanded early in the twentieth century during the nationalist movement and then was suppressed by the Dutch. In the 1920s a prominent Indonesian communist was Tan Malaka, a Stalinist who later abandoned that philosophy and became a "National Communist," focusing specifically on Indonesian needs. When independence was declared the PKI became active, opposing the democratic form of government that emerged after World War II. Among the most influential communists in Indonesia at that time was D. N. Aidit. He and other Communist Party members incurred Sukarno's wrath in a confrontation with government forces in Madiun in 1948. As a result of that defeat, Aidit along with other PKI members left Indonesia for China. However, they were back in the country and in favor with Sukarno in 1951, when the PKI made a comeback in Indonesia. Sukarno and Aidit became friends, and by June 1960 Aidit even held a position in the People's Consultative Assembly. But when the September 30, 1965, "Night of the Generals" took place, Aidit fell from favor quickly and fled Jakarta. He was killed in the bloodbath that followed that maneuver when the Communist Party was decimated.

Night of the Generals

The deciding incident in the battle for power between the PKI and the army occurred on the night of September 30, 1965, when seven of the army's high ranking officers were assassinated. These men were brutally murdered and their bodies thrown in an abandoned well called the "crocodile hole," located near Jakarta's airport. When the assassins approached the home of General A. S. Nasution, a prominent military figure and revolutionary hero, he was asleep in his bedroom. In one of the most publicized events related to the death of the military leaders, the assassins thought they saw a man trying to escape, and fired, killing Nasution's young daughter. This incident was decisive in drawing public support to the army and against the suspected killers—sympathizers and members of the Communist Party. The origins of this coup are still vague, but within Indonesia it was soon widely believed that the Communist Party was behind it, a belief that hastened the end of the PKI. There is another theory that a faction of the military staged the incident to discredit the communists and strengthen their own position. Neither theory has ever been proven.

The coup was suppressed in one day by forces under then relatively unknown Major-General Suharto (promoted to general on July 1, 1966). It was the aftermath of the coup that was decisive. Suharto's leadership in the moment of crisis gave him momentum and authority. In the following months he led the army in a campaign against the PKI, while Sukarno, his leadership dangerously threatened, exerted his influence to maintain control of the government. The struggle between Suharto and Sukarno paralyzed the government and created a power vacuum much like the one that had existed in 1945. This generated terrible consequences primarily in Central and East Java and Bali as well as in several other regions where anarchy prevailed. Hundreds of thousands of Chinese, as well as peasant members of the PKI in these locations, were massacred. In Javanese areas where the number of victims was the greatest, it was reported to be Muslim youth groups that took the lead in the slaughter as the bitter conflict between *abangan*—who had joined the Communist Party in the hope of having a better life—and *santri*—who opposed the Communist Party on its basic philosophy—divided the nation. The army could not, or would not, take serious steps to control the slaughter. Many Chinese were killed with the justification that they maintained ties with China and therefore were communists or at least sympathetic to communism. The underlying reason was probably more often a settling of old scores or hatreds against these members of the merchant class who had been given privileges under the Dutch and were still better off financially than most of the people in the rural areas. The growth of Islamic modernism, with its objections to less pure forms of Islam, was a primary cause of much bloodshed. There is the theory that the military was relieved to see the end of communism, as such a move could only strengthen its position in government. This has never been proven, but the aftermath of the Night of the Generals effectively ended the existence of the Communist Party in Indonesia. Suharto declared it illegal in 1966.

Immediately after the coup three men formed a working group that played a major role in governmental decision making. They were Suharto, the sultan of Yogyakarta, and Adam Malik. Suharto continued to gain strength as Sukarno's presidency weakened. On March 11, 1966, Sukarno signed a document giving extensive power to Suharto. This letter came to be known as Supersemar, an acronym for Surat Perintah Sebelas Maret (letter of March 11.) Within a year Sukarno was effectively ousted from office through the cooperative efforts of the youth organizations and the military—which had become the new power. On March 12, 1967, Suharto was named acting president of Indonesia. He was elected president on March 27, 1968. Sukarno died on June 21, 1970.

Suharto

The new regime under General Suharto consolidated power cautiously. In many respects he returned to the politics and style of the cabinets of the first three years of independence. He quickly restored relations with Western countries, and whereas Sukarno had once told the United States to take its aid and go to hell, Suharto actively sought U.S. and other Western assistance.

Under Suharto the Indonesian economy grew and the country enjoyed a higher standard of living than ever before. In sharp contrast to the years when the people did not have enough to eat, Indonesia now exported rice. Construction boomed in Jakarta and in other large cities throughout the country as foreign investment in Indonesian businesses escalated. Throughout Suharto's presidency significant numbers of Indonesians were added to the government payroll, and until the Asian economic meltdown in 1997, the standard of living for Indonesians in all social classes improved.

From the beginning of his first term, however, there were complaints of corruption, especially in regard to Suharto's friends and family. For example, in August 1968 a Suharto supporter named Ibnu Sutowo was named head of Pertamina, the Indonesian oil monopoly. In 1983 three of Suharto's daughters formed a business partnership, and by 1989 that organization controlled a profitable Jakarta toll road concession. In 1970 Suharto's half brother, Probosutejo, and close friend, Lim Siew Leong, a Jakarta billionaire, were allowed to corner the clove import market. Twenty years later Suharto's son Tommy was granted total control of that market. This was especially damaging as it caused considerable hardship to many small farmers who made their living producing cloves for the popular Indonesian *kretek* cigarettes. A number of government officials criticized Suharto's close friendships with several prominent Chinese businessmen and the opportunities he provided to them. Suharto angered many conservation organizations when he granted timber rights across much of Sumatra and Kalimantan to his golf partner and businessman, Mohamad "Bob" Hassan, a man who blatantly ignored environmental concerns. In 1982, for example, poor logging practices caused extensive forest fires to break out in East Kalimantan. These fires continued to burn for years, polluting the air throughout Southeast Asia.

Suharto's financial deals with Lim Siew Leong were especially irritating to Indonesian government officials. In spite of Indonesia's seemingly growing prosperity, as far back as 1988 the failing economy became a major concern when the Indonesian government announced that 36 percent of its income that year would go toward paying off the national debt. Criticism of government policies increased. But Indonesia's economy seemed healthy and little was actually done to curb Suharto's tendency to favor his friends and relatives, even as Indonesian banks became more involved in dangerous economic liaisons. Whereas these matters were not daily topics in international news circles, the issue that did attract the attention of the foreign press was Indonesia's takeover of East Timor. In 1975 Indonesian forces invaded East Timor and as a result attracted a great deal of negative attention.

East Timor

Perhaps the most controversial issue facing the Indonesian government during Suharto's regime was that of East Timor (officially, the República Democrática de Timor-Leste). The island of Timor was first visited by the Portuguese in 1515. Seven years later Ferdinand Magellan's ship, the *Victoria,* landed on the island and reported that it had been contaminated with syphilis. No one seemed to have anything positive to say about Timor. The island's climate is quite arid, the land is infertile, and the people who live there have a difficult time eking out a living. Nonetheless, by 1566 the Portuguese had built a fort there, which they maintained for ninety years, when they were ousted by the Dutch. Fighting between the two European nations kept control of the island up in the air for a number of years. The Portuguese sold their claim to Flores to the Dutch in 1851, but kept Timor. In 1913 the Dutch and Portuguese divided Timor, with West Timor going to the Dutch and East Timor to the Portuguese. Portuguese control of Timor lasted into the twentieth century.

Timor remained half-Dutch and half-Portuguese until Indonesia's revolution with the Dutch, when Indonesia took over the western half of the island. In 1975 the island was the site of a major upheaval when East Timor, with a population of approximately 750,000 Christians, was invaded by Indonesian troops.

Indonesian concern for East Timor began in earnest in 1974 during the Carnation Revolution in Portugal, when the right-wing government in Lisbon was replaced in a coup. As a result of this upheaval in Portugal, an anticolonial left-wing party replaced the Portuguese conservative government, and the new government decided to rapidly decolonize the country's overseas empire. This decision caused chaos in many of Portugal's former colonies.

Four centuries of colonial rule had done little to prepare East Timor for self-governance. In 1974 the colony claimed just one high school and fewer than ten college graduates, and the literacy rate was under 10 percent. Portugal had paid little attention to its colony in the Timor Sea. Portugal and Indonesia had actually held discussions about the future of East Timor, but problems arose before any agreement was reached. There were originally three opposing factions within East Timor. The first was the newly formed Fretilin Party, which was anticolonial and populist-oriented and vehemently opposed integration with Indonesia. The second, Timor Democratic Union (UTD), preferred gradual decolonization from Portugal. The third, the Timorese Popular Democratic Association (Apodeti), advocated immediate integration with Indonesia. In the first elections held on East Timor during the decolonization period, Fretilin, which supported an independent East Timor, and the UTD, which advocated a slow and controlled break from Portugal, outpolled the pro-Indonesian Apodeti Party. In 1975 the two groups opposed to integration into Indonesia (Fretilin and UTD) formed a coalition, but within a short while they were fighting between themselves. The result of this action was a bloody civil war in which several thousand people were killed and Fretelin emerged the winner. In November 1975, Fretilin declared the island an independent state. This announcement caused great alarm in Indonesia. The government had recently survived a brutal period in its history, one many Indonesians blamed on the Communist Party. Now this little half-island was showing strong signs of supporting communism, and the Jakarta government was not about to allow a communist government in the midst of its archipelago. On November 28, 1975, Indonesian military forces invaded East Timor, forcing Fretilin guerrillas into the mountains. On July 17, 1976, East Timor was incorporated into Indonesia as the country's twenty-seventh province.

Although Indonesia built roads and hospitals and established schools and a new university, in East Timor, the Indonesian government was ruthless in its treatment of the Fretilin Party and its sympathizers. In its attempts to eliminate the independence-seeking organization, Indonesian forces strafed villages, burned crops, and pursued guerrillas and their families into desolate mountain areas. From 1975 to 1980 an estimated 100,000 East Timorese died in fighting or from starvation and disease. (The Indonesian government reports 30,000 killed; foreign sources put the number at 200,000.)

An especially well-documented incident took place in November 1991 when a large crowd of East Timorese gathered to attend a memorial mass for a young man who had been killed outside the church where he had sought refuge two weeks earlier. He had spoken out against the Indonesian government and, fearing their reprisal, had fled to the church. After the memorial mass, a funeral procession walked to the cemetery. When the group arrived at the graveyard, soldiers suddenly appeared and started to shoot into the group of mourners. Many unarmed Timorese were killed, and the massacre was publicized internationally. A further embarrassment to Suharto occurred in 1996 when the Nobel Peace Prize was awarded jointly to Fr. Carlos Filipe Ximines Belo and Jose Ramos-Horta, both activists in the East Timor independence movement.

East Timor gained its independence on May 19, 2002. It is interesting to note that the new nation chose Portuguese as its national language and the U.S. dollar as its official currency. Neither Indonesian nor the rupiah is official today in East Timor.

In 1994 Suharto's methods became more overt, and he banned several major publications, effectively halting their criticism of his government's policies and the awarding of government contracts to his friends. In 1996 Megawati Sukarnoputri, daughter of Indonesia's first president, was the chosen head of the Indonesian Democratic Party (PDI). Suharto's supporters challenged her, and after several violent episodes a government supporter was named to replace her as leader of the increasingly popular PDI. In 1999 Megawati headed a new party, the Indonesian Democratic Party of Struggle (PDI-P).

Conditions worsened in Indonesia over the next three years, culminating in the collapse of the Indonesian economy in 1997. Riots and protests were almost daily occurrences on the streets of Jakarta and in other large cities throughout the country as the government failed to control the rapidly deteriorating economy. During this period ethnic confrontations escalated, with residents of Chinese heritage being singled out for especially harsh treatment. Reports of nepotism and cronyism continued to be regularly leveled against Suharto. Bowing to the inevitable, he resigned as president on May 21, 1998. Suharto was replaced by his vice president, B. J. Habibie.

Indonesia is the land of the *wayang kulit*—the Javanese shadow puppet dramas. The *dalang,* puppeteer, controls the puppets from behind a screen. He determines where the puppets move and what they say, but he is not seen. The *dalang* is familiar with mysticism. He has extraordinary skills and dexterity; not only does he make the puppets fly through the air but he determines the opinions they voice. He has great latitude with this, and often the puppets make politically incorrect statements that said by an ordinary citizen would bring down the wrath of the government. In the heyday of his presidency, Suharto was like a *dalang,* but his direction of the puppets became less effective as time went on, a situation exacerbated by the death of his wife on April 28, 1996. Madame Tien was from an old Javanese royal family and was thought by many Javanese to be the one with the effective mystical connections. After her death Suharto began to lose his control over the country—behind the screen as well as in front of it. In May 1998 he was forced to resign as president of Indonesia, ending his thirty-one-year reign.

Post-Suharto Years

Suharto's successor, Habibie, was instantly opposed by the majority of Indonesians, most notably the student organizations. They had been major players years earlier in ousting Sukarno and more recently in driving out Suharto. Several students were killed in riots protesting Habibie's presidency, which they viewed as a continuation of Suharto's policies of favoritism and family perks. Soon after he assumed the presidency, Habibie announced that he would hold elections before the end of his legal term (the remainder of Suharto's term). Presidential elections were held in early autumn 1999, and although Habibie was a candidate, he was not elected. It is of interest to note that Habibie supported two legislative measures that changed Indonesia's history. First, he lifted the ban on censorship in Indonesia, allowing foreign and national opinions to be printed freely in the press and broadcast on radio and television. Second, he supported the independence movement in East Timor, smoothing the way for that territory to become a new nation, separate from Indonesia. The latter move was not popular with Indonesia's military leaders, and it is interesting that Habibie took such a controversial stand on that issue.

The new president was a blind Muslim cleric by the name of Abdurrahman Wahid, popularly known as Gus Dur. The winner of the popular vote was actually Magawati Sukarnoputri, but the Consultative Assembly (Parliament) selected Gus Dur. A devout Muslim and an intellectual, he was faced with almost insurmountable problems. Not only was the economy still in a shambles, but also there were growing separatist movements in Aceh, Maluku, Papua, and Sulawesi, many of them intensified by Muslim-Christian conflicts. Gus Dur was not physically well and was a poor administrator. On top of this, money scandals and various reports of corruption wracked his months in office. So lacking in confidence in their president were the Indonesian people that on February 1, 2001, the Indonesian Consultative assembly voted 393 to 4 to begin impeachment proceedings against him.

Abdurrahman Wahid was impeached on July 23, 2001, and Megawati Sukarnoputri, the vice president and daughter of Indonesia's first president, Sukarno, was named the fifth president of Indonesia. She chose the head of the United Development Party (PPP), Hamzah Haz, a devout Muslim, as her vice president. (It is interesting to note that in 1999 Hamzah Haz had made the comment that no woman was fit to lead the world's largest Muslim nation.) Whereas Gus Dur was at odds with the military, Megawati has their support. She has reiterated her nationalist sentiments and opposition to any separatist movements within the country many times. Megawati is a moderate Muslim who came to power on the strength of her father's name. She has taken the highest office in her country at a time when religious-based civil insurrections have been added to Indonesia's overwhelming political and financial problems.

To add to these woes, on October 12, 2002, terrorists exploded a bomb outside a popular nightclub in Bali, killing 202 people. Prior to this incident, Bali had been considered a safe haven in a sometimes-volatile country. This shocking incident caused international condemnation and further economic concerns for Indonesia. Tourism in Bali had brought Indonesia millions in international currencies. After the bombing, tourism dropped off dramatically, thus eliminating what had been a substantial source of revenue for the country.

Indonesia is a diverse and fascinating land. From the earliest records, when rajas and sultans ruled the archipelago, through modern times, when the country strives to follow a democratic model, the archipelago has faced seemingly insurmountable problems. Ruling a country consisting of a solid landmass would be complicated enough, but controlling a nation comprised of thousands of islands ranging over several thousand miles and having such a wide diversity of people presents enormous problems. There is little doubt that 350 years of colonial rule had a major influence on Indonesia. Dutch colonialism, followed by the Japanese occupation during World War II and a growing spirit of nationalism that culminated in self-rule, combine to make its history unique.

References

Andaya, Leonard Y. *The World of Maluku: Eastern Indonesia in the Early Modern Period.* Honolulu: University of Hawaii Press, 1993.

Blair, Lawrence, with Lorne Blair. *Ring of Fire.* New York: Bantam Books, 1988.

Cakalele: Journal of Eastern Indonesia, Vols. 1–10. Honolulu. Center for Southeast Asian Studies, 1991–2002.

Hall, D. G. E. *A History of Southeast Asia* (3rd ed.). London: McMillan, 1977.

Hanna, Willard. *Indonesian Banda.* Philadelphia: Institute for the Study of Human Issues, 1978.

Lansing, Stephen J. *The Three Worlds of Bali.* New York: Praeger, 1983.

Miksic, John (ed.). *Borobudur: Golden Tales of the Buddhas.* Berkeley: Periplus Editions, 1990.

Pigafetta, Antonio. *Magellan's Voyage: A Narrative Account of the First Circumnavigation,* translated and edited by R. A. Skelton. New York: Dover Publications, 1994.

Ricklefs, M. C. *A History of Modern Indonesia.* Hong Kong: Macmillan, 1990.

Steinberg, David Joel, David K. Wyatt, John R.W. Smail, Alexander Woodside, William R. Roff, and David Chandler. *In Search of Southeast Asia.* New York: Praeger, 1976.

Van Niel, Robert. *Java under the Cultivation System.* Leiden: KITLV, Southeast Asia, 1992.

Websites

CIA website: http://www.cia.gov/cia/publications/factbook/geos/id.html

The following sites developed by Aad Engelfriet:

Photos, maps, and images of the Dutch East Indies: http://home.iae.nl/users/
arcengel/Indonesia/100.htm

Historical information according to ten time periods ranging from 100–1998:
http://home.iae.nl/users/arcengel/NedIndie/indexdei.htm

Historical and political detailed timelines from pre-1500–Summer 2001 in eleven
separate documents: http://www.gimonca.com/sejarah/sejarah10.html

CHAPTER TWO

Indonesia's Economy

HISTORICAL INFLUENCES

Indonesia's history provides an interesting insight into the country's current economic problems. Records of the earliest empires show that political regions in Indonesia were first organized along the lines of Buddhist and Hindu law. These kingdoms were followed by sultanates oriented toward Islamic law. All of these governments were based on rule by sovereign leaders or a political entity where one person headed the government for the duration of his or her life. This form of rule relied on a peasant class for labor and taxes to support a ruling oligarchy. Sectors of Indonesia were under some variation of this form of government from approximately the seventh century until it came under Dutch control in the seventeenth century. Rulers came and went, but the life of the peasant class changed little. These people provided the labor that made someone else wealthy and reaped little that bettered their own lives.

The Dutch colonial government took little direct control of the production of goods in the agriculturally rich parts of Indonesia. It was not their plan to dismantle the local political units, but rather to work through the existing regional officials who headed them. Members of this Indonesian elite were called *priyayi*. This method of operation, on the part of the Dutch colonial government, kept the Indonesian ruling class in the role of "collector of goods and labor." The difference for Indonesians under the Dutch was that the ruling class was now required to pay taxes and provide labor to the colonial government. To maintain their standard of living, these wealthy Indonesians were forced to demand goods and labor from their subjects that not only were sufficient to support themselves but were in amounts necessary to meet the Dutch demands on them as well. The *priyayi* were in an awkward situation. If they opposed the Dutch and refused to provide the products the colonial government demanded, they would serve no purpose in the Dutch process of collecting goods and services. In that case, they would have been without the income needed

Klungklung Palace, the center of government in South Bali before the island came under Dutch jurisdiction (Center for Southeast Asian Studies)

to maintain their conspicuous styles of living, and eventually these royal families would have been without power in their own territories. In such a scenario, the Dutch would probably have taken control of the workers, leaving the *priyayi* with no source of income to continue living their ostentatious lifestyles. Given that option, the *priyayi* continued their role as middlemen.

When the colonial government decreed that no Dutch citizen could rent land from local Javanese rulers to grow crops that would be in competition with government sale of such products on the open market, it caused hardship for the *priyayi*. The rental contracts between Javanese rulers and Dutch growers were often long-term arrangements. These contracts had usually provided the Javanese ruler with a large advance payment for land rental. In almost all cases these advance payments to the *priyayi* had been spent when this ruling went into effect early in the 1800s. In these situations the local ruler was faced with the dilemma of repaying the advance rental payments—money he no longer had. The way of handing this problem was to require more goods from the already overburdened farmer who was beholden to him. This plight was a major factor in the Java (Diponogoro) War from 1825 to 1830.

In 1830 a new Dutch governor-general, J. Count van den Bosch, was sent to Indonesia. He put into place a tax system called the cultivation system. At this time the Netherlands was involved in a war with Belgium as well as fighting the Java War in Indonesia, and Holland's coffers were low.

Under the cultivation system the Dutch required that agricultural products, such as coffee, tea, spices, indigo, sugar, and tobacco, be produced by Indonesians on land set aside for that purpose. Local rulers were to provide plots of land that peasant farmers would work. All produce from those parcels of land would be turned over to the Dutch. At first the peasants were able to keep up with the colonial government's demand for these agricultural products. However, as expenses back in Holland increased, so did the demand on the peasant farmer for increased production of sugar, coffee, tea, and tobacco. Although the cultivation system underwent adjustments and changes in the mid-1800s, at its onset approximately half of what a farmer made on his crops was paid out in taxes—in the form of agricultural products. The burden of plowing and harvesting crops on additional land often left the farmers with insufficient time to take care of their own crops. The result in many areas of Java was famine. The cultivation system was implemented primarily on the island of

Java—the most fertile and hence agriculturally productive island in the archipelago.

The Dutch did not continue to restrict their economic interests to agriculture. In the 1840s they were mining coal, and in the 1850s tin. By 1870 the Dutch government's policy of forced cultivation of agricultural products ended. Large-scale agriculture in Indonesia became privately owned as plantations replaced the cultivation system. In 1870 the Dutch passed the Agrarian Law. This law implemented a cash economy in Indonesia, and it was devastating for the peasant farmer whose land holdings hardly generated enough revenue to support a family. Consequently the cash-poor villager was soon living on credit. He went to two sources for money—the Chinese pawnbroker and the Arabic moneylender. The money borrowed was usually paid to a European landowner to rent land to grow food for his family. Laborers were paid wages on the plantations, and the estate owners paid taxes to the Netherlands government. A major product of the Indonesian plantations was rubber, the demand for which gained steadily after the introduction in 1908 of the Model T Ford automobile. The automobile industry also required Indonesia's most valuable resource—oil—which had been a major commodity on the world market since the 1890s. In 1890 a Dutch entrepreneur established an oil company in Indonesia that would become the highly profitable Royal Dutch Shell. At the turn of the century Royal Dutch Shell was drilling for oil in Kalimantan, on Borneo. The company eventually had oil wells throughout the country.

During the first half of the twentieth century the Dutch maintained firm control of Indonesia's resources—agricultural and mineral. Although Holland still reaped handsome profits from its colony in the East Indies, most of the money flowing into the Netherlands from Indonesia was used to finance military activity in those regions of Indonesia that were not under Dutch control, for example, suppression of rebellions in Aceh and Bali. Even with these expenditures, Dutch-owned rubber plantations and oil-drilling companies brought millions into Holland's treasury.

By the 1920s agricultural goods were almost completely replaced by rubber and oil as the major sources of income to the government. In this period the Dutch started to open Indonesia to foreign enterprises. A number of European companies operated plantations and businesses in Indonesia, paying taxes to the Dutch colonial government.

Forced labor from Indonesian peasants was no longer a method of raising money for the colonial government. The largest problem

Family processing rubber (Courtesy of Florence Lamoureux)

concerning the Indonesians at this time was the rapidly increasing population. From 1929 to 1938 the population of Indonesia increased by 15 percent while the production of food increased by only 3.5 percent.

World War II brought about changes in Indonesia as Japanese occupation forces replaced the Dutch as the "outside" nation controlling Indonesia's enormous supply of natural resources, especially oil. The Japanese desperately needed Indonesia's oil and minerals, but they had neither the time nor the labor force necessary to mine them. Instead they used Indonesian laborers to extract the rubber from trees and the minerals and petroleum from the ground. Like the Dutch, the Japanese did not share the profits from these resources with the Indonesians.

In the years immediately following World War II, Indonesians were too deeply involved in fighting their war of independence from Holland to address the issue of international trade, and in the late 1940s the economy of the young republic was grim. The Dutch had not trained Indonesians as engineers, surveyors, chemists, agricultural specialists, businessmen, civil servants, and medical personnel in sufficient numbers to oversee the needs of an economy that was heavily dependent on the export of natural resources and agricultural products. In some cases, when the Indonesians expelled the Dutch from a particular area, the villagers displayed their exuberance by destroying the factories and equipment that had belonged to that Dutch business. A case in point was a prosperous Dutch sugar cane plantation in East Java that also refined sugar in a factory located on the plantation grounds. The villagers celebrated the departure of the Dutch by burning the harvested sugar cane and smashing the heavy equipment used in the sugar refining process. When an Indonesian company eventually took over the land and the factory, a great deal of money had to be spent replacing equipment and preparing fields for planting. This scene was repeated time and time again at a high cost to the new Indonesian owners.

After independence, relations between the Dutch and the Indonesians remained strained. A number of acrimonious incidents arose, such as one in 1956 when Indonesia refused to pay about 85 percent of a payment Holland claimed it owed. It was later proven that most of this money was debt the colonial government had incurred and had transferred to Indonesia in agreements signed on the occasion of Indonesia's independence.

POSTREVOLUTION CHANGES IN ECONOMIC POLICY

The nationalists who had taken the reigns of government had no intention of following the economic policies of the Dutch. They considered such business practices to be elitist and lacking in consideration for the welfare of the people. It was therefore not surprising that when Sukarno became president he favored a socialist-based government rather than the Dutch capitalist-based model of mercantilism.

In some matters the government acted hastily with negative economic results. In December 1957 the Indonesian government took control of more than 245 Dutch businesses in Indonesia. The prosperous oil industry, however, was left partially under the control of foreign owners to ensure that there would be no break in the flow of oil production revenue into Indonesia. Sukarno's move to take ownership of all Dutch companies did not have the desired effect on the country's dismal economy. On the contrary, the civilian and military men who took over the operation of these companies for the government were inexperienced in international commerce and were unable

President Sukarno, the first leader of Indonesia after it became a republic in 1945, inspects his troops. (Hulton-Deutsch Collection/Corbis)

to maintain the level of profitability the companies had experienced under their former owners. As inflation lowered their salaries, the new proprietors resorted to accepting bribes. The lack of trained economists and businessmen in the new government was frustrating for the leadership, and in March 1957 a number of politicians were arrested on corruption charges. This element of dishonesty in government compounded the problem of graft and bribery already practiced in most of the troubled businesses.

In mid-December 1957, Indonesia's army chief of staff, General A. H. Nasution, appointed Dr. Ibnu Sutowo to the head of the state-owned oil company, Permina (Perusahaan Minyak Nasional—National Oil Company). In 1968 this company became Pertamina (the National Oil and Gas Company), and Ibnu Sutowo still headed it. By then, however, he was generally regarded as corrupt in his dealings with the government. Despite this, Pertamina was immensely profitable. Eventually dishonest business practices became deeply ingrained in the company, and in 1975 Pertamina was heavily in debt. The Indonesian government paid $10 billion that year to cover the company's deficit.

In 1957 Sukarno proclaimed martial law and put into effect a plan he called Guided Democracy. During the six years it was government policy, Sukarno manipulated a divisive combination of communists and military factions. He avoided including modernist Muslims in his inner circle. As the economy further deteriorated, Sukarno resorted to rule by slogan. In 1960 the slogan Manipol-USDEK was introduced. "Manipol" referred to the *political manifesto* stated in Sukarno's August 17, 1959, Independence Day speech; USDEK was basically an acronym for the 1945 Constitution, Indonesian Socialism, Guided Democracy, Guided Economy, and Indonesian Identity. By this time Sukarno was including the traditionalist Muslims of Nahdatul Ulama in his government, but he still shunned modernist Muslim organizations such as Masyumi. Sukarno had economic advisers—men and women who had studied abroad and made sound fiscal recommendations to him. There were also offers of assistance from the International Monetary Fund (IMF), but its suggestions were contrary to the tenets of communism, and Sukarno did not want to threaten his alliance with the PKI (Partai Komunis Indonesia—Indonesian Communist Party).

It is interesting to note that in 1959 a charge of corruption was levied against a young army officer named Suharto. He was found guilty and was demoted in rank.

Sukarno's Attempts to Control a Worsening Economy

By 1961 Indonesia was seriously arrears in its foreign debt payments, and by November 1962 the IMF restricted economic assistance to the Sukarno government. A few months later, in spring 1963, Indonesia devalued its currency (the rupiah = Rp) and implemented other economic controls to reinstate IMF support. In June of that year foreign oil companies were brought under the government-controlled oil company, Permina. That same year Indonesia joined the Organization of Petroleum Exporting Countries (OPEC).

In December 1962, in what seemed like yet another tactic to draw attention away from the country's failing economy, Sukarno declared war on Malaysia in what came to be known as the *konfrontasi* (confrontation). This conflict arose over disputed territories on Borneo. When Malaysia became independent from Great Britain, Indonesia had expected the British colonies on Borneo (now the Malaysian provinces of Sabah and Sarawak) to join the Republic of Indonesia.

This was not the case, and the two provinces remained a part of Malaysia even though they are not located on the Malay Peninsula. Sukarno felt that all of Borneo, except Brunei, should be Indonesian territory and thus initiated a border war with Malaysia to claim the Malaysian provinces that bordered Kalimantan, Indonesia's territory on Borneo. The PKI supported Sukarno's action, but the military was opposed to the move. There is evidence that the United States supported the Indonesian army on this issue. This had little effect on Sukarno, who was determined to proceed regardless of the opposition.

The *konfrontasi* was costly for Indonesia at a time when the country's economy was precarious. Inflation was out of control, foreign investment was down, and government corruption was rampant. It was during these years that Sukarno commissioned the building of several large statues and a sports stadium in Jakarta. These expensive and highly visible projects were touted as illustrating the power and glory of a mighty nation when in fact what they did was put a strain on already dangerously dwindling national finances.

The Unites States was concerned that communism was gaining power in Sukarno's government, and in December 1963 President Lyndon Johnson withdrew economic aid to Indonesia, although he approved covert aid for the Indonesian army. He saw the military force as a deterrent to communism in the archipelago. In March 1964 an angry Sukarno's response was to tell the United States to go to hell.

Indonesia's economy grew steadily worse as prices rose, intensified by food shortages. In 1965 prices increased by 700 percent—rice prices even higher than that. The government debt was estimated at 300 percent, and the salaries of government workers did not come close to keeping pace with the skyrocketing inflation. Army officers, especially, resorted to bribery and smuggling to make ends meet. In August 1965 Sukarno withheld Indonesian membership in such organizations as the World Bank, IMF, and Interpol while he encouraged alliances with communist countries in Asia.

Sukarno struggled to maintain a three-way alliance among the government, the Communist Party, and the army. This was never a successful union. The liberal PKI supported the peasants, the conservative army envisioned capitalist policies as the way to move the country forward, and Sukarno tried to keep peace between them while maintaining his nationalist ideals. Sukarno was a socialist, and the fact that he chose communism over capitalism as a means of drawing his country's beleaguered economy out of its downward spin was not surprising. Communism seemed to be the best political system to distribute the country's resources equitably. Sukarno needed desperately to improve the standard of living for the impoverished villagers who had been exploited under the Dutch. He had believed that independence would bring them a higher standard of living. But years of colonial rule, Japanese occupation, revolution, an ever-increasing birth rate and subsequent rapidly increasing population, the lack of trained personnel to fill essential government positions, an escalating level of corruption among government workers, and an increasing level of corruption between government workers and the military all contributed to Sukarno's failing government. Whether communist, mercantilist, or capitalist the new government was not equipped to deal with the many serious problems it faced. When Western governments became more and more critical of Sukarno and refused to lend Indonesia money, his response was to sever connections with the IMF, the World Bank, and Interpol.

The 1965 Coup

On September 30, 1965, seven military officers were murdered. (See Chapter 1, "Night of the Generals.") This incident caused panic in Indonesia, and a period of chaos followed. By mid-October fear had set in and inflation was out of control. Old scores between *santri* and *abangan,* military personnel and the communists, and peasants and ethnic Chinese were being settled by murder. In some areas of Java the rivers indeed ran red with blood. By the end of 1965 hundreds of thousands of communists, ethnic Chinese, and liberal Muslims (*abangan*) were dead. These killings were committed with the self-serving justification that the victims were communists and that their executions were carried out in the spirit of preserving the republic. After all, it was the PKI that spearheaded the killing of the army officers on September 30. Or was it? This theory was never proven true, or false for that matter. What did happen that night was the beginning of the death of communism in Indonesia and the assurance of the end of Sukarno's leadership of the Indonesian government. Major-General Suharto was the man who emerged in control of the government, who stopped the rioting and looting, and who sent troops to control lawless regions.

Suharto actually began his military career in the Dutch army and later served with the Indonesian revolutionary forces against the Dutch. Suharto considered Dutch government policies to be wrong, primarily because it was the Dutch who had instituted them. However, as the Suharto government developed, it came to resemble the capitalist colonial government in many respects. This was quite a contrast to the policies of the socialist Sukarno and had a dramatic effect on the economy.

ECONOMIC RECOVERY AND SUHARTO

In March 1966 Sukarno—who was still president—agreed to give Suharto extensive power, which the general immediately used to curb communist activities. In July Suharto asked the IMF to return to Indonesia and help the country with its financial problems. With the assistance of his foreign minister, Adam Malik, and his coordinator of economic policy, Hamengkubuwono, the sultan of Yogyakarta, Suharto's government made great strides in the economic recovery of Indonesia. In a conference in Tokyo in September 1966, Indonesian officials met with Western trade leaders, and the IMF granted Indonesia an eighteen-month moratorium on the payments of its debts. Early in 1967 the government guaranteed that there would be no future nationalization of property and that companies could send their profits abroad. Later that year, in March, the Indonesian People's Consultative Assembly (MPR) named Suharto acting president of Indonesia; this move stripped Sukarno of his power. At that time the Consultative Assembly met to select the president and vice president of Indonesia. In this respect it was similar to the U.S. electoral college, although the MPR has other responsibilities as well. Indonesia now elects its presidents directly and not through the MPR.

Suharto called his plan for governing Indonesia the New Order. Targeting economic rehabilitation and development, the New Order altered the course of Indonesia's domestic policies through a series of five-year plans Suharto labeled with the acronym Repelita. The aim of the New Order was to achieve these goals through a military-dominated administration that would include advice from Western-educated Indonesian economists. In the 1960s many young Indonesians traveled to the United States and other Western countries to study. An especially notable group attended the University of California at Berkeley, where its members studied economics. They became known as the Berkeley Mafia, or "technocrats," when they took up positions in Suharto's government. Their advice was generally sound, and had they been more forceful in expressing their opinion of the government's weaknesses over the years, the 1997 economic crisis might have been much less severe. But these economists were not as close

Suharto announces a new cabinet in 1966 (Bettmann/Corbis)

to Suharto as the military groups were. They certainly were not secure enough in their positions to criticize the awarding of government contracts to Suharto's family members and friends. Even as it became apparent that unorthodox deals were being made and that government contracts were circumventing the legally required channels, few government officials spoke out about this practice.

In August 1968 the oil companies owned by the army became part of Pertamina, creating a government monopoly on oil in Indonesia. In 1969 Suharto announced his first five-year plan—Repelita I. The primary purpose of this plan was to rebuild Indonesia's economy and to make the country self-sufficient in rice production. At that time 60 percent of the country's budget depended upon foreign aid.

Early in the Suharto years accusations of government corruption were heard, and by 1970 the voices were louder. For example, Suharto's close friend, Lim Siew Liong, and the president's younger half brother, Probosutejo, undersold many small clove farmers and were able to establish a monopoly on that market. Although spices are no longer exported to Europe in huge quantities, they are still a valuable domestic product. Cloves are a primary ingredient in Indonesia's *kretek* cigarettes. These popular clove cigarettes are smoked by Indonesians throughout the archipelago.

Repelita II, Suharto's second five-year plan, introduced in 1973, concentrated on providing food, shelter, and clothing for the Indonesian people. It would expand and equitably distribute social welfare benefits and provide more employment opportunities. However, the government's policies were becoming less democratic than they were at the beginning of Suharto's presidency. The double problem of falling oil prices and an unexpected drought that resulted in rice shortages gave the government cause for alarm. To make matters worse, Pertamina, the huge government oil company, defaulted on Canadian and U.S. loans, forcing the government to cover about $650 million in Pertamina's debts. A May 20, 1975, report to the Consultative Assembly stated that Pertamina's debts totaled over $10 billion. In March 1976, Ibnu Sutowo was relieved of his position as chief of Pertamina.

East Timor

To add to the government's economic woes, in December 1975 Indonesian troops invaded East Timor. At that time East Timor, a free portion of an island owned by Indonesia, was under the control of a left-leaning government. The Suharto government was conservative, and when a new Portuguese regime relinquished control of all of its colonies, the Indonesian government railed against the presence of a liberal (in this case meaning communist-leaning) nation among its islands. Indonesian forces invaded and quickly claimed victory in East Timor, but its rule there was short-lived. After much conflict East Timor became an independent country on May 20, 2002.

Early Charges of Government Corruption

Criticism of government corruption was becoming evident in the late 1970s as the army began to play an even more prominent role in Suharto's programs. Still, the people were more prosperous than they had ever been under Sukarno. They had put up with injustice under the colonial government, so the complaints of corruption and cronyism did not incense the populace to the point that they took any overt action. In addition to a higher living standard, few Indonesians wanted to make an issue of government dishonesty when a large share of the administration's support came from the military. The army kept the peace and had strong government backing. To oppose the military would most certainly attract the attention of the government, and that would not be without serious consequences.

Upon election to his third term, Suharto announced the government's next five-year economic plan, Repelita III. It emphasized a more equal distribution of wealth throughout the entire population and increased national stability. It also called for self-sufficiency in agricultural production. In the early 1980s oil production was on the rise and with it, government revenue. However, investment in Indonesia's businesses was declining due to increasing government restrictions on foreign investment. In the mid-1980s the government concentrated on growth in the manufacturing sector—textiles, shoes, electronics, and furniture to name some of the more prosperous businesses that exported goods. The GNP (gross national product—the amount of goods produced by a country in a given period) grew at an average rate of 7 percent per year from 1987 to 1997. Indonesia was considered to be an emerging industrialized economy.

Censorship of the Press

In 1984 Suharto's forth five-year plan, Repelita IV, was announced. It called for development of agriculture, especially aiming for self-sufficiency in rice production. It also promoted development of Indonesian industries, specifically industrial machinery production. Despite the country's prosperity, rumors of government dishonesty were on the rise, and in 1986 an Australian newspaper published an article on corruption in the Suharto government. Prior to this, incidents of nepotism and cronyism had been referred to indirectly, but no specific cases were cited. This was largely because of Indonesia's strict censorship of the press. The Suharto government carried suppression of the press to an extreme. For example, black felt pens were used on imported magazines to mark over "offensive" words and photographs, such as a picture of a woman wearing a bikini bathing suit. The government actually employed people to go through foreign newspapers and magazines for the purpose of inking out text and pictures considered to be offensive. There were also restrictions on videotapes and R-rated movies that were allowed into the country. This law resulted in a brisk business in black market R-rated films.

Nepotism

In 1988 a government audit revealed that over half of all government-headed businesses in Indonesia were financially unstable. In 1990 the Jakarta stock market fell sharply. In the midst of this worsening economic news the government granted Suharto's son Tommy a monopoly on clove imports. A significant number of small farmers had to sell their clove orchards as Tommy Suharto lowered prices to corner the market on this essential ingredient in Indonesia's *kretek* cigarettes.

In 1992 Suharto did away with the Intergovernmental Group of Indonesia (IGGA), a Dutch-based organization that had provided foreign assistance to Indonesia since 1969. When he outlawed the IGGA, Suharto remarked that the Dutch could go to hell, a comment reminiscent of an earlier financially troubled Sukarno. In 1993 Repelita V was announced as a plan to strengthen and consolidate development in every sector of the government and to prepare the nation to enter Repelita VI.

SEPARATIST MOVEMENTS AND VIOLENCE

The most serious economic matter facing the Indonesian government today is the constant threat of provinces and regions breaking away from the nation. The Indonesian government must come to a mutually agreeable solution to the dilemmas facing those regions seeking separate status or face the possible collapse of the nation. As noted in the brief summaries below, the turmoil in six locations in Indonesia is blamed almost exclusively on two factors. The first of these is an intense dissatisfaction with the unfair distribution of the resources and subsequent wealth in their provinces. The second is favoritism on the part of the government to outsiders—most often Javanese. In West Timor the trouble is directly related to the independence of East Timor, literally the other half of the island on which West Timor is located.

Aceh

Many historians believe that Islam came first to Indonesia through Aceh, in northern Sumatra, around 700. It was not for another nine or ten centuries that Aceh became part of what is now Indonesia—when colonialism was dominant in Southeast Asia. The British were the first to claim Aceh. However, the Dutch took it over from the British in 1824, agreeing to allow the region to maintain its independence. That agreement was short lived, and in 1873 the Netherlands invaded Aceh. It was a long, drawn out war that continued until 1942, the onset of World War II. When Indonesia was declared an independent nation in 1949, the Kingdom of Aceh was included as part of Indonesia although it had not actually been a Dutch possession. Later, in 1959, the government of Indonesia gave Aceh "special territory"

Muslim women praying in Aceh, Sumatra, February 2003 (AFP/Corbis)

status. This meant little other than some degree of autonomy in religious and educational matters. Although the government in Jakarta made concessions to Aceh, some Acehnese were still determined to have an independent Islamic state. In 1976 Tengku Hasan M. di Tiro established a new movement, Aceh Merdeka (Free Aceh). Since 1980 the Indonesian government has referred to this group as Gerombolan Pengacau Keamananan (GPK), which translates roughly as "bunch of disturbers of safety." Beginning in the late 1970s the government arrested many members of the Free Aceh movement and curtailed their activities. This ended in 1989, when a new group—the Aceh-Sumatra National Liberation Front (ASNFL)—appeared on the scene and carried out attacks against government troops and installations as well as the police.

Acehnese are most critical of the government's policy of entitlement to the region's resources—most notably Aceh's rich natural gas and oil reserves. They claim that not only does the central government reap most of the profits from these resources, but also most of the jobs in the oil and natural gas fields go to Javanese while the people of Aceh live in poverty. Another major complaint is with the government's transmigration policy, whereby people from high-density population areas on the islands of Java and Madura were relocated to less-populated areas of the country. The Acehnese are critical of the awarding of prime coastal and agricultural lands to Javanese transmigrants while they have little coastal property for fishing and prime land for their rice fields.

But perhaps the underlying issue in Aceh's discontent is religion. Unlike the Javanese, the Sumatrans tend to be devout Muslims. They are not fundamentalists, as evidenced by the major role that women play in their society. They are, however, quite different culturally from other Indonesians. Their language is not Malay based, and their adaptation of Islam involves incorporation of religion into economic and social justice.

Frustration had been brewing for some time, and in 1990 Indonesian security forces reacted to the actions of Aceh Merdeka and initiated an operation that resulted in extensive death and destruction. Amnesty International reported that between 1989 and 1992 approximately 2,000 people were killed in Aceh in military actions. The human rights group Forum, which oversees 75 nongovernmental organizations (NGOs) in Aceh, has compiled more than 650 reports of military atrocities in Aceh, including torture and death. The Free Aceh movement is now usually referred to as GAM (Gerakan Aceh Merdeka).

In an attempt to address these concerns, the Aceh autonomy law was signed in August 2001. It gave Aceh the power to determine its own judicial and educational systems and allowed it to increase revenues from oil and gas resources to 70 percent, twice the percentage previously allowed. In December 2002 another document was signed by Indonesian and Acehnese representatives assuring Aceh an even greater share of the island's resources. In May 2003 the agreement collapsed and Megawati ordered the Indonesian army to bomb Aceh.

Riau

Riau is another Sumatran province that resents the central government's use of revenues from its oil, natural gas, timber, agriculture, and ocean products. Riau province encompasses a sector of Sumatra located on the island's east coast and several offshore islands in the South China Sea—located along the well-traveled Strait of Malacca. Its people's complaint is similar to that of the residents of resource-rich Aceh and Papua—they provide the central government with products that bring tremendous revenue into the country, and in return they receive meager government funding for projects in their province. An August 2000 article in the *Christian Science Monitor* estimates the amount of oil Riau produces to be as high as 65 percent of Indonesia's total oil reserves. Caltex Indonesia is a major buyer of Riau's oil. The people of Riau, a significant number of whom live below the poverty line, resent the huge foreign company (Caltex is American owned) that brings in its own skilled workers and hires locals for only low-paying jobs. As a result of this dissatisfaction, the Free Riau Movement was established in 1998, when Suharto left office. The government has made some concessions in recent months, and Caltex has agreed to support sustainable development in the region. Whether these steps will be sufficient to appease the people of Riau remains to be seen.

Papua

The Indonesian province of Papua—formerly known as West Irian or Irian Jaya—covers the western half of the island of New Guinea. The other half is the independent nation of Papua New Guinea. Papua is rich in minerals, including copper and gold, and is similar to Aceh in several respects. A major similarity is Papua's use of arms to protest its status as an Indonesian province. When the Indonesian revolution against the Dutch ended, Papua, or Irian Jaya as it was called then, remained a Dutch possession. In 1962 it came under UN control, but in 1963, after Indonesian protest, it came under the jurisdiction of Indonesia on the condition that there would be a popular vote in 1969 to determine if the people of Irian Jaya wanted to be a permanent part of Indonesia. In 1969 it did become a province of Indonesia, although Papuans say that election was dishonest. Papuan protestors are calling for a rejection of that transfer and now demand that the United Nations revoke the 1969 election and declare Papua a free country.

In the early 1960s Papuans opposed to joining Indonesia formed the Free Papua Movement (Organisasi Papua Merdeka—OPM). The OPM has conducted guerrilla warfare for over thirty years, but until recently its efforts attracted little international attention. Like Aceh, most of the revenue from the sale of minerals in Papua is turned over to the government in Jakarta; and like the Acehnese, the Papuans resent the loss of money that would provide them with a higher standard of living. The Freeport copper mine in Papua is enormous, probably worth more than $35 billion. As is the case in Aceh, transmigration has brought thousands of Javanese to the province, where they now disproportionately outnumber the indigenous people and hold most of the prized civil service jobs. An element of religious concern is present as well, as about 60 percent of Papua's population are Protestant and most of the Javanese transmigrants are Muslims.

Incidents of torture and violence against Papuans have been reported, and they are often related to disagreements between local communities and foreign workers. One of the most publicized acts of violence was the death of independence activist Theys Hiyo Eluay. He was found dead on November 18, 2001, near the capital Port Numbay (formerly Jayapura). Eluay's body was found in his crashed car, and Papuan police said that preliminary evidence indicated Eluay was murdered. In February 2003, at court martial proceedings in Surabaya, an army officer testified that a private in the Indonesian army strangled Eluay when the independence leader refused to drop his efforts for a Papuan independence movement. Seven officers and soldiers have been brought up on charges related to Eluay's death.

Maluku

Violence throughout the archipelago is a tremendous drain on Indonesia's resources. Since its upsurge in 1998 no president has been able to bring this problem under government control, although the sobering effect of the Sulawesi and Bali bombings in fall 2002 seems to have slowed the incidents of violence in eastern Indonesia. The brutality in eastern Indonesia between Muslims and Christians has received a great deal of media attention, and the Indonesian government seemed unable to control the panic that permeated this region and affected both Christian and Muslim families. The island of Ambon witnessed especially horrible incidents of bloodshed and property damage. The situation was exacerbated by the influx of outsiders such as the anti-Christian militant group Laskar Jihad, which trained its members in warfare techniques on Java. This organization was active in many brutal attacks against Christians in Maluku, where continuous incidents of Christian–Muslim violence were reported on a regular basis during the period from 2000 to 2002. It is interesting to note that Laskar Jihad announced it was disbanding immediately following the Bali bombing incident on October 12, 2002. Indeed, the *Jakarta Post* on October 16, 2002, reported that about 700 members of Laskar Jihad left Maluku for their homes on Java a few days after the bombing. Despite this announcement, signs of Laskar Jihad activity were still

Members of the militant Muslim organization, Laskar Jihad, in Ambon, Maluku, October 2002 (Reuters News Media/Corbis)

evident in Maluku in summer 2003. At its height, this militant organization had about 3,000 volunteers in Maluku and about 750 in Central Sulawesi. The group denied their "disbanding" had anything to do with the Bali bombings. The Java headquarters of Laskar Jihad was located in a village about an hour and a half drive from Yogyakarta. An Islamic boarding school—a *pesantren*—was the militant organization's operational headquarters. Laskar Jihad was established in January 2000 for the purpose of opposing what its members perceived as a movement to form a Christian state within Indonesia. This state was believed to consist of Maluku, West Papua, and North Sulawesi. The leadership of Laskar Jihad further supported the theory that members of the former Republic of South Maluku, now based in the Netherlands, were behind this movement. Laskar Jihad claimed that the ultimate goal of the Christian group was to drive Muslims out of Maluku. The militant Islamic group labeled the Malukans, whom they claimed were killing Muslims, *kafir harbi* (belligerent infidels). To kill any of these infidels would have assured the slayers of martyrdom.

The high level of brutality on the part of both Christians and Muslims in Maluku has made it difficult to find a common ground where the opposing sides can come together.

Maluku, once known as the Spice Islands, was an early stronghold of the Dutch and one of the few regions where missionaries converted a significant portion of the population to Christianity. Maluku had actually declared its independence from Indonesia on April 25, 1950, calling itself the Republik Maluku Selatan (RSM, Republic of the South Moluccas). The Indonesian government tried to negotiate a settlement with the leaders, but when that failed, government troops were sent to Buru and Ceram. At that time, most of the young men of Maluku were soldiers serving abroad in the Royal Netherlands Army; thus they were not available to take up arms for the RSM. Consequently, the residents of Maluku were not able to turn back the Indonesian army. They appealed to the United Nations, stating that Maluku was supposed to become a free and independent state when Indonesia was granted its independence, but that matter was never settled. Eventually the United Nations Commission on Indonesia was disbanded, and the matter of Malukan independence was never resolved. Many Malukans migrated to Holland in 1957 when Sukarno exiled the Dutch from Indonesia. The RSM still exists in the Netherlands but has little international status.

Despite earlier differences, Christians and Muslims had lived in relative harmony for decades in Maluku. But the economic meltdown of 1997 triggered terrible violence in these islands, as it did in so many places throughout Indonesia. A growing problem is the flight of Christian refugees to neighboring Sulawesi. Although Sulawesi is predominantly Muslim, a sizable Christian population lives there, and all the elements are present for a religious rebellion similar to that in Maluku.

Sulawesi

Rebellion is not new to Sulawesi. The Permesta revolt that took place under Sukarno was one of the region's earliest protests. Permesta, a modernist Islamic group, later joined with religious movements such as Darul Islam and the PRRI uprising in Sumatra in the late 1950s. Like other areas of unrest, Sulawesi is rich in natural resources, nickel, gold, sulphur, and diamonds; and like Aceh and Papua, its people resent the fact that they profit little from the sale of their island's products. To some degree, increasing tensions in Sulawesi are attributed to the many Christians who come to the island seeking a safe haven from the violence and brutality in Maluku. The conservative Islamic regions of Sulawesi are not pleased with this influx of Christians, and there have been myriad incidents of violence. Laskar Jihad forces were, and most likely still are, present in Sulawesi and have attacked Christians there. Counterattacks by the Christian Red Force escalate the already volatile situation and have people asking when—and how—this will all end.

Sulawesi has had a history of supporting the central government. B. J. Habibie, Indonesia's third president, is from this island, and it is generally accepted that his poor showing in the 1999 election has curtailed Sulawesi's loyalty to Jakarta.

Kalimantan

Dyaks comprise the largest group of indigenous people of Kalimantan, Indonesia's province on Borneo. It should be noted that there are many groups of Dyaks, for example, upriver Dyaks, lowland Dyaks, and coastal Dyaks. Although today many Dyaks are Christian, their ingrained spirit-worshiping culture differs vastly from that of Islamic cultures. In 1996 and 1997 a number of families from Madura, an island off the coast of Java whose people are dedicated Muslims, were sent to West Kalimantan. This move was made through the country's transmigration program. The Dyaks hold the land and what it produces in the highest regard, and being required to share their place with outsiders was the primary cause of resentment that manifested itself in blatant interethnic violence. The incidents of murder numbered about 600, and more than 1,000 houses were destroyed by fire. The mayhem was so severe that 105,000 Madurese left the region and returned to Java and Madura.

West Timor

West Timor, still Indonesian territory, was the site of refugee camps that were established during the tempestuous period immediately after East Timor's vote for independence. At the peak of the fighting between East Timor and the Indonesian militias that had strongly opposed East Timor's bid for independence, East Timorese citizens either fled to the hills of their own country or were forcibly moved to the camps in West Timor. In September 2000, a year after the independence vote in East Timor, NGOs were assisting the refugees located in the West Timor camps who wanted to return to their homes in East

Timor. In protest against the East Timorese returning home, pro-Indonesian militia forces rampaged through the camps and brutally killed five United Nations workers. They also destroyed the offices of the UN High Commissioner for Refugees. Members of the militias were living in the West Timor camps, where they not only terrorized the refugees but also actively sabotaged East Timor's progression toward achieving independence at every opportunity. Although matters in West Timor are now somewhat quieter, the situation remains tense. It is unknown when life along either side of the Timor border will be peaceful.

Indonesia is making some headway in moderating the fervor of its separatist movements. Violence and dissatisfaction with the Jakarta government are still rampant in all of these regions, and until the people are given a bigger voice in the governance of their areas, the future of the nation will remain in jeopardy.

TRANSMIGRATION

Indonesia's transmigration program was ostensibly established to help the poor find work and to give landless families from overcrowded areas of the country the opportunity to farm. Government policy makers thought that balanced population distribution and regional development would not only provide a higher standard of living for the transmigrants but would result in an increase in the country's production of agricultural goods. The transmigration program became active during Suharto's Repelita III, beginning in earnest in 1979. It was scaled back starting in 1986, when the government faced budgetary constraints. The Dutch actually initiated a transmigration program in the twentieth century; it was under Suharto's New Order that it expanded dramatically.

Indonesia's transmigration program targeted people from overpopulated areas, usually Java and Madura, and moved them to locations with sparse populations. From 1969 to 1974 the government targeted 38,700 people for transmigration, and all but a few actually did participate in the program. The period 1974–1979 showed a big increase in transmigrants, but though 250,000 were targeted, only 118,000 moved. The program was most successful from 1979 to 1984, during which time 500,000 people were targeted for relocation and 535,000 moved. For the first and only time, more people migrated than were scheduled to leave their villages. By 1984–1989 the program had regressed, and of the 750,000 targeted for transmigration in those five years only 230,000 actually took part in the program. The figures for 1989–1994 are incomplete, but it is known that 600,000 Indonesians were targeted for migration during 1994–1999, though only 300,000 moved to a new location. In August 2000 the Indonesian government ended the transmigration program.

Although it was originally praised as a means of providing poor farmers with land and the opportunity for a better life, transmigration, like many of Suharto's government projects, had ulterior motives. For example, in 1994/1995 a development plan called the Integrated Economic Development Zone (Kawasan Pengembangan Ekonomi Terpadu—KAPET) was initiated. KAPET, a plan to develop the infrastructure necessary to obtain the rich resources in eastern Indonesia, was one of Habibie's ideas. It was visualized that relocating farmers, loggers, and mining transmigrants would supply the labor force for the region's agribusiness, timber, and mining companies. This plan proved unsuccessful for several reasons. After the 1997 economic crisis the International Monetary Fund provided the Indonesian government with funds to assist with the country's many grave financial problems. Those monies had strings attached; for example, the IMF required that the Indonesian government cut back on state-subsidized programs that were losing money. KAPET was one of those programs. Another problem was the animosity between the transmigrants and the timber companies. The transmigrants were mainly farmers, not company workers, and this difference in outlook gave rise to many problems. A third quandary was the antagonistic relationship between the transmigrants and the indigenous people. The resentment was present when the first migrants arrived, and it grew worse with the passage of time.

Although reasonably successful at first, transmigration never proved to be as popular as the government had hoped. Among the many reasons for this, perhaps the most important was the separation of villagers from friends and families. Family connections in Indonesia are extremely strong, with generation after generation of families living in the same villages and towns. The plan to move people to distant locations, where even occasional visits to their native villages would be expensive, was never well accepted. The policy became even more undesirable when the transmigrants realized that many of the new locations would not support additional agricultural demands. Obviously the people already living in those areas were not pleased with the arrival of outsiders whose livelihood would require a portion of the region's already limited farmlands. In regions where reasonable production requires a large spread of land, dividing that land to accommodate outsiders was not a program that appealed to long-time residents.

OVERSEAS EMPLOYMENT

A large number of Indonesians are employed abroad. The majority of these are men and women who cannot find gainful employment in Indonesia or who can earn much more money by working in a foreign country. In almost all of these cases the workers are sending a significant portion of their salaries back to their families in Indonesia. Most overseas workers hold positions in factories and mines or as domestic servants.

According to government migration statistics in 1979–1980, more than 7,650 Indonesians were working in the Middle East, 720 in Malaysia and Singapore, and over 2,007 in other countries. Five years later over 35,550 were employed in the Middle East, over 6,000 in Malaysia and Singapore, and more than 4,000 in other countries. By 1990–1991 the numbers showed another significant rise as the government reported 60,450 Indonesians were working in the Middle East, 18,500 in Malaysia and Singapore, and 5,100 in other countries. Notice the sharp increase in Indonesian workers in Malaysia and Singapore during that period. In 1994–1995 those Indonesians working in the Middle East numbered just under 100,000, in Malaysia and Singapore 57,300—more than three times as many as in 1991—and in other countries 19,100. By 1999–2000 Indonesians working in Malaysia and Singapore outnumbered those working in the Middle East, 187,600 to 153,900. That same year 63,000 were employed in other countries. These numbers vacillate over the twenty-one years for which figures are available, but 1983–1984 is the only period during which more Indonesian men than women were employed overseas. Under further review, the data for 1995–1996 and 1996–1997 show a tremendous jump in the number of men and women working in Malaysia and Singapore. The figure for overseas workers in those countries jumped from 46,800 in 1995–1996 to 329,000 in 1996–1997. This reflects the declining economic situation in Indonesia during that period. Given Indonesia's current economic situation, it is expected the country's diaspora will continue to increase.

1997 ECONOMIC MELTDOWN

In July 1997 a financial crisis hit Thailand that triggered an economic emergency across Asia. It was devastating to the economies of Korea,

Malaysia, and Thailand, but Indonesia was especially hard hit. The time was a particularly bad one for such a disaster, as a severe drought that year caused rice production to fall well below the country's need. In the fall of 1997 the Indonesian economy was so fragile that in October the Indonesian rupiah fell from a little over Rp 2000/US$1 to Rp 4000/US$1. Conditions worsened, and three months later the rate fell to Rp 10,000/US$1. In short, what an Indonesian consumer purchased for Rp 4,000 in October cost Rp 10,000 in January. Salaries did not rise accordingly, and riots and protest movements occurred throughout the country as the government took steps to counter the drastic economic downswing. Indonesia faced a bleak future.

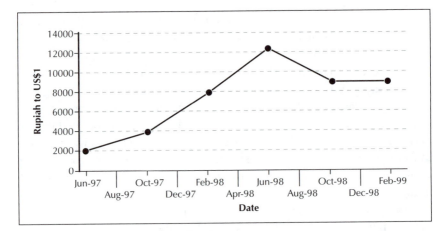

Figure 2.1: Comparison of the Rupiah and the Dollar, June 1997–February 1999

Source: FX Converter: http://www.oanda.com/converter/classic

The situation in Indonesia was so bleak that international financial organizations were called in to help. The IMF approved a $42 billion loan to Indonesia in November 1997, but to the surprise of many Indonesian economists, in January 1998 Suharto announced a budget contrary to IMF loan criteria, irritating the international financial organization. As food prices skyrocketed, riots broke out across the country. Incidents of violence were first reported in East and West Java, Sulawesi, Sumbawa, and Flores, but they soon spread across the country. In spite of this, and almost as though they were out of touch with the people, in March 1998 the MPR elected Suharto to a seventh term. Students were the first to register violent disapproval. Protest movements erupted on campuses throughout the country. In Jakarta there were violent riots, including a number of rapes. The object of the brutality was often the Chinese. This was reminiscent of the days following the September 1965 Night of the Generals. The Chinese had fared better than the Indonesians under the Dutch colonial government, and although that was more than half a century ago, ethnic Chinese are still targeted for violence when Indonesia is in perilous times. As angry mobs torched and looted stores and roamed the streets, international newscasts beamed satellite pictures of the rioting around the world. The lack of government control of the worsening situation gave prospective investors cause for concern and further hampered any hope for a quick end to the country's financial woes.

Issues Suharto's Government Failed to Address

On May 2, 1998, Suharto resigned the presidency and was succeeded by his vice president, Baharuddin Jusuf (B. J.) Habibie. The new president worked with the IMF and used its funds to support banks threatened with closure due to massive withdrawals. Many banks had loaned money without securing adequate collateral and were teetering on the verge of collapse. Still the violence continued to increase. The student protestors, especially, saw Habibie as Suharto's crony and were adamant that a new, uncorrupt government be established in Jakarta. The violence spreading across the country seemed certain to escalate as the June 1999 elections approached.

Until the Asian economic crisis in fall 1997, the Indonesian economy had grown at approximately 7 percent annually for thirty years despite significant government corruption. In less than four decades, the country had gone from an agriculturally based economy to an industrial economy. Agriculture was still vital to the country, and although the number of workers in the agriculture sector declined due to improved farming methods, the government continued to provide subsidies to the farmers, primarily in the form of fertilizer. The use of technology, however, had not improved agricultural yields enough to keep up with the growing population, and farmers still relied heavily on government support.

Although Indonesia had some success in bringing down its birthrate, overpopulation remained a drain on the country's resources. A major problem developed when agricultural lands would be divided again and again as new generations of children inherited increasingly smaller acreages of property from their parents. As the size of a family's rice fields became smaller, it was evident that not everyone could stay in the village and work the land. Consequently, large numbers of

Indonesian president Suharto (center) and Vice President B. J. Habibie (right) arrive at the presidential palace in Jakarta to announce Suharto's resignation as Indonesia's second president. (AFP/Corbis)

young men and women moved to urban areas to look for work. This caused an excessive labor force to accumulate in cities, and the result was massive unemployment and ultimately expanding ghettos.

At first the industrial sector, concentrating on export goods such as clothing, processed food, and furniture, had considerable success. But policies such as minimum wage and competition from other Asian nations resulted in a lowering of income from those products. There is little question that until fall 1997 the number of Indonesians living in poverty had declined during the Suharto years. It was also clear, however, that President Suharto and his cronies, conglomerates, and politically connected businessmen friends who had far more than their share of the country's wealth were soon going to have to face up to the problem of growing unemployment in the country's large urban centers.

Possible Solutions

Economists met and agreed to make many changes, but economic reform in Indonesia depended in large part on the restructuring of the country's banks. In November 1997, sixteen banks were liquidated, a move that caused panic among depositors who feared loss of their funds. As a consequence, mass withdrawal of money from many Indonesian banks ensued. There was no deposit guarantee in Indonesia's banks at that time, and the adverse effect of the crisis affected even Indonesia's established financial institutions. (U.S. banks insure accounts up to a set amount, thus protecting their depositors' money.) At the end of 1998 Indonesia's Central Bank initiated a full deposit guarantee, although many saw this move as too little too late. Earlier, in January 1998, the Indonesian Banking Restructuring Agency (IBRA) was set up to oversee the restructuring of threatened banks and to manage funds for bank reorganization. It was estimated that the cost of the restructuring would be Rp 300 trillion (US$30 million); how to finance it was a sensitive issue. The government wanted to issue bonds to cover over three quarters of the amount, but the MPR objected. There seemed to be a lack of either political agreement or government policy.

How did Indonesia go from being such an economic success story to economic chaos? Economists cite a number of reasons. The one most often repeated is that the government was simply too involved in business. Suharto's cronies and family members were given far too many "good business deals" rather than allowing the marketplace to make that determination. Clearly corruption in government was a primary factor in the 1997 crisis. Later, when Habibie became president and the press was subject to less stringent restrictions, the stories of nepotism and cronyism were widely publicized. This made it more difficult for the government to divorce itself from the country's economic problems.

In the 1980s and early 1990s vast amounts of money from overseas were invested in Indonesian businesses. Then in fall 1997, when the rupiah fell, the stability of Suharto's government came under a scrutiny that it had previously avoided, and people were alarmed at what they learned. The government had failed to heed its own financial advisers, who had warned that there was a serious need for more effective regulations on business and commerce. The "in" conglomerates, cronies, and relatives saw these ideas as restrictive, and the technocrats did not have the power to overrule them. Money alone could clearly not fix Indonesia's economic woes. More effective controls were needed during the Suharto regime—controls that did not favor a few select businesses regardless of whether or not these businesses were good for the economy and the people of Indonesia. To get the economy back on track would require an honest government that was supportive of extensive changes in Indonesia's business policies and a judiciary that would back up those changes.

THE JUDICIARY

In summer 2002 Dato Param Cumaraswamy reported that the state of Indonesia's justice system was worse than he expected. Cumaraswamy, a Malaysian lawyer, was conducting a ten-day investigation of Indonesia's judiciary's independence for the United Nations. He further stated that the UN often had asked that a representative be sent to Indonesia, for the international organization frequently sensed that the judicial system was in trouble. This was particularly the case under the Suharto government, when state intervention in court cases was common. The UN report concluded that there was widespread corruption in the courts and urged the government to make elimination of these dishonest men and women its highest priority. It also stated that corruption in the courts, although excessive under Suharto, continued to escalate through mid-2002. It is speculated that the cause for this would likely be that the country's lawyers and judges are commonly trained in the large universities on Java. Upon completion of law school these men and women return to their home provinces, taking with them the ways and methods of the urban Java courts. Thus, the practice of judicial corruption is carried throughout the island chain in much the same way.

The nongovernmental organization Indonesian Corruption Watch (ICW) conducted a study of courts in Jakarta, Medan, Surabaya, and Yogyakarta (all cities on Java). The ICW concluded that although victims varied from city to city, the manner in which judicial officials extracted money followed a general pattern. When a criminal case was filed, court officials asked for a fee—the amount requested depended on the wealth of the person involved. Once court proceedings began lawyers might choose judges, but the most potentially profitable cases were almost always handled by district court chiefs. Verdicts could then be negotiated through the prosecutor or directly with the judge. When judges postponed a verdict, it was often an indication that the defendant should meet with the judge to provide "special compensatory consideration." The procedure was similar in civil courts, with additional fees requested to show gratitude to judges. Corruption in commercial courts might include fictitious creditors and the appointment of court receivers. Here, as in the criminal and civil courts, money could hasten or slow down a case and could raise or lessen charges, which could result in prison or city arrest. The ICW commented that the high level of corruption in the courts could only be controlled through public knowledge of the activities of Indonesia's lawyers and judges.

The UN report supports the ICW's plea for public control of the judiciary, citing that for three years no court had allowed law students or judiciary watchdogs to have copies of their rulings—this despite the fact that court rulings are supposed to be public records. The ICW and UN investigator Cumaraswamy concurred on the high degree of corruption among the members of Indonesia's legal profession. Both noted that along with other problems, procedures for qualifications for admission to the bar were not adequately provided. In short, the legal profession lacked regulations, and lawyers lacked discipline.

In his report to the UN, Cumaraswamy noted that Indonesia's economic and political elite could carry out any crime with impunity—it would be just a matter of price to have charges dismissed.

The sad state of the judiciary is viewed by many as one of the major causes of the 1997 economic meltdown in Indonesia. Failure of judges to rule against illegal government organizations and activities intensified, and criminal activity rose through the upper levels of government, setting the scene for grave economic problems down the line. Had Indonesia's judges been open and fair-minded in their decisions, many of the illegal activities of government officials and the Suharto family would never have reached the proportions that they did. Indonesian judges have long looked the other way as contracts favoring Suharto's friends and families were approved and sanctioned as legal.

Not all news about the judiciary is bad. The BBC News World Edition dated September 4, 2002, reported that Akbar Tanjung, speaker of Indonesia's parliament, was sentenced to three years in prison for his diversion of $4.5 million in state funds. Media polls had shown that 60–70 percent of the people of Indonesia thought he was guilty, and the case garnered considerable publicity. Tanjung appealed the court's verdict, and according to Indonesian law he cannot be jailed until the case is settled. In contrast to the verdict in the Tanjung case is the case of Suharto's son Tommy, who got off with a fifteen-year jail sentence for murdering a judge. Ridding the state courts of corruption will clearly be a major undertaking and will probably go on for some years to come.

THE WEALTH OF SUHARTO'S FAMILY AND FRIENDS

On June 1, 1998, an investigation into Suharto's personal wealth began with the Supreme Court's probe into the personal wealth of all government officials. A great deal has since been written about corruption in the Suharto government and the favoritism shown to his family and friends. According to George Aditjondro, a scholar at the University of Newcastle in Australia who has written extensively on Suharto family wealth, Suharto's establishment of a large number of charitable foundations provided the means for the family to accumulate such vast wealth. These foundations (*yayasan*), ostensibly organized to support charitable causes, were in reality vehicles through which the Suharto family could avoid taxes and accumulate riches. Donations brought in most of the revenue to these organizations, which were neither audited nor open to public inspection. Suharto issued a presidential decree that private and public companies must make donations to these foundations. For example, in 1978 all state-owned banks were required to give 2.5 percent of their profits to two foundations—Dharmais and Supersemar. Supersemar dispersed 84 percent of its funds to Suharto family projects. Suharto actually had to sign any checks over $50,000 paid out by these foundations, so he was aware of these foundations' expenditures. A 1992 decree required each taxpayer or company making over $40,000 per year to donate 2 percent of its income to another of Suharto's foundations—Dana Sejahtera Mandiri. When one of Suharto's foundations took over a bank, that bank's donation increased its contribution to a Suharto *yayasan* to 8 percent of its profits.

On numerous occasions state-owned companies formed joint ventures with members of the Suharto family. The Suharto children held monopolies on distribution and import of most major goods. They obtained low-interest loans by strong-arming bankers and then reneged on the loan payments. One business associate estimated that the Suharto children neglected to pay taxes on $2.5–$10 billion in income. In a well-known case, the company managing government roads became a shareholder with Siti Hardiyanti Rukmana, Suharto's daughter (more often known as "Tutut") in a private toll road company that charged fees from drivers on government roads. Suharto regularly ignored the constitutional requirement that parliament approve any use of public funds and continued to issue presidential decrees and ministerial decisions that favored his family and friends. Following is a brief chronology of some of the business interests of Suharto's family and friends. These items were reported in *Time Asia* magazine's May 24, 1999, issue in an article titled "Suharto, Inc." and in a March 23, 2000, speech by George Aditjondro titled "The Global Tentacles of the Suharto Oligarchy." (Aditjondro, formerly on the faculty of Australia's Newcastle University, has published extensively on the Suharto family's wealth.)

- In 1969 Suharto agreed to a wheat import and flour-milling monopoly for his close friend, Lim Siew Leong, "Uncle Liem" to the Suharto children.
- In January 1970 due to student protests, Suharto set up a commission to investigate corruption in government. The commission reported that corruption was indeed rampant in government; however, only two cases were prosecuted and then the commission was disbanded.
- In 1970 Lim Siew Leong and Suharto's half brother, Probosutejo, were granted a clove import monopoly.
- In the mid-1980s two of Suharto's sons, Tommy and Bambang, acquired considerable stock in Pertamina, the state-owned oil company. Their firms apparently received 30–35 cents for each barrel of oil sold during 1997–1998. That would have totaled

approximately $50 million. Just before Suharto resigned, Pertamina cancelled many of its contracts with the Suharto family's petroleum-related businesses. At that point Pertamina saved $99 million in one year.

- A June 13, 1988, article in the *New Yorker* magazine reported that a representative of a stationery company that supplied paper to the Indonesian Ministry of Education and Culture suddenly lost its contract when one of the Suharto children bid for supplying that ministry with stationery.

Next to oil, the most profitable businesses for the Suharto children were the monopolies they held on importing plastic and tinplate. Two of the Panca Company's four directors were Suharto's sons, and a third was his foster brother. Tinplate is essential in the manufacturing of canned goods, and once the Suharto family gained control of that market, tinplate could be obtained only through Panca Holdings. One of Suharto's sons, Sigit, and Suharto's friend Bob Hasan, who is known for his control of the timber market, co-owned an enormous company that held timber concessions, tea plantations, and a monopoly on Nissan cars.

- In 1989 a government audit showed that two thirds of Indonesia's government-run businesses were financially unsound.
- In 1990 Suharto's son Tommy was given a monopoly on the clove trade.
- In 1998, after Suharto left office, an investigation of Bob Hasan, Suharto's friend who had been essentially in charge of all of Indonesia's major timber concessions, was investigated. Forestry groups that had not been controlled by the Suharto government demanded that Hasan return $2.8 billion in forestry fees he had collected from 1991–1998. When he resigned, Suharto's salary was $1,764 per month. At that time the total of his six children's wealth was estimated at almost $5 billion.

Bribery and extortion are commonplace in Indonesia. An acquaintance of the author's had an experience with bribery while living in Indonesia. It took place in the Sukarno-Hatta Airport in Jakarta in March 1995. When reentering Indonesia from a trip to mainland Southeast Asia, the traveler was unable to produce a return ticket to the United States. Knowing she would be returning to Indonesia after a few weeks of traveling in mainland Southeast Asia, she had left the ticket in her residence in Indonesia. When her travels to Laos, Thailand, and

Myanmar were completed and she returned to Indonesia, the immigration official at the airport told her that without a return ticket to the United States she could not reenter Indonesia. She was then ushered into a small room where a uniformed official explained the importance of her having a ticket back to the United States. Her explanation that she had one, but not with her, fell on deaf ears until she realized what was happening and asked the official, "How much?" His response was, "How much do you have?" After trying to pay in rupiah (she had only about the equivalent of $5 in Indonesian currency with her), she finally offered him $30 US, which he accepted. Her passport was stamped, and she was allowed to go through the immigration and customs counters to spend another three months in Indonesia.

AFTER SUHARTO

There is little question that Suharto's policies undermined the economy of Indonesia. Those policies had eroded the government for years, so that even when Habibie replaced Suharto in 1998 and implemented a number of reforms, the economic situation did not stabilize. Habibie was thought to be too closely linked to Suharto, and the people wanted a complete change at the head of their government. This concern, coupled with a scandal regarding payments from a bank in Bali to cover his political party's election expenses, made Habibie even less popular with the people.

Gus Dur replaced Habibie, but though a brilliant man and respected theologian, he was unable to control the escalating secessionist movements in Ache, Maluku, Papua, and Sulawesi. He, too, was involved in a money scandal of his own making, connected with payment of government funds to one of his employees. However, it was probably his inability to stop the rapid growth of the increasingly strong secessionist movements that brought about his impeachment.

Magawati Sukarnoputri, Gus Dur's vice president, took the reins of government in summer 2000 when Gus Dur was forced to step down. Magawati has declared that she will seek the judicial reform needed to oversee the legislative change that is essential to put the economy back on track.

The Indonesian economy is slowly improving, but it now faces the new dilemma of Western nations' hesitancy to invest in a country with strong ties to fundamentalist Islamic nations that conceivably could be tied to terrorism. The October 12, 2002, bombing in Bali underscored this concern. Megawati is literally playing a balancing act within

Presidential candidate Megawati Sukarnoputri (left) raises the hand of Indonesia's newly elected president, Abdurrahman "Gus Dur" Wahid. (AFP/Corbis)

her own country, trying to please both liberals and fundamentalists while holding the secessionists at bay and getting the economy back on track. The international economic decline brought about by the September 11, 2001, terrorist attacks in the United States has further harmed the Indonesia economy as well.

Since Suharto's resignation in 1998 the Indonesian economy has slowly improved, with the rupiah now hovering around 8,800 to the US$. Foreign investment has picked up, and international business conglomerates seem more willing to invest in Indonesian enterprises. However, the problems Megawati faces are still overwhelmingly economic ones. If she is able to stabilize the Indonesian economy and control escalating food and oil prices, many related issues will become more manageable. This is a big "if," and although charges of corruption against her are still less notorious than those associated with her predecessors, they are becoming more prevalent. Will the twin problems of economic depression and dishonesty that brought down her father's government as well as the governments of Suharto, Habibie, and Gus Dur end Megawati's presidency as well? Presidential elections will be held in 2004, and Amien Reis, speaker of the People's Consultative Assembly and a strong candidate for president, may prove more powerful than Indonesia's first woman president.

References

Aditjondro, George J. "Chopping the Global Tentacles of the Suharto Oligarchy: Can Aotearoa [New Zealand] Lead the Way?" Speech, Aukland, New Zealand, March 23, 2000.

Bonner, Raymond. "A Reporter at Large: The New Order—I." *New Yorker,* June 6, 1988: 45–79.

_____. "A Reporter at Large: The New Order—II." *New Yorker,* June 13, 1988: 71–91.

Colmey, John, and David Liebhold. "Suharto, Inc.: It's All in the Family." *Time,* May 31 1999. Available online at http://www.TimeAsia.com05/24/99.

Hall, D. G. E. *A History of Southeast Asia* (3rd ed). London: Macmillan, 1977.

Ricklefs, M. C. *A History of Modern Indonesia.* Hong Kong: Macmillan, 1990.

Schwarz, Adam. *A Nation in Waiting: Indonesia in the 1990s.* Boulder: Westview Press, 1994.

Websites

"Chronology of the Crisis," paper by an Indonesian economist: http://www.asian-affairs.com/Indonesia/soesastro.html

Department of the Parliamentary Library of Australia, "The Indonesian Economy: What Went Wrong," by Hadi Soesastro: http://www.aph.gov.au/library/pubs/cib/1999–2000/2000cib17.htm

Human Rights Watch: http://www.hrw.org/reports/world/indonesia-pubs.php

Indonesian transmigration: http://dte.gn.apc.org/ctrans.htm#figs
Indonesians working overseas: http://www.migrationinformation.org/indo_
    table2.cfm
Suharto's five-year development plans, Repelita I–Repelita VI: http://www.
    indonesia-ottawa.org/Handbook99/contmpid_R.htm
Sukarno's government policies of Manipol and USDEK: http://www.lexisnexis.com/
    academic/2upa/Ias/cfIndonesia.htm
United Nations and Indonesia Corruption Watch reports on Indonesia's judiciary:
        http://www.geocities.com/aroki.goe/0208/INA-sinbonjudiciary–0207.html;
        http://www.geocities.com/aroki.goe/0208/INA-judiciaryworse.html
U.S. Embassy in Jakarta: http://www.usembassyjakarta.org/
U.S. State Department: http://www.state.gov/r/pa/ei/bgn/2748.htm#econ

CHAPTER THREE
Indonesian Institutions

GOVERNMENT AND POLITICS

Before monarchies and sultanates were established in the Indonesian
archipelago, the people gathered in safe and agriculturally productive
regions. They eventually chose leaders as well as fellow villagers to
serve on local councils. These units functioned as food-growing and
distributing entities, and as protective and law-making units. Village
councils determined division and use of land as well as water rights,
perhaps the most important rulings they made. Determination of the
use of water resources continues to be a major role of local Indonesian governments today. Villages grew and absorbed other villages,
becoming centers for trade and cultural activities. The ruling elements
of these population centers developed and were eventually labeled as
monarchies or kingdoms, with the strongest individuals becoming
rajas or kings.

Rajas and Sultans

The earliest recorded large governmental units in Indonesia were
monarchies. The first kingdoms were probably small, but they
amassed power as they increased in size. Chinese archival records in
the sixth century indicate trade with such kingdoms as Srivijaya and
later with the Sanjaya, Kediri, and Majapahit kingdoms (see Chapter
1). These empires were located mainly on Java and on the coast of
south Sumatra, and in other places where the fertile soil made it possible to grow agricultural products and favorable harbors encouraged
trade. India was an early influence on Indonesian culture, and it was
on this country's laws and government policies that the rajas of
Indonesia based their governments.

With the introduction of Islam in the thirteenth century, Hindu and
Buddhist leaders were sometimes converted to the new religion. At
other times, wars were fought between Hindus and Muslims to determine the ruling power. Eventually in most of the archipelago, sul-

Corner of a Balinese village temple with rice terraces in background (Center for Southeast Asian Studies)

tanates replaced kingdoms, and sultans superseded rajas. Sultans passed their titles on to their sons and, like their Hindu and Buddhist predecessors, waged wars to gain powers. The arrival of the Dutch in the seventeenth century did much to limit the power of Indonesia's sultanates. Even so, the village remained the basic political unit in Indonesia, with the village farmer the backbone of the economy.

Early European Influence and Colonial Government

Sultanates were well established when the first Portuguese and Dutch traders arrived in Indonesia. Incidents of interaction between Portuguese and Dutch sea captains and local sultans are well documented. Neither the Portuguese nor the Dutch were primarily interested in proselytizing; instead, their attention was on cultivating good relations with local government officials, with whom they wanted to arrange the purchase of local products. Their goal was to gain the advantage in the lucrative trade in spices and other exotic goods of the region. Thus it was commerce that initially drew the first Europeans to Indonesia, not religion.

After the Portuguese left Indonesia the Dutch gained control of the business of the exporting and importing of goods in the archipelago.

Although ships from other countries still traded within the island chain, the Dutch were the predominant commercial entity. Dutch merchants soon realized the tremendous power the Indonesian aristocracy had over the peasant farmers, and before long they were conducting their business through these ruling families. They collected any taxes they levied and goods they wished to purchase through this elite class simply because it was the most efficient way to conduct their affairs. For 200 years the Dutch confined their activities mainly to commercial ventures, but eventually these Dutch businessmen became drawn into disputes between local rulers. In most cases the Dutch-supported ruler won the dispute, thanks mostly to the superior arms supplied by the Dutch, and as a result the Dutch East India Company (VOC) became involved in local politics. The VOC began to provide capital to its selected elite to help establish a favorable regime. When this practice became more entrenched the VOC began to lose money. Fearing loss of income from its rich colony, on January 1, 1800, the Dutch government took control of Indonesia from the VOC. This marked a change in the manner of conducting business and the collection of goods and taxes, although the Dutch colonial government continued to work with local Indonesian rulers.

The Dutch administered their colonial government in Indonesia by posting men from the Netherlands to civil service positions in the colony. They trained very few Indonesians as government officials. Later, when the Dutch no longer controlled Indonesia, the lack of trained civil servants was a serious problem for the new republic.

Planning for an Independent Nation

The Dutch government continued to handle administrative and business matters pertaining to its Indonesian colony until the start of World War II. In the early twentieth century the Netherlands became less stringent in its demands and adapted a more lenient stance with Indonesia, allowing Indonesians to have access to education and to play a minor role in business enterprises. This changed dramatically with the arrival of the Japanese occupation forces in March 1942. The new administrators brought Japanese soldiers to oversee the government, but as the war went on they were needed in the battlefields. When these men moved out of administrative positions, Indonesians replaced them. These workers made up the small cadre of administrators available to serve the new Indonesian government at the end of the war.

Under the best of circumstances, Indonesia would be an extremely difficult country to govern, with its approximately 6,000 inhabited islands spread over 3 million square miles and its approximate 225 million people belonging to over 100 cultural groups. Before the Dutch colonized Indonesia—and treated the chain of islands as a single political unit—the islands were only loosely organized politically, and their inhabitants operated along language and ethnic divisions with local rulers setting trade policies and agreements. Indeed, political boundaries throughout Island Southeast Asia were much different prior to European colonization. For example, the island of Borneo was not divided into three countries—Indonesia, Malaysia, and Brunei—as it is today. Before Great Britain claimed North Borneo as its territory, that region was closely tied to the Philippines, with which it shares a common culture. Some of the current political boundaries in Southeast Asia that are based on European divisions are still disputed.

Immediately following World War II, on August 29, 1945, a constitution prepared by the Congress of the Indonesian National Political Consensus (PPPKI—Permufakatan Perhimpunan-perhimpunan Politik Indonesia) was adopted and Sukarno was declared president of Indonesia. The preamble to the 1945 constitution reflects the people's urgency to be a free nation. It reads:

> With independence being the right of every nation, colonialism must be eliminated from the face of the earth as it is contrary to the dictates of human nature and justice.
>
> The struggle of Indonesia's independence has now reached a glorious moment, having led the Indonesian people safely to the threshold of independence for an Indonesian state which is free, united, sovereign, just and prosperous.
>
> With the blessings of God Almighty and impelled by the noble idea of a free national life, the Indonesian people do hereby declare their independence. Further, in order to establish a government of the State of Indonesia which shall protect the whole Indonesian people and their entire homeland of Indonesia, and in order to advance their general welfare, to promote the intellectual life of the nation, and to contribute to implementing order in a world founded upon independence, eternal peace and social justice, Indonesia's national independence shall be formulated in a Constitution of the State of Indonesia, which shall have the structural state form of a Republic of Indonesia with sovereignty of the people, and which shall be based upon: belief in one God, humanity, unity, deliberation for representation and social justice for all Indonesians.

As mentioned previously, there were few civil service workers available to serve the new government, and their only roll models had been

Dutch colonials and Japanese military personnel. Neither Europeans from a small country with a like population nor an army of occupation had Indonesia's best interests at heart, and both made a poor paradigm after which the new government could pattern itself. Both had come only for the country's resources; governance of the people and their welfare was not a primary concern. Post–World War II Indonesia faced trying times. To make matters worse, government in-fighting became the norm in the new nation as military, separatists, communists, nationalists, and religious extremists vied for political power.

The Government of the Young Republic of Indonesia

When the Dutch left for good in 1949, the new Republic of Indonesia adopted a constitution that provided for a parliamentary system of government. Indonesia had an earlier constitution, written in 1945, that relied more on consensus than on voting. The 1949 constitution is more in the style of Western constitutions that are based on elected officials and majority rule.

The 1949 Constitution and Pancasila

Under the rules of the 1949 constitution an executive would be selected who would be responsible to the parliament. At that time there were many political parties, all espousing their own philosophies. Due to the revolution with the Dutch and the difficulty in establishing a sound government, it was not until 1955, when the government was sufficiently organized, that the first countrywide election was held. So many political parties gained seats that coalitions within that first parliament were almost impossible to establish. As a consequence little was accomplished as party leaders scrambled to firm up alliances. Before long, religion became a major issue among the elected representatives. Sukarno opposed any plan to have the country come under Islamic law, and a philosophy called Pancasila became the basis of the Indonesian government. *Pancasila* comes from Sanskrit, meaning five principles. The five tenets of Pancasila are:

1. Belief in the one and only God
2. Just and civilized humanity
3. The unity of Indonesia
4. Democracy guided by the inner wisdom in the unanimity aris-

ing out of deliberations among representatives (consensus, as in village decision making [gotong royong])

5. Social justice for the whole of the people of Indonesia

By adopting these tenets, freedom of religion was assured to all Indonesian citizens.

As the 1950s progressed the country's economic conditions worsened. Religious groups were dissatisfied, and perhaps the most serious matter was the rising question of secession among many regional areas. Residents of northern Sumatra were unhappy with the government's failure to designate Islam as the national religion and objected to parliament's overwhelming number of Javanese delegates. Aceh, a province in northern Sumatra, produces large amounts of oil, and its people resented the fact that so much revenue from its sales went to Java. Other regions, such as the oil-rich province of Riau, expressed dissatisfaction with the government and wanted to be independent. Maluku, a strong Christian area in eastern Indonesia, had been sympathetic to the Dutch during the revolution and wanted to govern themselves. Sulawesi, a region rich in natural resources and with a history of opposition to Javanese rule, resented having to conform to laws essentially made by the Javanese, who dominated the parliament.

Guided Democracy

In November 1956 the Constituent Assembly (the Indonesian legislative body of government) met to draft a permanent constitution. That group was dissolved three years later without having been able to produce such a document. Between 1949 and 1957 Indonesia's parliamentary body had established seven new governments. Each was dissolved with little accomplished. Sukarno desperately needed to take control of the government. Frustrated with the inability of the divided parliament to function, he called for "Guided Democracy," a government where decisions would be made by consensus and not by "half of the parliament plus one." Sukarno wanted to nullify the 1949 constitution and revive the 1945 constitution that he and other nationalists had put into effect immediately after World War II, when he was first named president. This document provided considerable power to the chief executive. His plan included cabinet representatives from the major parties that would be advised by various regional, religious, and labor groups. Parliament was not to be eliminated, but its duties modified. Guided Democracy would give Sukarno substantial power, allowing him to change government policies as he deemed necessary. On February 21, 1957, Sukarno announced his policy of Guided Democracy. It involved the establishment of a National Council whose members he would select. Political parties and elected representative bodies were to be eliminated, and Sukarno announced that decisions would henceforth be made in the old-fashioned way—by consensus (*gotong royong*). To guarantee his control of the government, Sukarno declared martial law on March 14, 1957.

Guided Democracy was not accepted gracefully. Conditions outside of Java became chaotic as antigovernment riots erupted in Sumatra and Sulawesi. Seeking scapegoats for his failing government, on December 1, 1957, Sukarno targeted the Dutch in Indonesia, announcing the nationalization of over 240 Dutch businesses. Four days later he announced the expulsion of approximately 46,000 Dutch citizens from Indonesia. This move was especially unpopular in eastern Indonesia, where the Dutch had significant success in converting Indonesians to Christianity and many of the people had opposed Sukarno's policies from the onset of his government. Many Indonesians from Ambon left the country with the Dutch and took up residence in Holland, where there is a large Ambonese community today. In 1950 a group of eastern Indonesians set up the Republic of South Maluku and proclaimed themselves independent from Indonesia. A year later, Indonesian troops occupied Maluku. Since 1966 a South Maluku Republic government in exile has been in existence in the Netherlands.

In February 1958, when a rebel group in Sumatra called the PRRI (Pemerintah Revolusioner Republik Indonesia—Indonesian Revolutionary Republic) declared a revolutionary government, Sukarno ordered government planes to bomb them. The PRRI fighters were strong Muslims, and they were soon joined by Permesta rebels from Sulawesi, also supporters of Islamic reform. The government forces were too strong, and despite PRRI's best efforts, by May 1958 they were defeated. There is evidence that the United States supported the PRRI and Permesta rebels in part to protect American oil fields in the region and in part to halt the spread of communism in Indonesia. Islamic groups such as Masyumi and Darul Islam were sympathetic to the rebels' cause, but they were not among the groups close to Sukarno. Their influence on government was no match for either the communist party or the military. The world knew little about those organizations at that time, as the foreign press was concentrating on

Sukarno and the manner with which he was handling the country's economic problems. Too little attention was given to the growing influence of Islam—modernist and traditionalist. Much of the peoples' discontent with the PKI, especially, but also with the army was fomented by fundamentalist Muslims. The influence of this element of the population had been kept at a minimum under the Dutch, but an independent Indonesia, where many of the people supported religious zealots, underwent an increase in the antigovernment activity of a number of modernist Islamic groups.

In July 1959 Sukarno dissolved parliament and announced that the government would revert to the 1945 constitution, a document that gave the president greater control and had decisions made by consensus—not election. As mentioned earlier, this enabled him to expand the legislative body by adding more members from the provinces, as well as 200 other members to represent various organized groups, often referred to as functional groups. These consisted of organizations of professionals, students, women, labor, and also the military.

During the early 1960s Sukarno became more and more anti-Western in his outlook. In his effort to appease all political factions his slogan in early 1960 was "Nasakom," which stood for *nationalisme, agama* (religion), and *komunisme* (communism). On January 7, 1965, Sukarno ordered Indonesia's United Nations delegates to walk out of the UN in protest of that organization admitting Malaysia as a member. At that time Indonesia was deeply involved in a confrontation with Malaysia over disputed lands on Borneo.

Within the Sukarno government the competition between military forces and communists grew steadily fiercer as both tried to maintain an advantage with the president. They viewed Sukarno as the crucial element in controlling the government, and each wanted the other out of the picture. The president needed them both, and he played them against each other in order to maintain his tenuous control of the government. He would defy the West, withdraw from the UN, and do whatever it took to keep the peasants and the PKI with him. The military could not withdraw from government for fear that the communists would be the main influence on the president. As for the religious groups, Sukarno apparently did not consider their influence equal to that of the army or the communists. It was a strange alliance for all three elements—Sukarno, the communists, and the military—and although economic conditions grew steadily worse, this arrangement continued until the abortive coup on September 30, 1965, the Night of the Generals (see Chapter 1).

Although many assumed that the Indonesian Communist Party (PKI) had instigated the coup, others blame some units of the army along with outside Western anticommunist elements that feared the growth of communism in Southeast Asia. Whoever originated the coup, the results were extreme as hundreds of thousands of Indonesians were murdered under the guise of cleansing the country of communism. Many more were imprisoned without trials, and as a result the PKI was essentially eliminated in Indonesia—at that time the fifth most populous country in the world.

The Role of the Communist Party

The Communist Party was a presence in Indonesia while the country was still under Dutch rule. In May 1920 Perserikatan Kommunist di India (the Communist Association of the Indies) was established. In 1924 this group changed its name to Partai Komunis Indonesia (PKI; in English, the Indonesian Communist Party).

Modernist Islamacists opposed the PKI from the beginning for its adherence to the communist tenet of nonbelief in God. This rift dogged the PKI and its role in Indonesian politics through 1965. The independent government's first anticommunist rebellion occurred in Madiun on Java in 1948. The issue was PKI opposition to Sukarno's and Hatta's willingness to accept Dutch terms to end the revolution. The rebellion was squashed, and in the years following the revolution the PKI was careful to work with the Sukarno administration as much as possible in order not to lessen its role in government.

Between 1960 and 1965 PKI support grew among Indonesia's peasant population as the communist organization worked for land reform that favored the poor farmer. With PKI backing labor, the organization's activity increased on sugar and rubber plantations. The fact that these plantations were frequently owned by members of Indonesia's military elite further increased the tension between military and communist groups.

The PKI, the army, and the Muslims were in a three-way contest for control of the government, which in the early 1960s was clearly under the leadership of Sukarno. The PKI had the support of the *abangan*— the poor peasants—who were the bulk of Sukarno's supporters and who viewed communism as a means of improving their lives. The army was largely composed of the famous Freedom Fighters, heroes of Indonesia's independence who quickly became entrenched in government enterprises that favored themselves and their families. The modernist

Muslims had been gaining power in Indonesia since Dutch implementation of the Ethical Policy had allowed more religious freedom and educational opportunities to Indonesians. As discussed earlier, they were opposed to communism on the basis of its antireligious doctrine.

There was some overlapping of these groups, but communism clearly did not mesh well with either the army or the modernist Muslims. At one point Sukarno actually named Aidit, head of the PKI, as a member of the MPR, intensifying the rift between the three factions vying for a major role in government.

The end of the PKI came in 1965 when blame for the abortive coup was directed almost solely at the communists, resulting in a murderous sweep of PKI members and others throughout the archipelago. Not only the military, but also fundamentalist Muslims were especially aggressive in attacking people they thought to be communists. In the period following the coup, large numbers of Indonesians who were considered by the government to be procommunist were sent to prison camps, among them Indonesia's preeminent author, Pramoedya Antara Toer.

Suharto outlawed the Communist Party in Indonesia in 1966. The mid-1970s independence movement in East Timor had a strong element of left-wing politics and caused some Indonesians, especially members of the military establishment, to oppose independence for the formerly Portuguese region. Recent Indonesian presidents, however, have given less credence to the concept that communism is a threat to their governments. The end of the Cold War was a dominant factor in the increasing lack of interest in communism in Indonesia. Since the late 1980s there has been little concern in Indonesia that communism would be an alternative form of government there.

The Role of the Military in Politics

From the very beginning of Indonesia's fight for independence the Angkatan Bersenjata Republik Indonesia (ABRI—Armed Forces of the Republic of Indonesia) played a major role in shaping the country's future. Comparable to Colonial America's Minute Men, Indonesia's Freedom Fighters (*pejuang kemerdekaan*) fought the Dutch for independence from colonial rule. Many an Indonesian obituary today prominently and respectfully states that the deceased was a *pejuang kemerdekaan*. Ironically a substantial number of these soldiers had been in the Dutch army prior to World War II; the most prominent of them was President Suharto.

In the aftermath of the revolution some members of the Indonesian army assumed leadership roles in the establishment of the new government. However, as Sukarno struggled to form a stable administration the army found itself in competition with the Communist Party for control of the country.

By 1958 Sukarno ordered the army to put down insurgencies among Indonesian groups who opposed his policy of Guided Democracy. The most prominent of these rebel groups were the PRRI (Indonesian Revolutionary Government) in Sumatra and the Permesta revolutionary movement in Sulawesi. Both the PRRI and Permesta movements were supported by Masyumi, a modernist religious movement that opposed Sukarno's close connection to the communists. Four years later, in 1962, the army was reluctantly involved in an invasion of Malaysia—the *konfrontasi*—at a time when Sukarno was trying to divert attention from horrendous economic problems at home.

When seven high-level army officers were murdered in the September 30, 1965, coup the attention of the Indonesian people shifted dramatically and favorably to the military. A somewhat odd alliance between the military and modernist Muslims emerged, mainly because both organizations wanted communism purged from their country, albeit for different reasons. Suharto, the emerging leader of the country and a major-general in the army, was not a *santri* (devout) Muslim but an *abangan* (traditionalist) Muslim. However, he saw the alliance as necessary to rid the country of all vestiges of the PKI. During his time in office Suharto walked a fine line between a military-controlled government and a modernist Islamacist one that wanted the military to have reduced political clout.

Under Suharto the role of ABRI increased, especially when *dwifungsi,* a policy actually started under Sukarno, became a major political course of action. *Dwifungsi* means dual function and refers to the Indonesian army's twofold role as both a defense and a sociopolitical force. At the height of Suharto's years in office the army held seventy-five nonelected seats in parliament; by 2000 that number was reduced to thirty-eight, and beginning in 2004 the army will hold no assigned seats in the legislative body.

The army prospered under Suharto as many military personnel ran for public office and when elected enjoyed the privileges that powerful political friends could provide. It was not until 1997, when both the onset of the economic crisis and problems surrounding the East Timor independence movement became more widely known, that the army began to lose power.

Back when Suharto ordered the invasion of East Timor, in 1975, the army became deeply involved in that arena. Many military men died fighting the rebels in East Timor, and they saw millions of dollars in government funds bring spent there. Because of this, ABRI was totally unable to accept the Habibie government ruling that granted East Timor its independence. This inability to accept the loss of a region they felt had claimed the lives of so many of their comrades and such an enormous concentration of Indonesia's resources for twenty-five years was manifested in a reign of terror that has not yet fully subsided.

When Gus Dur took over the Indonesian presidency in 1999 he made an effort to further control the Indonesian armed forces. However, he found it a herculean task as problems relating to separatist movements escalated in Ache, Maluku, and Papua, all with overtones of military involvement.

Megawati is thought to be a friend of the military, however, it was during her term that it was decided that ABRI would have fewer seats than it has claimed in the DPR for decades. In the scheduled 2004 election, the thirty-eight seats held by the military will no longer be set aside for them. Although there are protests against this action, the proof of the intent will be seen in 2004.

Suharto's "New Order"

Prior to becoming Indonesia's leader, Suharto had spent his entire career in the army. It is not surprising that he encouraged the belief that the Night of the Generals was a communist plot to overthrow the government. His determination to support this theory is evidenced in the fervor with which suspected PKI members were targeted for violence. Following the attempted coup, Indonesia's economy was in ruins, and it was soon apparent that Sukarno could not bring order out of the chaos. On March 11, 1966, Sukarno signed a document officially giving Suharto a wide range of power, the intent being that Suharto would bring stability to the country and the government. This was an auspicious move for Suharto, who continued to gain popularity over the weakening Sukarno. In March 1967, a year and a half after the coup, the People's Consultative Assembly (MPR) named Suharto acting president. Many of Sukarno's supporters were by that time arrested or dead, and Suharto had been instrumental in the selection of new members to the MPR.

The new government took control and immediately began imple-

Pramoedya Ananta Toer, Indonesia's most renowned author (AFP/Corbis)

mentation of the policies it labeled the "New Order." Relations with Western countries and the United Nations resumed, and the border war with Malaysia came to an abrupt end. Initially Sukarno tried to hold onto his power by treating the coup as an isolated incident of no great importance. Suharto would have none of that. He was a military man whose opposition to communism was well documented. Once Suharto was named president, Sukarno faded quickly from the public view. Suharto kept those elements of the Sukarno government that suited him, but he changed many policies and in effect established the patterns for the present political system in Indonesia.

Suharto took over the nation in a troubled time. Three hundred and fifty years of colonial government, four years of Japanese occupational government, four years of self-government while fighting a revolution followed by sixteen years of an Indonesian government with a steadily failing economy preceded his presidency. In spite of doubts about his abilities, Suharto proved to be up to the task. By the late 1960s the Communist Party ceased to exist in Indonesia, and in 1969 Irian Jaya, the western half of the island of New Guinea, which had been controlled by the Dutch until 1962 and by Indonesia through the United Nations from 1963 to 1969, was named an Indonesian province. Indonesia seemed on its way to becoming a stable and economically sound nation.

Suharto's intolerance for communism was exhibited in many ways. In 1969 the Indonesian government ordered the imprisonment of a number of suspected communist sympathizers, among them the author Pramoedya Antara Toer, who had been imprisoned by the Dutch in the late 1940s for his support of the Indonesian revolution and who is today the country's most eloquent and best-known writer. The Suharto government accused Pramoedya of being a communist and incarcerated him on the prison-island of Buru from 1969 to 1979. It was during this imprisonment that Pramoedya wrote the *Buru Quartet,* a series of four books that follows a Dutch-educated Indonesian who faces the inequity of the Dutch colonial government.

In the 1970s, negative comments about Suharto's government began to be heard. Among the most common accounts were reports of corruption. But despite stories of nepotism and dishonesty, the country was relatively stable, and outwardly the economy seemed healthy. There had been so many miserable years that Indonesia's people seemed willing to accept a certain level of corruption in exchange for a higher standard of living and peace.

Suharto's New Order differed significantly from the rule of the

Japanese and of Guided Democracy. His policies were more like those of the Dutch, who had attempted to control the people rather than involve them in decision making. (Interestingly, early in his military career Suharto had been in the colonial forces.) Though Suharto had not been active in the nationalist movement, he had played a major role in the Indonesian Revolution. As Lieutenant-Colonel Suharto, he led the forces that briefly recaptured Yogyakarta from the Dutch on March 1, 1949. Suharto had not attended university; he was a military man who believed in the power of the military and top-down leadership more than democracy.

Throughout the Suharto presidency Indonesians had seemed willing to tolerate the sort of small-scale corruption that made it possible for someone earning a low salary to supplement it with charges for questionable services. For example, a driver might encounter a crude roadblock on a remote road in front of a rural family's house. When the driver stopped he would be expected to pay a small fee to be allowed through the barrier. In the cities police frequently stopped drivers and demanded instant payment for minor traffic infractions that the driver may or may not have committed. Giving a few rupiah to the rural family or paying off the policeman would be easier and cheaper than dealing with the roadblock on the way down the road or paying for the ticket the policeman would issue. This is in contrast to the large-scale government corruption discussed in Chapter 2.

Governments since 1998

When the 1997 economic crisis resulted in Suharto's resignation on May 21, 1998, his vice president, B. J. Habibie, replaced him. Habibie was not a popular president. He was perceived as Suharto's puppet, and the people had had enough of Suharto.

University students, especially, opposed Habibie, and when students were killed in several protest demonstrations Habibie's ability to govern was severely affected. His short term in office was further compromised by much-publicized brutal riots in the Chinese sector of Jakarta. Especially shocking were pictures of Chinese women being brutally raped. These photographs were posted on computer websites and instantly made available around the world. Habibie was not free of money scandals either, as evidenced in the Bank Bali scandal. In that incident Habibie was accused of being involved in a scheme to use International Monetary Funds (IMF) earmarked for the country's economic recovery to aid his political party. By December 1998 acts

Indonesia's third president, B. J. Habibie (AFP/Corbis)

of violence and protest demonstrations had escalated dramatically throughout the country. Realizing that it would be disastrous for the nation to continue on its present course, the MPR voted to hold the scheduled 2002 presidential election in 1999, two years early. Habibie was the Golkar Party's candidate in that election, which he lost to Abdurrahman Wahid (Gus Dur), a candidate for the National Awakening Party (PKB). This election gave the Islamic parties their first elected president.

Gus Dur

Indonesia's fourth president, Abdurrahman Wahid—known to all as Gus Dur—was elected on October 20, 1999. Megawati Sukarnoputri, the Democratic Party (PDI-P) candidate, won the popular vote, but the MPR chose Gus Dur. His presidency was greeted positively in most circles. The fifty-nine-year-old, blind, devoutly religious head of the Islamic organization Nahdlatul Ulama brought a new element to government. His honesty was not in question and he had no connection to Suharto or his cohorts. Gus Dur is a traditionalist Muslim, but one who accepts some modernist theories. This fact made him agreeable to all of the religious parties at the time of his election. However, Gus Dur's government was soon in trouble. His weakness lay primarily in his inexperience. He shunned advice from more knowledgeable colleagues, and he, too, was soon rumored to be immersed in money scandals. He reportedly misused funds from the sultan of Brunei and in a second embarrassment was purported to have given government money to one of his employees. Heightening these problems was the fact that he did not have the support of the military, a matter that hastened his downfall. The relationship between Indonesia's military and Muslims tends to be contentious, and the military contingent of the electorate would have preferred Megawati to Gus Dur as president. Megawati was perceived as pro-military although not pro-Suharto. Separatist movements grew more violent during Gus Dur's time in office, and it soon became apparent that if a change in government were not quickly undertaken, it would be in danger of collapsing. Abdurrahman Wahid, a beloved man but incompetent governor, was the first Indonesian president to be impeached.

Megawati Sukarnoputri

On July 23, 2001, Megawati Sukarnoputri, the daughter of Sukarno, was named the fifth president of Indonesia. A moderate Muslim, she took office with the support of both the legislature and the military. Megawati immediately made clear her opposition to the separatist movements. Her strongest attribute at first seemed to be her ability to choose competent men and women to head units of her govern-

Megawati Sukarnoputri, Indonesia's fifth president (AFP/Corbis)

ment. In the time Megawati has been in power, the economy has become more stable, and although violence is still prevalent in many provinces of Indonesia, efforts are being made to calm these situations. Terrorism, as evidenced in the October 12, 2002, bombings in Bali and the August 5, 2003, Jakarta bombing, have added to her problems.

It is too soon to pass judgment on her government, but if Megawati can curb the violence in Maluku, Papua, and Aceh and maintain her good relationship with the military, the fundamentalist Muslims, and her government colleagues she may make more headway toward government stability than any of her predecessors. She recently said she would be a candidate for president in 2004.

Structure of Government in Indonesia Today

The structure of Indonesian government is complicated. The main state political organs are the House of Representatives (DPR), the People's Consultative Assembly (MPR), the presidency, the Supreme Advisory Council, the State Audit Board, and the Supreme Court.

Every five years 500 members are elected to the House of Repre-

Portraits of presidents Wahid, Sukarno, and Megawati for sale at a sidewalk shop in Yogyakarta (Center for Southeast Asian Studies)

sentatives (Dewan Perwakilan Rakat—DPR), or as it is sometimes referred to, the parliament. All Indonesian citizens over eighteen may vote, as may younger married citizens. The Indonesian people elect members to represent them in this parliamentary body through their political parties. At this time only 462 members are actually elected to the DPR; the remaining 38 are currently members of the military and the police who were appointed, not elected. These thirty-eight members will hold their seats only until the 2004 election. In August 2002 the MPR amended the constitution to end the provision of non-elective DPR seats for the military and police.

The MPR is comprised of all 500 members of the DPR as well as 195 representatives of the provinces and members of designated special groups. Indonesian law dictated that the MPR have 700 members; however, when East Timor withdrew from Indonesia it left the MPR with five fewer members. Thus, the current actual membership of the MPR is 695. The MPR has two charges. The first is seeing that the government adheres to the constitution. The second is providing guidelines for policy. In the same August 2002 session that the MPR voted to end parliamentary seats for the military, it also voted to end MPR election of the president and vice president. These officials will now be elected directly by the people and no longer by the MPR.

The president selects the members of the cabinet. Upon request, the Supreme Advisory Council (Dewan Perwakilan Agung) advises the president on political, economic, sociocultural, and military issues. Members of the Supreme Advisory Council are nominated by the DPR and appointed by the president for a period of service of five years.

The principal function of the State Audit Board (Badan Pemeriksa Keuangan) is to inspect the government's finances. The findings of the State Audit Board are reported to the DPR.

The Supreme Court is the judicial branch of government, and it ranks equally with the legislative and the executive branches. The Supreme Court was restructured in 1968 to meet the conditions set out in the 1945 constitution—to be free from government intervention in the pursuit of justice. The Indonesian judiciary came under heated criticism during the years following the 1997 economic crisis. It was reported that corruption in the courts added significantly to Indonesia's economic problems.

Political Parties

The number of political parties in Indonesia has increased dramatically in recent years, but seven parties receive the most votes and are therefore the most influential in the formation of government. They are: Golkar (the party of Suharto, whose members are mostly government workers), led by Akbar Tanjung; the Indonesian Democratic Party of Struggle (PDI-P), led by Megawati Sukarnoputri; the National Mandate Party (PAN), led by Amien Reis; the National Awakening Party (PKB), led by Mathori Abdul Djalil; the United Development Party (PPP), led by Hamzah Haz; the Justice and Unity Party (PKP), led by Eddie Sudrajat; and the Crescent Star Party (PBB), led by Yusril Ihza Mahendra.

In the 1999 election the PDI-P won 153 seats, Golkar 120, the PPP 58, the PKB 51, and the PBB 13. Four other parties won from five to thirty-eight seats in that election.

Government from the provincial units down to the municipal level mirrors the organizational structure of the national government. There are 30 provinces and 354 regencies in Indonesia. Governors head the provinces; municipal levels of government are headed by regents or mayors. Relations between the legislative, executive, and judicial bodies on the provincial and regency levels follow a similar pattern to that of the national level. Below the municipality is the district, headed by a *bupati* who is appointed by the mayor or the governor. Next come townships, each of which is headed by a *camat* who is appointed by the *bupati*. Last is the village, headed by the *kapala desa,* who is appointed by the *camat* with the agreement of the villagers. In some cases villages are divided into hamlets or *banjar* that have elected leaders. In Bali this group controls the use of water, essential to the rice terraces.

Other government units are the military and the police. The military in Indonesia have long been regarded as having a social as well as a defense role. As mentioned previously, since the downfall of the Suharto government the position of the military in the Indonesian government is considerably less powerful. The expression "*dwifungsi,*" standing for the double duty of defense and social development, was first applied to Indonesia's military in the 1950s.

The Politics of the Separatist Movements

Perhaps the most serious matter facing the Indonesian government today is the ominous threat of provinces and regions breaking away from the nation. Problems are especially serious in Aceh, Papua, Maluku, Sulawesi, Kalimantan, and West Timor (see Chapter 2, "Separatist Movements and Violence"). Papua and Aceh are seeking to be independent of the central government, and the political and economic implications of such a move on the part of either of them would be catastrophic for Indonesia. Some arrangements have been agreed upon between the Jakarta government and Aceh, but the matter is still not completely settled. Sectarian violence in Maluku and Sulawesi is under more control since the October 2002 Sulawesi and Bali bombings and the downsizing of the terrorist group Laskar Jihad. Terrorist activity is currently precariously contained in Kalimantan and West Timor.

The government has been loath to consider separate status for any of its provinces, but as corruption in government became more commonplace, several regions in Indonesia have demanded control of their own political and economic affairs. Aceh, an oil-rich and strong Muslim province in North Sumatra, had long wanted to be separate from the central Indonesian government. The Acehnese want to control the region's vast oil reserves and have a government more in sync with Islamic law. For decades the region has provided tremendous revenue to the Indonesian government through its extensive petroleum reserves without comparable government assistance. In 2003 Aceh was granted a greater return on the sale of its resources, but whether this move will be sufficient to stem the long-existing dissatisfaction of the Acehnese with the central government in Jakarta remains to be seen. After the economic meltdown in fall 1997 Sulawesi, Papua, and Maluku joined the ranks of regions expressing their desire to follow the lead of East Timor and secede from Indonesia.

Governed as one entity during the colonial period, the people across the chain of islands differ in many respects. As noted in Chapter 1, in northern Sumatra the people are primarily devout Muslims while in Ambon at least half of the population is Christian. In Papua many people are still spirit worshipers. In addition to religion, folklore and language also differ markedly across the country. It would be difficult to govern such a diverse population under the best of circumstances, but with the government coming under criticism for dishonest and faulty economic policies, it was even worse. When cronyism, nepotism, and corruption charges were lobbed against the Suharto regime in 1996, forest fires resulting from poor government enforcement of logging regulations were burning out of control in the timber-rich Kalimantan province. Ethnic violence was on the rise. An especially fierce confrontation broke out in Kalimantan between the indigenous Dyak people and the Madurese (people of Madura, a small island off the east coast of Java) who had come to the region under the government's transmigration program.

Terrorism and 9/11

Indonesia suffered tremendously in the Asian economic meltdown in fall 1997. The situation took a further turn for the worse when distrust in political leaders resulted in four presidents taking over the reins of government in three years, three of them leaving office before completing full terms. As noted in Chapter 2, regional conflicts increased in number and intensity as the economic situation worsened.

The next setback to Indonesia's economic revival was the al-Qaida terrorist attacks on the United States on September 11, 2001. As anti-Muslim sentiment increased in the West, religious differences became more pronounced in Indonesia. Regions where people of different beliefs had lived side by side for generations became scenes of chaos and horror. Then, on October 12, 2002, a bomb exploded in a Bali nightclub in the popular tourist area of Kuta Beach. This was an especially shocking event as Bali had always been considered a "safe" place, one where visitors need not worry about terrorist activity. Over 200 people from twenty-one countries were killed in that blast. Blame for this incident was placed on the fundamentalist Islamic group Jama'ah Islamiyah. Bombs also exploded that same night in Denpasar, Bali, and in North Sulawesi. These explosions resulted in far less damage than the Sari nightclub bombing at Kuta Beach, though they were also the work of terrorists. These incidents, along with the August 5, 2003, Jakarta hotel bombing, drew international attention to religious troubles in the archipelago. The government has been unable to control the violence in most of these locations. Each new president has attempted to bring peace to the country, but the population is so widely dispersed and so diverse and poor that the people seem to forgo logic and rationality when faced with senseless violence.

RELIGION

Islam

Although Islam differs from country to country there are basic tenets to which all Muslims adhere. Islam is a monotheistic religion. Allah is God and Muhammad his chief and last prophet. In addition to Muhammad, Islam has other prophets: Noah, Abraham, Isaac, Ismail, Jacob, Moses, David, and Jesus. All Muslims follow the teachings of the Koran (*Qur'an*), the Muslim holy book, which is composed of the words of God. Muslims also revere the *Hadith,* a collection of the sayings and actions of the prophet Muhammad. The *Hadith* is often controversial. For example, in a region where Islamic law (*sharia*) is practiced a severe punishment may be meted out based on the *Hadith.* Such judgments may cause dissention between traditional and modernist Muslims. Traditionalists oppose outside interpretation of the Koran, preferring to accept the words of Allah as written down by his prophet Mohammad and not anyone else's interpretation of those words.

The mosque is the Muslim's place of worship. It may be large or small, but the mosque is almost always topped by a dome and spire. At the apex of the spire is either a new moon and star or Arabic writing proclaiming the glory of Allah. Mosques have no specified priests or pastors. The *imam* leads the prayers at the mosque, but he has no religious authority.

There are two primary branches of Islam based on the teachings

Mosque in Medan, Sumatra (Courtesy of Florence Lamoureux)

of those who followed Muhammad: Sunni and Shi'a (or Shi'ite). The Sunni have a strong belief in Allah's control over their lives. The Shi'a believe one's fate is up to him/herself. Sunni Islam is practiced by the vast majority of Muslims because it purports the belief that the Koran is a final revelation of Allah and no words or interpretation should be connected with it. Shiá Islam, in contrast, believes that an *imam* may receive divine revelations and therefore can add to the Koran. About 90 percent of all Muslims are Sunni. Indonesians follow the Sunni beliefs. All Muslims follow the five basic pillars of their religion, which are:

1. To state verbally that there is only one God and that Muhammad is his prophet
2. To pray at five designated times each day
3. To fast from food, liquid, and sexual relations from sundown to sunup during the month of Ramadan
4. To give alms to the poor
5. To make the pilgrimage to Mecca (the haj) once in a lifetime if at all possible

The fifth requirement, the *haj,* is made to remind the traveler of the anguish suffered by Abraham and his family.

The *sharia* is the law of Islam. It is based on the teachings of the Koran and is the guiding principle of most social activity. Indonesia is not governed by the *sharia,* although all Muslims are aware of its basic ideology and it is frequently a factor in the decision making of daily life.

The Coming of Islam to Indonesia

Islam came to Indonesia in the early thirteenth century. By 1515 a Portuguese traveler reported that it was prevalent in eastern Sumatra and on the eastern and central coasts of Java. By the time the Dutch colonial government established its headquarters at Batavia in the early 1600s, Islam had spread to the interior realms and villages of Sumatra and Java.

The Dutch sought goods for trade, not souls for religious conversion, and the rulers of Java—and other regions to a lesser extent—complied with the Dutch demand. The local Javanese rulers were not, for the most part, devout Muslims; instead, they practiced a blending of Sufi Islam with their traditional Hindu and mystical beliefs. An Indonesian interested in fundamentalist Islam at that time would have been exposed to the teachings of religious leaders from the Middle East—who were discouraged from coming to Indonesia while the Dutch controlled the region. Indonesians who might have wanted to become more entrenched in Islam during colonial times had neither the opportunity nor the time to do so. Although the Dutch were not particularly interested in converting Indonesians to their religion, neither were they eager to encourage the workers in their colony to learn more about a religion that was associated more closely with the Middle East than with Europe. The question arises as to the influence of the Dutch colonial government on the spread of Islam. Would the religion have become more deeply embedded in Indonesian society had the Dutch not become such a strong presence in Indonesia so quickly and had they not remained there for over three centuries? In considering the introduction of Islam into the region, the case of the Philippines is an interesting one, similar to some extent to Indonesia. It is clear that the arrival of the Spanish, who came to the Philippines to colonize but brought with them friars to convert the Filipinos to Catholicism, checked the growth of Islam there, limiting its spread to the southern islands. The northern Philippines today is devoutly

Catholic while the southern territory is devoutly Islamic. Islam never made a significant headway where the Spanish colonizers were strongest.

The contrast between Indonesia and the Philippines is interesting. Although the Spanish did not want Islam to spread northward and interfere with their proselytizing, the Dutch in Indonesia wanted to control its spread not so much out of religious concern as due to apprehension over Islam's perceived effect on their control of the peasant labor force. For an answer to the question of colonial influence on the spread of Islam in Indonesia, one should look at Islam in Indonesia during the Ethical Policy period and beyond.

As discussed in Chapter 2, in the early twentieth century the Netherlands relaxed its commercial demands on Indonesia. One of the most marked and influential changes resulting from the so-called Ethical Policy that took place was the rapid growth of modernist Islam. Until then the form of Islam practiced in Indonesia had not adhered precisely to the tenets of the religion. This was the religion that the Javanese elite preferred. They maintained much of their Hindu ritual as well as their traditional beliefs. However, as Muslim clerics who had studied in Mecca and Egypt returned to Indonesia they brought with them a more conservative form of Islam, one that held strictly to the rules of the religion. Several of these "modernist" scholars came to Sumatra, and as a result of their teaching West Sumatran society was considered to be at the heart of Islam in the Malay-speaking world through the late 1920s. Prior to World War II as the nationalist movement grew, so too did modernist Islam. Although they were not mutually exclusive, these two groups worked separately. Both wanted independence for Indonesia, but their perceptions of a post-independence Indonesia were quite different.

Throughout its political history the Republic of Indonesia has accommodated the devout Islamic element of the electorate as it represents a significant number of votes. President Sukarno was half Javanese and half Balinese, and although he professed to be Muslim, he was never especially religious. During his presidency, Sukarno did not include a significant number of members of the modernist Islamic groups in his government. Their dissatisfaction with Sukarno grew as he became drawn more closely to the Communist Party—a group that shunned belief in God. President Suharto is Javanese, and his religious beliefs, like those of many Javanese, are a mixture of Islam, Hinduism, and mysticism. Suharto, more *abangan* than *santri,* worked with the fundamentalist Muslims, but he never supported them. Habibie was president for such a brief and troubled time that he had little time to indulge his religious beliefs. He is a Muslim, but being from Sulawesi, he did not share Suharto's penchant for the mystical. Habibie is an intellectual with a Ph.D. in engineering from a German university. He encouraged organizations that supported Islam and intellectual activity. Gus Dur is Javanese, and when chosen to be president he was head of Nahdlatul Ulama (NU), an Islamic group anxious about the growth of modernist Islam. The NU gives some support to modernism but still wants to preserve Indonesia's traditional Islamic practices. Megawati is a moderate Muslim and, like her father, is not supported by modernist Muslims. However, similar to her predecessors, she recognizes the power of the fundamentalist Muslims. Her vice president, Hamzah Haz, is a devout Muslim and critic of those who are not. It is clear that fundamentalist Islam plays a major role in Indonesian politics and society, and any effective ruler must be aware of the cost of excluding modernist Muslims from governmental decision making.

When taking religion into account one must be aware that Indonesia has the largest Muslim population in the world. It numbers over 170 million, or about 88 percent of the country's inhabitants.

As stated earlier, Muslims in Indonesia are often regarded as either *abangan,* less religious, or *santri,* devout. These designations have recurrently been the cause of tension in Indonesia. Two primary Islamic organizations in Indonesia reflect the beliefs of the people: Members of the aforementioned Nahdlatul Ulama are traditionalists who want to conserve Javanese beliefs through their religious practices. They are interested in proselytizing and maintaining a traditional religious education. In contrast are the Muhammadiyah. They believe in strict adherence to the tenets of Islam. Although they support government as well as Islamic schools, they want to bring Islam into all aspects of Indonesian life.

There are four important Muslim holidays in Indonesia. The first, called Hari Raya (often referred to by its Arabic name, Idul Fitri), is a three-day holiday that comes at the end of the fasting month of Ramadan. At this time it is customary to visit one's parents and other relatives. New clothes and feasting are part of the celebration. A second important holiday, Maulid, celebrates the birth of Mohammad. The third, Isra Miraj, honors the prophet's final journey to heaven. The forth holiday is Eid ul-Adha. It commemorates the prophet Abraham's willingness to sacrifice his son to God. This holiday comes at the end of the *haj* pilgrimage period and is celebrated with prayer and *selamatan* (feasts).

Circumcision

The circumcision (*sunat*) ceremony for young boys aged approximately eight to thirteen is a cause for great celebration in Indonesian Muslim communities. It is considered the child's entry into the Islamic community. There is usually a big feast, a *salamatan,* with many guests. Often a *sunat* ceremony is held for several boys who have been circumcised at one time. In recent years there has been a movement to circumcise boys within forty days of their birth, as directed in the Koran, although this is counter to Javanese tradition.

Marriage

The marriage ceremony between two Muslims is also an Islamic rite of passage. Marriages are frequently arranged, but a woman must agree to be married to the man selected by her parents. Although a woman may be represented by a guardian at the actual ceremony, she is considered equal to her husband. Immediately following the wedding the couple pays their respects to their parents. The groom gives his new wife gifts of gold or a Koran. In some cases the bride is also given the traditional dress and veil that are worn by women when they pray. Wedding clothes are dictated by tradition, and the elaborate hairstyles and makeup for the bride involve hours of preparation. A legal service between the families usually takes place in the mosque. A social affair similar to the reception following a Christian wedding follows in a nearby facility.

Funerals

Muslim funerals involve the cooperation of the entire village. Friends and relatives perform such ritual tasks as bathing the deceased and praying for her or his welfare. It is important to the entire community that the family has sufficient funds to cover burial costs. Bodies are buried quickly after death—within a day if possible. Different ethnic groups follow different funeral practices. In Bali the bodies of Hindu men and women are cremated in accordance with their religion. In Sulawesi the Toraja people follow a very different and unusual ritual. Since their funerals are costly, sometimes a Toraja's body is kept for several months while a family raises the money needed to finance the large, expensive funerals and feasts that must be provided for the guests. At the beginning of the ceremony, the body of the deceased is

Muslim cemetery in Madura with rack for body awaiting burial (Center for Southeast Asian Studies)

brought to a special building, where it remains during the feast. In preparation for the feast, water buffaloes and other animals are slaughtered. The killing of these animals is part of the ceremony and is viewed by all the guests. After the festivities are over the body of the person for whom the funeral is being held is carried to a cave in a nearby cliff. A wooden figure is placed outside that cave, signifying that the person is interned inside. Even though today most Toraja are Muslim, they still follow this traditional funeral practice.

The Mosque and the Family

Much of a family's life revolves around the local mosque. Children go there to attend classes in Arabic and religious studies. Women's groups meet there, as do other social organizations. Food and clothing are distributed to the poor at the mosque, and the men go there on Fridays to pray. The *imam,* the leader of a local Islamic community, is at the mosque to assist the people who attend the various functions there. Wedding rituals are held at the mosque, as are Koran reading competitions. Indeed, the mosque is the center of the community and of a family's social and religious life. The mosque's public address system calls the faithful to prayer five times each day. Anyone in the vicinity of the minarets' loud speakers cannot ignore the summons in Arabic, *"lã ilãha illã Allãh Muhammadan Rasel Allãh,"* which means, "There is no god but Allah, and Muhammad is the messenger of Allah" (Eksiklopedi Tematis Dunia Islam, 2002, vol. 3, p.17).

Christianity

About 8 percent of the population of Indonesia are Christian, with the largest concentration found in eastern Indonesia. One sees churches throughout the country, and Catholic schools are common in urban areas. Violence in Maluku has been publicized as a major Christian–Muslim problem in that region; however, accurate assessments of the severity of the situation are not readily available. The Christian population in Maluku is predominantly Protestant as their ancestors were converted by the Dutch. In Flores, Timor, and Sumba, however, the people are mostly Catholic. These islands were actively proselytized by the Portuguese.

Catholic church in West Timor (Courtesy of Florence Lamoureux)

Hinduism and Buddhism

Hinduism was introduced from India and is still practiced on Bali. Throughout the rest of Indonesia one observes Hindu statues and monuments in varying stages of disrepair but sees very little in the way of traditional religious practice. For example, Bali's form of Hinduism does not have the caste system that is so prevalent in India. Hinduism accounts for the belief of approximately 2.4 percent of Indonesia's population.

Buddhism, introduced first to Sumatra from India, is less prevalent, with less than 1 percent of the population calling themselves Buddhists. Most Indonesian Buddhists live on Java.

EDUCATION

Education is a priority in Indonesian families, and even in the most difficult of times, they will find money for school expenses. Education was the exclusive right of a privileged class for too long, and modern-day Indonesians understand that their children's futures and the future of their country depends on education.

Government/Public Schools

Upon its independence one of the first steps the Indonesian government took was to organize a public education system. Schools were established for primary, intermediate, and secondary levels under the government's Ministry of Religious Affairs. Originally six years of primary education was required; this number was later increased to nine years. The new government decreed that classes be taught in Indonesian, although in some schools local dialects are still used, especially in the early primary grades. Current figures show that about 15 percent of Indonesia's schools offer instruction in local languages.

Under Suharto's New Order the government took over more of the cost of public education and built thousands of new schools. More books and educational materials were supplied, and an effort was made in rural areas to reach children who had not had the opportunity to go to school. By the end of 1990 the government estimated that 91 percent of all 7–12-year-olds were attending primary school, compared to 62 percent of all boys and 58 percent of all girls in 1970. The same report shows that just less than 8 million students were enrolled in intermediate schools and 4.7 million were attending high schools in 1990.

Nine years of formal schooling are now compulsory in Indonesia. In 1990 approximately 92 percent of eligible primary school children were enrolled in school. In 1991 almost 1.5 million Indonesians were registered in degree programs at public and private universities and colleges across the country. The literacy rate of the country in 1990 was 85 percent. Prior to the Asian economic crisis in 1997 most children attended school, but the cost of required school uniforms, books, and supplies (for which families are solely responsible) has now placed public education out of the reach of some families. Tuition is charged for both government and Islamic schools; monthly elementary school tuition runs approximately $6.25 at government schools and $25 at Islamic schools. Fees run higher for middle schools and high schools. This, and the fact that in hard economic times it is not unusual for children to work in the rice fields or otherwise contribute to the family income, has affected school enrollments although no current data is available that gives precise figures.

Government school facilities in Indonesia are often inadequate, sometimes without running water and often lacking basic building maintenance. Teachers are poorly paid and must often work in unwholesome environments with a paucity of educational materials. Books are at a premium, and it is rare for students to have copies of textbooks. Conditions are somewhat better in the Islamic schools. In high schools and universities some texts are still in English, although more and more are being published in Indonesian.

Early Educational Institutions

During most of the Dutch colonial period, education for the masses did not exist. Only a few children of the elite ruling class on Java were allowed an education. In the early twentieth century, however, when the Dutch implemented their Ethical Policy, schools for Indonesian children began to appear under the auspices of the colonial government as well as through the work of dedicated individuals and several nationalist and religious groups.

Raden Adjeng Kartini

Raden Kartini was a Javanese of noble birth. At the time she was growing up there were almost no educational opportunities for women in Indonesia. The Dutch schools were limited to Dutch children and the sons of Indonesian elite. Kartini established a primary school exclusively for girls in 1903. After independence the national government took over the matter of public education, and girls were granted equal educational rights with boys.

Taman Siswa

In 1922 Ki Hadjar Dewantara established the first Taman Siswa (Garden of Pupils) school in Yogyakarta in Central Java. Ki Hadjar Dewantara had been exiled to the Netherlands from 1913–1919, and while there he became interested in education. He established Taman Siswa as an alternative to colonial and Islamic schools. These schools were immensely popular, and by 1932 there were over 165 Taman Siswa schools in Indonesia. Taman Siswa schools still exist in Indonesia though their numbers decreased with the establishment of government-sponsored public education.

Muhammadiyah

At the same time Taman Siswa was introduced to Indonesia, modernist Muslims were establishing schools as well. In 1912 Kyai Haji Ahmad Dahlan, an Islamic scholar who had studied in Mecca, established Muhammadiyah (the Way of Muhammad). Because it purported modernist Islamic views that traditionalist Muslims in Java opposed, the organization grew slowly. However, by 1925 there were fifty-five Muhammadiyah schools in Indonesia. That same year Muhammadiyah education was introduced to Minangkabau society on Sumatra, where it flourished. By 1938 the organization had 1,774 schools along with numerous mosques and libraries all supporting the tenets of modernist Islam.

Budi Utomo

Budi Utomo was another organization that supported education. Founded in 1908, it reached its peak membership of 10,000 in December 1909. Its members' concern was the loss of Hindu-Buddhist elements in Javanese culture. Budi Utomo was more a political entity than an educational organization. However, its founder, Dr. Wahidin Soedirohoesodo, made a great effort to provide financial support for Javanese elite to study classical dance and gamelan. He also supported a Western style of education, as opposed to the Islamic style promoted by the modernists in Muhammadiyah. Budi Utomo was disbanded in 1935.

It was during this same period that a few bright, young Indonesian scholars attended colleges and universities in the Netherlands. Among them were men and women who opposed not only the colonial government in Indonesia but the ruling Indonesian class as well. These people formed the core of the Indonesian independence movement, and their strong desire for mass education was reflected in the new republic's constitution.

Pesantren

Pesantren, meaning "religious boarding schools," have a long history in Indonesia, back as far as the Majapahit empire. The curriculum at these religious schools is based on the Koran. However, *pesantren* offer the range of curriculum required by the government education system. The scholars who first established these schools were orthodox Muslims, and when modernist Islam came to Java in the 1900s they made every effort to oppose it. Until mass education became available, *pesantren* were the only institutions where Indonesians could obtain an education, and they were restricted to males. A mainstay of their course offerings was—and still is—Arabic. The fact that these schools were the sole providers of education to Javanese for over a century and that their education was based on the teachings of Islam explains why many of Indonesia's leaders—products of this education system—support a government based on religion.

Today these schools are chiefly for secondary and university-level students. The Indonesian government acknowledges four types of *pesantren.* The first is the traditional school, where students board and study under a *kyai* (teacher) who develops the curriculum. The second has secular and religious courses and sometimes uses its own curriculum and sometimes one developed by the Ministry of Religious Affairs. The third type follows the Ministry of Education model plus offers a traditional religious education. The fourth is primarily a boarding home. Residents at these *pesantren* attend either regular government schools or *madrasah,* and the *kyai* offers religious classes in the evenings. Tuition at *pesantren* is variable, depending on the school's reputation. They are considered private schools, and children must apply to them as in any private institution.

The Islamic organization Nahdlatul Ulama controls many *pesantren.* It was formed in East Java in 1926 as an opposition group to the modernist Muslims. Most of Nahdlatul Ulama's founding *kyai* were from rural areas of Indonesia where traditional Islam was favored. Indonesia's forth president, Abdurrahman Wahid, is a member of a prominent Nahdlatul Ulama family and himself a leader in this traditional Islamic organization.

The number of *pesantren* in Indonesia jumped from over 4,700 in 1980 to 9,000 in 1996; student enrollments in that period went from about 800,000 to 1,900,000, with the largest growth rate in the 1990s. A significant number of graduates from these schools went on to establish their own *pesantren*, thus reinforcing the teachings of the school many times over.

Madrasah

Madrasah means school in Arabic; they are Islamic-based institutions that concentrate on primary and secondary education. In recent years these schools have incorporated the Indonesian Department of Education's curriculum, making for easy transition between *madrasahs* and government schools. *Madrasah* schools are popular, as their costs are lower than those of government schools.

Christian Schools

Catholic schools are fairly common in Indonesia, especially on Java. Classes are usually taught by nuns, and the curriculum is quite demanding. Many devout Muslims send their children to these schools because of their high level of academic performance.

References

Fox, James (ed.). *Indonesian Heritage Series: Religion and Ritual*. Singapore: Editions Didier Miller, 1998.

McBeth, John, and Dini Djalal. "A Puppet on a String." *Far Eastern Economic Review*, August 2, 2001: 12–18.

Mydans, Seth. "Indonesian Rulers Mix Politics and Mysticism." *New York Times*, September 2, 2001. (Printed in the *Honolulu Star Bulletin*, September 2, 2002: F5.)

Ricklefs, M. C. *A History of Modern Indonesia*. Hong Kong: Macmillan, 1990.

Rigg, Jonathan (ed.). *Indonesian Heritage Series: The Human Environment*. Singapore: Editions Didier Miller, 1996.

Schwarz, Adam. *A Nation in Waiting: Indonesia in the 1990s*. Boulder: Westview Press, 1994.

Websites

Government structure: http://www.indonesianet.com/hilight/higovern.htm

Human rights: http://www.pbs.org/newshour/bb/asia/july-dec99/indonesia_7–8.html

The Indonesian 1945 constitution: http://www.indonesiamission-ny.org/
    issuebaru/HumnRight/1945cons.htm
  http://www.insideindonesia.org/edit65/fealy.htm
The military in Indonesia: http://www.fas.org/irp/world/indonesia/abri.htm
Pancasila: http://www.Info-indo.com/history/pancasila.htm
The Qur'an, *hadith,* and the prophet Muhammad: http://www.arches.uga.edu/~
    godlas/primsourcisl.html

CHAPTER FOUR
Indonesian Society and Contemporary Issues

THE FAMILY

The family is the primary unit in Indonesia. From infancy through old age an Indonesian remains close to his or her parents and siblings. Prior to independence, generations of families tended to stay in the same village. In the twentieth century, as more people became educated and opportunities were limited in the villages, many villagers relocated to urban areas. However, even family members who have moved away return to their villages to visit as often as they can, and always for the Idul Fitri holiday at the end of the fasting period of Ramadan. Respect for one's parents and grandparents is a basic feature of Indonesian culture. Respect is often shown to a parent or a respected elder by kissing the back of the person's hand on first encountering them after an absence. It is expected that children will do as their parents tell them. Opposing their wishes indicates a lack of respect and would result in admonition and, in severe cases, ostrasization.

In recent years there are many fewer arranged marriages in Indonesia, but the practice does still exist, especially in rural regions. Even in cases where men and women select their marriage partners, family approval is of utmost importance. Once a couple agrees that they will marry, their parents get together to make the arrangements. If for any reason either the potential bride or groom breaks the engagement, that person's parents lose face. Although there is considerable marriage across ethnic groups, many older people still frown on it, expecting their offspring to marry someone in the same tribal group. Also, a household with husband and wife practicing different religions would be exceptional, though with modern mobility, this too is changing.

Another aspect of Indonesian life that is changing is the wearing of traditional clothing. Although it is not uncommon to see women in traditional dress, they are more and more often seen in Western clothing. Traditional dress for an Indonesian woman is a sarong (*kain*), a piece of cotton cloth about a yard wide and two and a half yards long, fastened around the waist and falling to the ankles. The cloth is usually an intricately patterned batik; batik designs are made through a method of hand-printing by coating with wax the parts of the fabric not to be dyed. An overblouse called a *kebaya* is also worn. A *kebaya* may come to a woman's hips or to mid-thigh. *Kain* and *kebaya* are worn on ceremonial occasions such as weddings, and at these events the women's *kain* would be elegant batiks and their *kebaya* made from the finest diaphanous fabric. Traditional dress for men is a sarong. Men will usually don these plaid wraparound garments in the evening after they bathe. This is casual dress, and men do not wear sarongs to formal affairs or to their offices. For formal occasions, however, men usually wear long-sleeved batik shirts, and they always wear the black fez hat, which they call *peci* (pronounced "peachy"). This is also a mark of nationalism and patriotism. The *peci* is worn by all men at any time, but always at formal activities.

Family Planning

Until post–World War II infant mortality in Indonesia was high. It was not uncommon for a woman to have ten or more children, several of whom would not live to see adulthood. Large families were necessary to work the rice fields (*sawah*), and the death of babies and small children, while deeply mourned, was a fact of life. With the discovery of antibiotics and other modern medicines, fewer babies and young children died, and Indonesia's population reflected this phenomenon. As the country's population increased, so too did its dependency on government resources and international aid, and Indonesia was forced to import food, most notably rice. The shortage of rice continued until the introduction of "miracle rice" in the 1970s. This strain of rice was developed through research at the International Rice Research Institute (IRRI) in Los Banos in the Philippines. Intense efforts to increase rice yields were undertaken principally to deal with the serious matter of burgeoning populations in post–World War II Asia. The new rice plants had higher yields and went a long way toward solving Indonesia's problem of self-sufficiency in rice production. However, unforeseen problems arose. Fewer people were needed to work the *sawah*, and more and more young men and women were leaving the villages and looking to the towns and cities for work. The result of this exodus to the cities was a growth in urban ghettos and the resultant problem of increasing urban crime. The Suharto government was keenly aware of the problems related to overpopulation, and its solution was to institute a policy called "Two Is Enough" (Dua Cukup). This program encouraged the use of birth control and other family planning methods and was quite effective. From 1974–1991 the birth rate in Indonesia dropped 5.6 percent. Indonesia's population still increased, but less dramatically. Population growth in 2001 was estimated at just 1.6 percent.

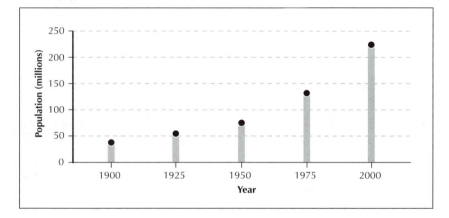

Figure 4.1: Indonesia's Population 1900–2000

Source: http://www.library.uu.nl/wesp/populstat/Asia/Indonesia.htm (Jan Lahmeyer)

Although Islam does not encourage family planning, Suharto made it a priority in his administration. The case was made that smaller families would allow children more advantages, such as education. More education would mean better jobs, which would result in higher incomes. This would benefit an entire family. In short, fewer children meant a higher standard of living for everyone in the household.

Women

Indonesia is rapidly becoming an industrial nation, and women are working in factories in increasing numbers. Even before this era, women were the backbone of Indonesia's economy as small-scale marketers and farmers. Prior to the arrival of international industries, such as Goodyear and Nike, a family's income relied on what could be produced by its members and what profit could be made from the sale of these products in the market. Selling produce, meat, and eggs not consumed by the family supplied much needed income. Industrialization has brought change to Indonesia, and especially to women. Many who had been working as domestic servants have been attracted to factory work, and some were forced to leave school to take menial factory jobs in the aftermath of the 1997 economic meltdown. Many industries are relocating to Indonesia, and almost all of them are actively seeking women workers for low salaried positions. For the woman with little education, a job in a garment or shoe factory might seem more appealing than being a maid. However, not all factories are concerned about the welfare of their workers. In many instances where poor salaries and sweat-shop conditions exist, disillusioned women have learned that the industrial sector is not a panacea.

In spite of industrialization, women who sell their goods in the marketplaces are still very much in evidence. It is traditional work for women, and the market vendors will remain a mainstay of the Indonesian economy for many years to come. This is underscored by the fact that women have less access to education than do men.

Even so, a substantial number of Indonesian women do seek degrees in higher education, and a significant number study abroad. Many Indonesian women hold professional positions. In the mid-1990s approximately 44 percent of all physicians and 63 percent of dentists in Indonesia were women. Women comprise half of all of the nation's primary teachers, and only slightly fewer teach secondary school. The figures for women in government are less encouraging: In 1996 women held 12.8 percent of the seats in parliament, but in 1999 that number dropped to 8.8 percent.

According to an October 2000 speech by the U.S. ambassador to Indonesia, Richard S. Gelbard, "women in Indonesia make up over half of the country's work force." These remarks were made at the Indonesian Women's Workers Conference in Jakarta in a speech titled "Working Women in Indonesia." Despite the range of occupations they hold, women's salaries still are well behind those of men, and their jobs are less secure. In the aftermath of the 1997 economic meltdown, women were fired from their positions in the manufacturing, financial, and trade sectors at a much higher rate than men were.

When women object to unfair treatment in the workplace, the result can be shocking. Two incidents provide examples of violence that resulted when women protested conditions in the factories where they worked and where the workers were primarily women. In 1993 a woman was tortured and killed when she objected to the firing of her fellow workers at a watch factory in the vicinity of Surabaya. Her story was the focus of a play, *Marsinah Menggugat,* which was performed not only in Indonesia but in several U.S. cities as well. In 1994 there was another murder. This time a woman, Titi Sugiarti, was killed for protesting working conditions in a textile factory outside of Bandung. Her crime was attempting to organize a strike to improve working conditions for the women employed at that company. In neither of these cases were the persons responsible brought to justice, and women labor leaders continue to be arrested and imprisoned.

Indonesian women marry on average at 18.5 years old, and they have an average of 2.56 children. A woman's life span is about 65.3 years. Although the average girl will spend six years in school, only 9.1 percent will attend university. All women over age eighteen may vote, and all married women (and men) may vote regardless of age.

On April 12, 1998, the *Indonesian Observer* reported that 20,000 Indonesian women die every year due to childbirth-related problems. This is about 393 women for every 100,000 live births. The *Observer* further stated that this number is fifty times higher than in developed countries, and three to six times higher than in other Southeast Asian countries such as Malaysia, Thailand, and the Philippines. However, almost 90 percent of pregnant women receive prenatal care. HIV and AIDS are on the increase in Indonesia. In March 2002 the Indonesian government initiated a program to control the spread of AIDS. Among women, the virus is most commonly seen in the sex trade. In Jakarta the percentage of cases of HIV or AIDS among prostitutes is reported to be around 17 percent, and in some regions of Papua it is thought to be as high as 26 percent among village women not involved in prostitution. Control of the spread of this disease is exacerbated by the refusal of many Muslim men to use condoms. Government reports on the number of cases in Indonesia have been unreliable. In 1996, for example, the government announced that there were 390 people suffering from HIV or AIDS in the entire country. In contrast, a study by a University of Indonesia research group set the number at between 12,000 and 31,000. It is certainly unrealistic to accept that fewer than 400 people in a country of over 224 million people suffer from these diseases, which have spread so rapidly throughout the world.

One of Indonesia's most influential women was Raden Adjeng Kartini. Born in 1879, this educated daughter of a Javanese aristocrat became well known for her efforts to bring about equal rights for all Indonesian women, not just those of noble birth. Her erudite correspondence with a Dutch woman was eventually published as *From the Darkness Comes Light.* Her birthday, April 21, is an Indonesian holiday—Mother's Day. Kartini is best known in Indonesia for starting a

Muslim schoolgirls, Madura (Courtesy of Florence Lamoureux)

school for girls at a time when only boys were educated. Her father, a member of the Javanese elite and an educated man, wanted his daughter to be educated. The young princess likewise felt compassion toward other less fortunate women and wanted them to have the same opportunities to learn that she had.

The role of Muslim women in Indonesian society is of interest in the West, especially since 9/11. Certainly more women wear the headscarf today than did thirty years ago, but it is still rare to see an Indonesian woman completely covered in a *burka*. Women are active in programs at their village mosques, but in most cases this does not preclude their activity in other organizations. In cases of fundamentalist Islam, however, this is different. Strict Muslim women usually spend their time with other women and are kept separate from men on many occasions. For example, at weddings and other ceremonies, men gather in one room and women in another. A devout Muslim woman would not touch a man who is not a family member. This was recently observed when a well-educated Muslim woman who had done graduate work abroad invited her university professor from thirty years earlier to come to her home near Jakarta. Although genuinely delighted to see her former teacher, she was forbidden by tenets of her religion from shaking his hand.

Within Indonesia are countless women's organizations, ranging from religious to military in their focus, and many of them have considerable political influence. Indonesian women have clearly shown that there is strength in numbers, whether through military wives' clubs, market cooperatives, or labor unions. Indeed, given the constraints of Islamic law, Indonesian women can sometimes best make their voices heard through these women's organizations.

Muslim men are allowed up to four wives—if all are treated equally. This is not a practice that most women accept gracefully, and it is often through participation in these women's organizations that a women faced with this situation finds the sympathy and courage to deal with this awkward dilemma.

THE VILLAGE

Next to the family an Indonesian owes loyalty to the village. In rural areas village people work together to plant and harvest rice. Rice is served at every meal, even if potatoes, bread, or noodles are on the table as well. Village councils meet to determine who will work in the *sawah* and when. Once the rice is harvested it is divided among those who worked to plant, harvest, and thresh it. Prior to the green revolution, rice plants were not as easy to harvest, and often small amounts of rice were left in the fields after the threshing. This grain was gleaned by the poor of the village, who came in after the harvest and gathered the rice left on the ground. It was one way the village cared for the less fortunate among them. Caring for the poor is a basic tenet of Islam, and it is imperative that the less fortunate villagers—widows, the disabled— be cared for by the more fortunate. Indeed, the more prosperous a family, the greater their obligation to assist the less fortunate among them. Although *sawah* are usually individually owned, it is the custom for rice farmers to help each other with planting and harvesting. This policy of *gotong royang* is ever present in Indonesian society.

Like so many other aspects of Indonesian culture, village life is changing, and if a person earns enough money he or she may purchase rice and not have to face the back-breaking task of working in the fields. If a person of such means remains in the village he or she would still par-

Women and children in a rural fishing village (Center for Southeast Asian Studies)

ticipate in the many rituals related to the growing of rice. The villager who moves to the city, in contrast, cannot do this. By not participating in the planting and harvesting of rice, urban dwellers are less exposed to the village rituals, and their ties to the old ways tend to weaken.

Much tradition is imbedded in producing, preparing, and eating rice. For example, it is customary to serve yellow rice (*nasi kuning*) in the shape of a cone on special occasions. The cone must be "broken" by the person being honored, who does so by taking the first serving of it. Rice in Indonesia is more than a staple food; it has a connection to almost every aspect of life. The author witnessed an interesting incident in West Java several years ago when two five-year-old girls were playing with a set of toy dishes. They were pretending to prepare and cook a meal when a foreigner suggested that the children be given a few spoons of uncooked rice to make their play more realistic. She was told that this would be frowned upon in Indonesian culture. Rice is too meaningful to the Indonesians and too tied to their rituals for children to play with it. Other foods yes, but not rice.

Village Work away from the Rice Fields

Of course the planting and harvesting of rice is not the only work done in the village. There are merchants who own a variety of shops, gas stations with mechanics, doctors, dentists, teachers, and depending on the size of the village, individuals who teach classes outside of the formal classroom in music, dance, and other arts. As already noted, women market vendors are a significant source of income for many families. An interesting businessman is the village barber. He may ply his trade in a shop or with a stool for his customer located under a convenient tree in the village marketplace. He is a good example of the entrepreneurial villager who fills a need in the village while keeping his overhead costs as low as possible. The shoe repair man is an equally enterprising businessman. He may be seen in the village marketplace with his glue pot, knives, and pieces of old tires. He cuts the rubber to fit the sole of the worn shoe and attaches it with strong glue. There are many such workers on the streets of Indonesia. They perform services that everyone requires—including food vending and repair work—and because they have almost no overhead they are able to do their work for very little money. If something breaks and it is at all possible to repair it, there is probably a *tukang* (worker) in the marketplace who can fix it. This ingenuity provides a living wage for many an otherwise unemployed man or woman.

The Village Market

A popular gathering place is the market (*pasar*). Here one finds not only shoppers, but also vendors, beggars, businessmen and women, and less savory characters such as pickpockets. A wide variety of goods and services are available in an Indonesian *pasar*. Farmers bring their produce, meat, and eggs and display these items in booths or on the sidewalk. Often it is women who do this, and it is not unusual to see a nursing mother deftly making change as she sells vegetables or fruit. The market is a place to rid oneself of unwanted items as well. Old shoes, clothing, pots and pans, books, and an assortment of second-hand household and personal items are for sale.

Goods ranging from cosmetics to electronic equipment can be found in an Indonesian market. Toys from China, often broken or flimsily made, are on display everywhere. (One suspects that the better grade of Chinese products is sent to the developed countries.) Dry and paper goods are available, but they are most frequently sold in shops, not directly on the street. Often the shopkeepers are Chinese and have owned their establishments for generations. Gold jewelry stores are prominent and are almost exclusively Chinese owned. Many Indonesians refuse to trust banks, preferring to buy gold as a means of saving their money. It is always redeemable, and Indonesian gold at 22 carats is a valuable commodity. This is a practice that transcends all levels of society: From the servant to the wealthy landowner, gold jewelry is considered to be a safe investment. Failing banks and unsettled economies over the decades have no doubt contributed to this practice. Restaurants and professional offices are also located in the marketplace, as are a wide variety of prepared foodstuffs that vendors sell from small individual carts. These men and women cook curries, meatball soups, and other delicacies while the buyer waits. If you want takeout you have to bring your own container, as the cook must rinse each dish and use it for the next customer. Paper plates are much too expensive, although meals that lend themselves to such unique packaging are often served on banana leaves. Spoons are provided for soups, but sticky foods are often eaten with one's fingers.

Markets are transportation centers, and at their peripheries one sees dozens of horse carts, trishaws, and a wide selection of motorized vehicles. Drivers wait here for the next shopper who will need a ride back home. Driving is hectic around the marketplace, and there are many accidents. This situation has been intensified in recent years as a plethora of cars and trucks of all sizes attempt to negotiate the narrow and busy marketplace streets and alleys. Men with goods in containers balanced on either end of a bamboo pole carried across one shoulder also are a common sight along these streets and alleys, though admittedly not as much in evidence as they were in the past.

THE CITY

The contrast between rich and poor is much sharper in Indonesia's cities than in the villages. The spirit of *gotong royong* does not protect the unemployed city dweller to the same extent that it protects the villager. This further emphasizes the importance of family proximity and of maintaining a close relationship with one's relatives.

The shopping mall is a popular phenomenon throughout Indonesia's cities. Large and small, these busy arcades might spread over a large area or be housed in a multilevel building with courtyards and escalators—which may or may not be in working order. Their patrons are teenagers, middle-class men and women, and senior citizens who come not only to shop but to enjoy the glitz of the music, lights, and multitiered stores that contrast to the more simplified—and less expensive—village markets. Just as in the United States, malls house movie theaters and fast-food restaurants—among them Dunkin

Parliament grounds with reflecting pool and sculpture (Center for Southeast Asian Studies)

Donuts, Kentucky Fried Chicken, and McDonalds—along with other commercial enterprises. Indonesian shopping centers provide their visitors with a wide variety of stores and restaurants as well as photocopying shops and other technology service-oriented businesses. Malls are popular meeting places, and just as in the United States, teenagers are the mainstay of them. There have been several serious fires in Indonesian shopping centers. Fire regulations in Indonesia are not strictly enforced, and fire-fighting equipment is not as readily available as it is in Western countries. The multiple-level malls are more apt to suffer from serious fires, and lack of insurance coverage often means that destroyed shopping centers are not rebuilt.

The larger cities are filled with expensive hotels and restaurants that cater to the people, both wealthy Indonesians and foreigners, who come to do business. The successful urban dweller may be a business person, a lawyer, a physician, a secretary, a salesperson, a blue-collar laborer, or a government official. As is the case in many Asian cities, the available workforce outnumbers positions. Jobs in the cities often require skills that the marginally educated villager lacks. The result is an increasing urban population of undereducated, underemployed people. City rules and regulations further limit opportunities for this potential workforce. The recent prohibition of manual and motorized trishaws on inner-city streets eliminated jobs for many men who formerly survived on income generated by transporting people short distances. Sidewalk vendors are sometimes allowed to set up their stands, but in most cities' downtown districts this also is prohibited. Many vendors defy this law, plying their trade with one eye out for the police. The lack of work for this unemployed and underemployed strata of society has produced a growing number of desperate people who have been drawn to gang membership and drug sales and use.

Use of Illegal Drugs

The Indonesian government provides little data on the use of drugs, though government sources admit it is a growing problem. In the Australian newspaper *The Age,* reporter Tom Hyland in Jakarta wrote on January 4, 2003, that drug use in Indonesia is on the rise, with ecstasy being the drug of choice. As is often the case, drug users who inject substances suffer the additional scourge of HIV or AIDS when they share needles. *The Age* article stated that in a health clinic on Bali, a test done on ninety-eight people who inject drugs showed that all but five of them tested positive for HIV. A study done in Jakarta, where drug use is most common in nightclubs, showed similar results. Henry Yasodinigrat, an Indonesian member of an antidrug lobbying group and member of the government's National Narcotics Agency, made this comment in *The Age* article: "There is not a school or district anywhere in the country where drugs are not used."

The same article quotes a health worker as saying that there is a "caste system" among Indonesian drug users. The middle class uses ecstasy, and the lower classes use *shabu-shabu* (a form of methamphetamine). High-grade Sumatran marijuana is available to the user with enough money. With drug use on the rise, the problem calls for strict control, but according to one antidrug campaigner quoted in *The Age,* "the syndicates have a lot of money to buy officials." A U.S. State Department report in 1999 claimed that ecstasy abuse is a major problem in Indonesia. It went on to note that there has been a drastic increase in methamphetamine use among teenagers, young professionals, and prostitutes in recent years. And a December 1, 2002, article in the *Jakarta Post* by David and Joyce Djaelani Gordon reported that of 120,000 persons infected with HIV/AIDS, 43,000 were intravenous drug users.

With the government's budget already too meager to cover such concerns as the high infant mortality rate, malaria control, tuberculosis, and unclean water, fighting drugs can fall between the cracks. Despite this, Indonesia's official tolerance of drug sales and use is zero. Amnesty International reports that in October 2001 Megawati called for the increased use of the death penalty for drug traffickers and drug dealers.

Control of drug sales and use is difficult in the wealthiest of nations. Indonesia's myriad political and economic dilemmas require that the money available for all government programs be divided many ways, leaving little for drug use prevention and treatment and for the control of the import of illegal drugs.

Anti-Chinese Sentiment

Resentment of the wealthy by the poor has been prevalent in Indonesia's urban areas since colonial times. This hatred is often manifested in violence toward the Chinese community. Many Chinese held lucrative positions in Indonesia during the colonial period, when the Dutch allowed them to buy and sell goods, enabling the Chinese to become an entrenched merchant class. The Chinese also were allowed to own shops, while Indonesians were denied that privilege. The Chinese were rarely farmers, and therefore they were not forced to produce large quantities of agricultural products to meet Dutch quotas, as were the Indonesians. Later, as money lenders, the Chinese became even more unpopular with many Indonesians, who viewed them as a privileged class while they, the people of that land, were not given the same advantages. This was evidenced in the 1998 riots in Jakarta when Chinese shops were burned and Chinese women raped. Rampaging gangs roamed the city streets, angry at a system that denied them the material goods their wealthy neighbors possessed.

Indonesia's cities have many of the same problems of cities around the world, but their problems are currently intensified by continuing economic troubles that result in high unemployment and low salaries.

TRADITIONAL ARTS AND ENTERTAINMENT

The cultures of Indonesia's islands vary widely and their differences, as manifested in their arts and entertainment, reflect the diversity of the country.

Two of Indonesia's best-known traditional occupations concern the decorating and weaving of cloth, namely batik and ikat. Another is the assembly of traditional musical instruments for the Indonesian game-lan, or percussion orchestra, which accompanies *wayang kulit* per-formances, the shadow-puppet theater that is perhaps the artform most associated with Indonesia. Dance, stone and wood carving, metal work, and painting round out the archipelago's collection of traditional arts and entertainments.

Batik

Indonesian batik is among the finest in the world. The process of out-lining patterns on fabric in wax and then dying unwaxed portions in selected colors has long been an art in Indonesia. The artist starts with the lightest color and moves on to the darkest, covering the col-ored portions with wax to protect them before the piece of cloth is dipped into the next colored dye. This is traditionally women's work, and many Indonesians consider the best batik makers to be in Cen-tral Java. There are a variety of complex designs that these workers follow, some small and delicate and others big and expansive. Tradi-tional batik colors are brown, black, and dark blue, although mod-

Batik (Center for Southeast Asian Studies)

ern shoppers find batiks in many different colors. Traditional batiks are often considered to have mystical qualities and are prized as such. A length of high-quality batik sells for well over $1,000, although there is a wide selection of moderately priced pieces ($15–$50) in Indonesian markets.

Ikat

Ikat is made by dying strands of cotton before weaving them into cloth. Making this fabric—processing the cotton, dying it, and weaving it—is extremely labor-intensive; consequently, ikat is not produced in large quantities for general consumption. Like batik making, weaving ikat is primarily women's work. The best examples of ikat are found on the islands of Sumba, Flores, and Roti and, to a much lesser extent, on West Timor. On these islands one can still see colorfully dyed stands of cotton drying on lines and shrubbery and women with backstrap looms turning out traditional patterns. As is the case with batik, certain ikats are believed to have magical powers. These are handed down from parent to child. Also like batik, antique pieces of ikat can be very expensive. Both batik and ikat patterns can be made by stamping or silk-screening designs onto fabric. These are much less expensive and are obviously not authentically produced batiks and ikats.

Gamelan Instruments

The art of making the gongs used in the percussion orchestra, the gamelan, is carried on by special blacksmiths, many located in Central Java. The brass instruments are still created in the traditional manner, usually by families where the process of pounding the red hot metal to specific thickness and size has been handed down from father to son. In addition to gongs, the gamelan orchestra consists of drums and brass plates of varying sizes suspended across a frame and played somewhat like a xylophone. There are also flutes and the *rebab,* the only stringed instrument in the orchestra. During *wayang kulit* (shadow puppet) performances, female vocalists usually accompany the gamelan musicians. Their voices enhance the details of the story being told by the *dalang* (puppet master). The gamelan is played not only at *wayang kulit* performances but also at dance performances and myriad other activities and events. Its distinctive music is associated with Indonesia.

Gamelan musicians perform on Bali. This orchestra is composed mainly of percussion intruments. (Paul Almasy/Corbis)

Shadow Puppets

Probably the most enduring form of Indonesian family entertainment is the shadow puppet show. A puppet master (*dalang*) manipulates the leather puppets (*wayang kulit*). He—the *dalang* is almost always a man—adroitly controls the puppets that he displays between a bright light, traditionally a gas lantern, and a screen that may be as simple as a large square of white cloth. Members of the audience may watch the performances from either side of the screen, choosing to view the dexterity of the *dalang* and see the colorful puppets at rest, as well as being active, or to enjoy the mystical effect of the shadows. A tal-

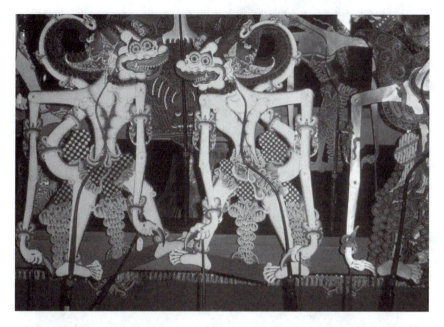

Wayang Kulit, three-dimensional leather puppets used in Indonesian theater productions (Courtesy of Florence Lamoureux)

ented *dalang* can move several puppets at the same time. A gamelan orchestra accompanies the puppeteer and the chorus as they relate the story the puppets are acting out on the screen.

A shadow play may go on for several hours, all night, or even days. Great battles and tender family scenes are portrayed with equal dramatic presence. The accompaniment of the gamelan adds to the mystical atmosphere the *dalang* is creating. Each brightly painted puppet is unique. Their manner of moving indicates to the audience if they are refined (*halus*) or course (*kasar*). Although it would take an outsider many performances to notice the many subtle differences between the mannerisms of good and evil characters, Indonesians are able to do this when they are children. In addition to flat leather puppets (*wayang kulit*) there are theater performances using three-dimensional wooden puppets, called *wayang golek*. They are held by a wooden rod and are most often seen in West Java. A third but much less common puppet is the *wayang kelitik*. These are flat wooden puppets that are also held by a rod fixed to the bottom of the puppet. *Wayang kelitik* are rarely used in performances today. However, they can still be found in Jakarta's antique shops. The two most popular

Wood carving of Rama and Sinta, characters in the Ramayana
(Courtesy of Florence Lamoureux)

stories of puppet theater, *The Ramayana* and *The Mahabarata,* have their origins in India.

The Ramayana

The *Ramayana* tells the story of Prince Rama, who is banished to the forest with his beautiful wife, Sinta, and his brother, Laksmana. When Rama and Laksmana continue deep into the forest looking for a golden deer that Sinta saw and wanted them to bring to her, disaster strikes. Sinta is kidnapped by the evil giant Rawana, and Rama's attempts to rescue her occupy much of the story. Well-known characters in this epic are the monkey Hanuman and the mythical bird, the Garuda, who assist Rama in his quest to rescue Sinta. The *Ramayana* has multiple endings. In one ending Sinta is reunited with Rama. In another she is rejected by him as she may no longer be pure. In a third Sinta must undergo a trial by fire, which she does to prove her purity.

The Mahabarata

This ancient tale is one of intrigue and family rivalry. It features the long-existing animosity between the Pandawa and Kurawas families. At various times in the past each family has had the upper hand over the other. The *dalang* tells the story of past intrigues and difficulties each family encountered. The scene for much of the story is the several-day battle that takes place between the two related clans. The Pandawa brothers emerge victorious, and the eldest brother becomes king.

The *Mahabarata* is more popular in Indonesia than *The Ramayana,* though characters from both stories are immensely popular and can be seen carved in stone and wood and frequently portrayed in paintings and sculpture. Adaptations of both *The Ramayana* and *The Mahabarata* are heard on radio and seen on television and in dance performances. *Wayang kulit* is a form of entertainment that transcends generations, and it is not uncommon to see grandmothers and infants sitting on the grass, watching the performance. There is little protocol imposed on the audience as people eat, talk, sleep, and generally have a good time at such affairs.

Wayang Wong and other Dance Forms

In *Wayang wong,* an elegant style of dance drama, the *Ramayana* and *Mahabarata* epics are told with dancers on a stage, not shadow puppets on a screen. This style of dance was the precursor of *wayang orang*, a more popular version of dance drama than the classical *wayang wong*. *Wayang wong* is performed only by the most talented and best trained dancers. Their every movement reflects the class and elegance of the characters they are playing.

Java and Bali are rich in many arts. Yogyakarta, a city in Central Java, boasts several fine academies where classical dance is taught. Popular on Bali are performances of *topeng* (masked) and *legong* (performed by young girls) dances. Javanese and Balinese art forms are much more widely known internationally than the less well publicized forms of art and entertainment on other islands, although performance arts such as the *randai*—a dance form that depicts Islamic stories and incorporates martial arts (*silat*) in Sumtra—are gaining international fame.

The Kris

The kris is a traditional ceremonial dagger with a distinguishing wavy blade. It is believed to have strong mystical powers, and the Javanese who are fortunate enough to own them as family heirlooms treat them with great respect. Only expert artisans create krises, and the art of doing this, like most such crafts, is passed down in a family. Not only the kris itself, but the process of making it is also heavily imbued with spirituality. A fine kris is a work of art and highly prized. Owners periodically remove them from their special storage cases and carefully clean them. These knives are still seen frequently on ceremonial occasions such as circumcisions or weddings. Their presence gives status to the owner and lends a classic prestige to the occasions where they are worn. The kris is most often evident in Javanese culture.

Painting

Painting has been an art form in Indonesia for many years, but it became especially popular in the nineteenth century. Today there are extensive artist's colonies in Yogyakarta and the surrounding area, in Central Java, and in Bali.

Perhaps the most readily recognized of Indonesian painting styles is the traditional Balinese style wherein artists fill their canvases with details of daily life and mythology. Balinese painting changed markedly in the 1930s when a movement called Pita Maha revolutionized the form of Balinese painting. Bright colors and inked outlines characterized the new style. In the 1950s Balinese painting underwent another change as artists began to use flatter colors and emphasized body contours. Bali's best known painters include I Gusti Nyoman Lempad and Dewa Nyoman Batuan. Several European artists, including Walter Spies and Hans Snel, worked in Bali and influenced painting styles there.

Apart from Bali, many other Indonesians gained prominence as painters. Perhaps the most widely known of these painters is Affandi, an expressionist. Another painter of that genre is Popo Iskandar, who became active in Bandung art circles. Iskandar's sharp colors and animals command attention in galleries across Indonesia. A respected source of information on art in Indonesia is *Art in Indonesia: Continuities and Change,* by Claire Holt.

There are many painters, wood and stone carvers, and sculptors in Indonesia. Certainly Bali has men and women who are skilled in all of these arts and more. Add to these the Balinese dancers and musicians and Bali is unquestionably Indonesia's most creative island. Yogyakarta on Java is a close second to Bali with a large community of performers and artists in residence. Many of the Yogyakarta artists are under the patronage of the sultan of Yogyakarta, whose palace (*kraton*) houses numerous works of art and hosts innumerable dance and *wayang* performances. Many classes in dance and music are taught on the palace grounds. (To learn more about the many arts throughout Indonesia, consult the websites listed in the References section at the end of this chapter.)

POPULAR CULTURE

In contrast to traditional forms of culture are such popular activities as foreign films, martial arts, and other sports. Films are an especially well liked pastime with young and old alike. It is reported that President Magawati was in a theater viewing the animated American film *Shrek* when the MPR named her to replace the impeached president Gus Dur. Although fundamentalist Muslims are critical of the influence of foreign films and videos, this form of entertainment remains extremely popular with Indonesians.

Indian films are well liked in Indonesia, as are Chinese martial arts films. Many Indonesian filmmakers use *silat* (Indonesian martial arts) techniques in their films. Classes in this art of self-defense are popular with young Indonesian men. The randai dance from Sumatra utilizes *silat* moves in its performances.

Soccer is perhaps the most common and popular sport in Indonesia. One sees children and adults kicking the black-and-white patterned ball around vacant lots everywhere in the country. Indonesia participates in the Asian Games, a regional athletic competition started in New Delhi in 1951, and does well in them. The country's worldwide reputation for excellence in sports is in badminton, where it often wins Olympic medals. In the 2000 World Olympic Games in Sydney, Australia, the Indonesian badminton singles contender for the gold medal lost to a Chinese player. The Indonesian doubles team, however, did take the gold medal that year.

Among adults, nightclub entertainment is significantly attractive, as is gambling. However, Islam forbids both of these pastimes as well as drinking alcohol. As a result, people who participate in these activities tend to do so surreptitiously.

A recent style of music that is growing in popularity in college campuses is *nasyid.* It is categorized as Islamic music and is sung by groups of devout Muslim university students. The melodies are somewhat reminiscent of 1970 Western-style pop music, but the lyrics, which extol the virtues of Islam, are usually pointedly anti-Western.

Three other popular styles of music in Indonesia are *kroncong, dangdut,* and *pop barat. Kroncong* is similar to Western music, but it incorporates some gamelan sounds. *Dangdut* has its origins in Indian music. *Pop barat* (literally Western pop) is decidedly Indonesian but based on rock-and-roll music from Europe and the United States.

The music of the Indonesian gamelan orchestra is certainly not considered to be pop music, but it is well liked by Indonesians of all ages. Gamelan music is regularly broadcast on radio stations all across the island chain and is available on CDs and cassettes. These are best-sellers with tourists visiting Indonesia, who are often attracted to the haunting sounds of the gamelan.

In addition to the forms of entertainment noted previously, Indonesia has water parks, museums, art galleries, botanical gardens, symphonies, and theaters that feature ballet and dramatic performances. The country's best-known water park is Ancol. It is located in Jakarta near the harbor area and boasts the usual pools and slides that are found in similar amusement centers around the world.

There are a number of museums of all sizes and specialties throughout Indonesia. Several excellent museums located in Jakarta are the Indonesian National Museum, the Textile Museum, the Wayang Museum, the Jakarta Historic Museum, Taman Mini (Indonesians Miniature Park), and Sunda Kelapa, the harbor park. The art gallery

Taman Ismail Marzuki houses an excellent collection of Indonesian art. Although there are numerous galleries throughout Indonesia, Taman Ismail Marzuki is one of the best. Contemporary artists also display their paintings at Ancol.

An excellent place to view the arts and crafts from the Indonesian islands is Taman Mini in Jakarta. Built at the request of Madame Suharto in 1975, the park features a number of small museums, each in the form of a house unique to the architecture of a specific island. Inside these houses are people dressed in the traditional clothing of that region, performing one or more of the crafts for which the people living there are noted.

The city of Bogor, located about forty miles inland from Jakarta, is the site of the country's predominant botanical garden, Kebun Raya (great garden). Visitors encounter an enormous range of tropical trees, plants, and flowers as they walk along the garden's many winding pathways. Those in the garden at sunset are often fortunate enough to see Kebun Raya's impressive community of large nocturnal fruit bats leave their perches in garden trees and set out in search of food. The bats make this flight all together, and it is quite startling to watch their departure from the garden. Other animals can be found there as well: Several varieties of snakes, scorpions, centipedes, and even a large monitor lizard are among the garden's inhabitants. Kebun Raya is not only a tourist attraction but, more important, a thriving research center. Botanists, horticulturalists, and plant pathologists from all over the world come to Bogor to do research.

Theaters in Jakarta feature Western as well as Indonesian dramas and dance performances. Because of the country's many diverse ethnic groups, the arts—whether music, theater, fine arts, ceramics, or textiles—differ from region to region. Westerners are most familiar with the exquisite paintings, wood and stone carvings, and dance from Bali. However, such unique items as textiles woven with gold thread from Sumatra, ships cloths from Nusa Tenggara, ceramics from Lombok, and silver jewelry from Yogyakarta are known throughout the art world as valuable commodities. Indonesia has a tradition of interest in the arts that remains strong today.

LITERATURE

Some of Indonesia's most poignant writings—poetry, novels, short stories, and newspaper editorials—were produced by nationalist writers prior to and following the Indonesian revolution. After independence, their short stories and poems could be found regularly in Indonesia's leading newspapers and magazines. In 1986 a four-book set of short stories by Indonesia's best authors was published in Jakarta under the title *Cerita Pendek Indonesia* (Indonesian Short Stories). Among the authors whose works are included are Umar Kayam, W. S. Renrda, Nh. Dini, and Mochtar Lubis. Unfortunately, considering the outstanding writing available, relatively little Indonesian prose or poetry has been translated into English. Some of Indonesia's best-known books and poems that are available in English are the poet Rendra's *Ballads and Blues: Poems;* journalist/author Mochtar Lubis's *Road without End, Twilight in Jakarta,* and *Tiger!*; and the novelists Iwan Simatupang's *Drought* and Pramoedya Antara Toer's *The Fugitive, The Earth of Mankind, Child of All Nations, Footsteps, House of Glass,* and *Girl from the Coast.* In addition to these books, the Jakarta publishing house Lontar has an extensive listing of contemporary Indonesian prose and poetry in English.

THE PEOPLE

Indonesia's motto, "Unity and Diversity," is most appropriate. A traveler across the island chain will encounter Indonesians who speak many different languages, who have contrasting physical attributes, and whose cultures are in sharp contrast.

Javanese

The Javanese people constitute the largest ethnic group in Indonesia. By their name it is evident that they live primarily on the island of Java, although Javanese hold government positions throughout the country. They were the people of the great empires—Kidiri, Sanjaya, Majapahit, Mataram. The Javanese were Buddhists in the heyday of Borobudur and Hindu when Prambanan was built. When the Javanese converted to Islam and began the Mataram empire, those who retained the Hindu faith moved to Bali, where Hinduism remains the dominant religion today. The Javanese have their own complex language, one with levels of words and terms that must be used when addressing people of higher or lower class, a concept not unlike the Hindu caste system. Most Javanese are not followers of modernist Islam, but many—especially in Central and East Java—practice a religion that combines elements of Hinduism, Islam, and mysticism. Former President Suharto subscribed to such a religion.

The dance and music of Java compete with those of Bali as being the most refined and difficult to master in Indonesia. Students from all over the world come to Yogyakarta to study gamelan and court dances. Many performers study at the palace (*kraton*) of the sultan of Yogyakarta, whose support of revolutionary forces during the war for independence won his family the right to retain the sultanate. The sultanate in Yogyakarta is the only one recognized by the Indonesian government. In some other places, such as Ternate, the resident of the sultanate and heir to the title still is called sultan, but he is not officially recognized as a representative of the Indonesian government. As mentioned previously, Yogyakarta has also produced some of the country's most illustrious painters and writers.

The Javanese dominate politics in Indonesia, partly because of their sheer numbers. Although Java constitutes only about 7 percent of the land in Indonesia, it contains about 65 percent of the population, 45 percent of whom are Javanese. The Sundanese of West Java make up about 14 percent of Indonesia's population. The people on Java have more access to large cities, the arts, politics, educational institutions, and exposure to international influences than do other Indonesians. Outside of Java, the general opinion of Indonesians about the Javanese is that they are refined but tend to be conceited.

Sundanese

The Sundanese of West Java were especially active in the revolution against the Dutch, and many Sundanese freedom fighters lost their lives in the revolution. Sundanese often use *wayang golek* (wooden three-dimensional rod puppets) in their performances, although all forms of the popular puppets are found in West Java. The climate of West Java is conducive to growing vegetables, and consequently the diet of Sundanese people includes a larger variety of vegetables than is found in most other parts of the country. Sundanese dishes frequently include carrots, cauliflower, and potatoes as well as the greens found throughout the rest of the country. As a general rule, Sudanese are more devout Muslims than the Javanese.

Madurese

The small island of Madura is located off the coast of Java. Madurese culture is similar to Javanese, but the Madurese tend to be very devout Muslims. The island's traditional sport is bull racing, often featured in tourist brochures. Madura's population is dense for the island's size, comprising about 7 percent of Indonesia's total population. For this reason the people of Madura were often targeted for Indonesia's transmigration project.

Balinese

Balinese culture is probably the most widely recognized internationally of any in Indonesia. Hinduism permeates all facets of life on the island. In contrast to the rest of Indonesia, where Islam prevails, pork and ham are regularly served. Artists of all types thrive—wood and stone carvers, painters, writers, musicians, dancers, architects. It is not unusual to come upon a parade of colorfully dressed men, women, and children observing the anniversary of a temple. Cremations—elaborate and plain—with large papier-mâché bulls burning while ritual dances are pereformed, are another common sight. Roadsides in Bali are almost always decorated with graceful bamboo weavings that sig-

A Balinese cremation (Courtesy of Florence Lamoureux)

nify a ceremony is being held or will soon be taking place. Offerings of flowers are everywhere, from small baskets outside of shops to decorations of elaborate colored rice arranged in tiered pyramids and carried in baskets on women's heads.

The most sacred of Bali's temples is Besaki, located on the slopes of Gunung Agung (Great Mountain), which is Bali's highest mountain and an active volcano. Gunung Agung erupted in 1963 and caused extensive damage; however, the temple compound—which consists of several temples built in tiers ascending the mountain—has been restored to its former glory and is again open to all who wish to visit the sacred Hindu site. Perhaps the most well-known temple in Bali is Tanah Lot; it is certainly the most photographed. In contrast to Besaki's high elevation, Tanah Lot is located on a large formation of rocks by the edge of the sea. Its pagoda-like shape is often depicted in tourist brochures, especially at sunset. Both Tanah Lot and Besaki are popular tourist spots and are usually crowded with visitors and Balinese alike.

Because Bali is the tourist center of Indonesia, luxury hotels abound and surfers can be found on the popular beaches. Bali is tolerant of outsiders, probably because they do so much for the economy. The October 12, 2002, bombing of a nightclub in Bali resulted in a sharp decline in that island's tourism, a tragic setback for Bali's economy.

Sumatra

Sumatra is a large island that shares one of the busiest waterways in the world with Malaysia. The Strait of Malacca flows between the northern coast of Sumatra and the southern tip of the Malay Peninsula. A number of different ethnic groups, including the Batak and the Minangkabau, live on the island.

Batak

The Batak are among the most distinctive of the people of Sumatra, in part because Batak society was not exposed to Western culture until the late 1800s, so the people retained their traditions well into the Dutch colonial period. Batak culture mixes the customs of spirit worshiping and Indian components with Christianity. Batak weavings and other crafts of the Lake Toba region of Sumatra are highly prized. The Batak are divided into three main groups—the Koro, Timurs, and Pakpaks, all of whom live around Lake Toba in northern Sumatra.

Samosir Island is located in the middle of the lake, and all Batak trace their ancestry to Samosir, a popular site for archaeological work in Indonesia. Batak history is sparse but includes animistic practices that were manifested in human sacrifice and cannibalism. Present-day Batak are now predominantly Christian.

Minangkabau

The Minangkabau are a matriarchal Muslim society on Sumatra. An often repeated legend of the Minangkabau is one concerning their defeat of a powerful enemy. Anticipating a battle with opposing forces, the Minangkabau challenged them to a contest: their water buffalo against the enemy's, winner take all. Rather than select one of their larger animals, the Minangkabau chose a nursing calf and kept it from its mother for two or three days. When the enemy put its water buffalo into the arena where the match was to be held, the Minangkabau set the very hungry calf free. Seeking to nurse, it immediately ran under the adult animal, thinking it was its mother. The crafty Minangkabau had attached a sharp spike to the young calf's head, and when it ran beneath the adult animal it slit open the beast's underbelly, killing it. This is why the roofs of Minangkabau houses are shaped like the horns of the water buffalo. The Minangkabau people were among the first Indonesians to accept the tenets of modernist Islam. They did this while remaining a solidly matriarchal society.

Sulawesi

Toraja

In Central Sulawesi, the Toraja people still perform public ritual slaying of a water buffalo and other animals at a ceremony for the dead and still put wooden images of their deceased relatives (*tau tau*) on display outside burial caves in nearby cliffs. Funeral ceremonies are so expensive that sometimes a family must resort to the traditional binding of a body in fabric for months before sufficient funds can be raised. Relatives from far and near return to South Sulawesi for these elaborate and expensive ceremonies. Also unique to the Toraja are their intricately crafted houses with roofs shaped like the prows of canoes. Today the Toraja are Muslims, but their traditional folkways of dealing with death and burial are still observed.

Buginese

The Bugis people are also located in South Sulawesi. They are renowned for their ship building and seafaring nature. Although the Bugis are Muslims, they have been long associated with pirating on the seas throughout the archipelago.

Flores and Sumba

The island of Flores, a port of call for Portuguese merchants, centuries ago adopted Catholicism, and its inhabitants retain a strong Christian culture. In contrast to the mosques in other areas of Indonesia, Catholic churches dot Flores and nearby Sumba. Portugal had a significant effect on the language, architecture, and culture of Flores, and many families there still have Portuguese names. At one time Flores and Sumba were major providers of sandalwood, although most of the aromatic trees were cut down long ago. Today both are renowned for their ikat textiles.

Kalimantan

Kalimantan is Indonesia's portion of the island of Borneo, which also contains the countries of Malaysia and Brunei. Two peoples, the Dyaks and the Punan, make up the primary ethnic groups of Kalimantan. Whereas present-day Dyaks are usually rice farmers, the Punan are gatherers of forest resources. The two peoples complement one another and maintain good trade relationships.

Dyaks

Kalimantan is home to many groups of Dyaks, who for centuries were predominantly jungle dwellers. However, exposure to contemporary cultures has attracted a significant number of Dyaks to towns and cities. Dyak folklore is rich in tales of plants and animals, and other aspects of their culture reflect this dependency on the native flora and fauna. Up until World War II some clans were headhunters, and they fought with other Borneo peoples. Their traditional dwellings were longhouses that held entire villages. Some longhouses still exist in Kalimantan's rainforests. The Dyaks in Eastern and Central Kalimantan are usually Muslim, while those in the East have converted to Christianity. Inland dwellers maintain many animistic beliefs.

Punan

The Punan people are forest dwellers, preferring the jungle to the villages and cities of Borneo. Their reputation for immense and detailed knowledge of Borneo's inland plants and animals is legendary. The Punan still use blowpipes to hunt game and gather forest fruits and vegetables, roots, and herbs. However, their lives are changing as more outsiders enter the Punan regions and bring Western culture with them. The Punan are located throughout Kalimantan. Like other Dyaks, urban dwellers tend to convert to Islam; inland inhabitants remain animists.

Papua

Formerly known as Irian Jaya, Indonesia's portion of the island of New Guinea is home to several diverse ethnic groups.

Dani

The Dani, the largest ethnic group in Papua, live primarily in the Baliem Valley located high in the Maoke Mountains. Dani men are frequently photographed wearing the traditional penis sheath, a long gourd that covers a man's genitals. Until the past twenty to thirty years the Dani were isolated from Western culture and lived as they had for centuries. They have a system of agriculture that involves the cultivation of taro and sago and the raising of pigs. They also have developed a remarkable irrigation system and have managed to control malaria. These two factors have made their region the most densely populated in Papua. For the most part, the Dani have converted to Christianity.

Asmat

The Asmat people of southeastern Papua still believe that power from the spirits is essential for the continuance of life. Such power is obtained through the naming of inanimate objects as well as animals. For example, if a man names a weapon for a deceased warrior, that weapon can carry the power of the warrior. Conversely, if the person uses a name in a negative way, the effects can bring him misery. By contrast, urban Asmats are often Christians.

The Asmat are well known in Western art circles for their wood-carvings. These are now in high demand, especially as the traditional carving techniques and coloring of the wood with distinctive reds, whites, and blacks are carried on less and less by young Asmat artisans.

The Indonesian islands range across myriad waterways—the Indian Ocean, South China Sea, Java Sea, Celebes Sea, and the Straits of Malacca and Makassar, to name just the largest of them. The customs and folkways of the people who live thousands of miles apart developed quite differently. It would be a lengthy undertaking to describe each different ethnic or language group here; however, the reader wishing information on a specific group is encouraged to consult the References section at the end of this chapter and the Annotated Bibliography at the end of this book for websites giving more information on the islands and specific ethnic groups.

THE ENVIRONMENT

Environmental issues are a major concern in Indonesia. Law enforcement is an almost impossible task in remote areas of the country, and payoffs and corruption play a big part in some of Indonesia's worst environmental transgressions.

In recent years forest fires have been a major cause for concern. The forests in Kalimantan especially have burned out of control on many occasions. Usually these fires can be traced to carelessness at logging camps, but natural causes such as lightening are also to blame. In 1997 alone forest fires in Indonesia resulted in $3 billion of damage. The logging camps are located so far from any cities or towns where fire fighting equipment might be located that once started, they can burn uncontrollably for days, months, and even years. This adds to the disaster of overlogging, a serious problem in Kalimantan.

During Suharto's presidency the destruction of the Indonesian rainforest was a major concern, and Bob Hassan, a cohort of Suharto, was one of the major profiteers from overlogging Indonesia's rainforests. Indonesia is home to a significant number of the world's endangered plants and animals. The orangutan is native to Sumatra and some places on Borneo, but despite the heroic efforts of Indonesian scientists, the animal is disappearing. Their habitat is rapidly being destroyed by logging companies encroaching on their forests and by growing villages extending their parameters. The animals also have been illegally sold as pets. Several years ago the Indonesian government established a policy that such animals must be returned to the

Baby orangutan at animal rehabilitation center on Sumatra (Courtesy of Florence Lamoureux)

wild. Under this law, baby orangutans were taken from their owners and brought to rehabilitation camps. There they were taught to live in the jungle. The animals were trained to stay high in the trees so that tigers and other predators could not reach them. Some trainers did this by putting the young animals on a loosely woven bamboo structure. When the animals would come down to the ground they would get a mild spank on their bottoms. To reinforce the value of staying in the trees when the animals were returned to the jungle, the trainers installed a platform at a high elevation and stocked it daily with bananas and other fruits. An orangutan was considered to be successfully rehabilitated when it no longer came back to the platform but was able to find food on its own.

Other endangered animals in Indonesia are the Javan rhinoceros and the Sumatran tiger. Both are almost extinct. One of the primary reasons for the loss of these animals has been illegal trafficking in animal parts. The rhino's horn and the tiger's penis are both thought to be powerful aphrodisiacs and will bring large sums of money on the Asian market.

Rare orchids and other exotic plants are also regularly shipped out of Indonesia illegally. The geography of the archipelago makes smuggling a relatively easy task, and although the Indonesian government attempts to control such activity, it is almost impossible to do so. It is interesting to note that in recent years pharmaceutical companies have become interested in tropical rainforests as a possible source of new medicines. There is a genuine concern that if these forests are not protected, possible cures to serious diseases may be lost.

Indonesia has more animal species than any country in the world. Of the country's 515 plus species, approximately 126 bird, 63 mammal, and 21 reptile species are threatened with extinction. Indonesia's tropical forest is second in size only to that of Brazil. It is estimated that the logging industry alone will deplete 132 million acres of prime rainforest land in Indonesia by 2025.

The Indonesian government has established a number of protected areas, among them Komodo National Park, the environment of the infamous komodo dragon. This island is so far off of the beaten path that overuse by people is not yet a serious problem. Another protected park is Gunung Leusser National Park on Sumatra. In addition to being the location of an orangutan rehabilitation facility, the park's jungles provide an environment for the amazing rafflesia plant, with its three-foot-wide flowers and unbearably awful smell. A few tigers and rhinos roam the depth of this park's jungles, where they are protected by their isolation.

There are many other protected regions in Indonesia. In 1995 the country boasted 164 nature reserves, 44 game reserves, 54 recreation parks, 13 marine recreation parks, 4 grand forest parks, 13 hunting reserves, 10 marine nature reserves, and 24 national parks.

An escalating problem in protected areas is the removal of firewood. Indonesian villagers cook over open fires that require a constant source of fuel. Prohibiting people from entering a forest where they have traditionally gathered firewood is not only unpopular but a difficult rule to enforce. The government is attempting to involve villagers living in close proximity to protected areas in its conservation efforts by initiating educational programs that teach them how to turn tourism to their advantage. Ecotourism is growing in popularity in Indonesia, and it is believed that if local people can see a profit for themselves from this business, they will do their share to protect the flora and fauna that bring the tourists to their locations. It is a new concept but one that has the potential to go a long way toward saving Indonesia's precious resources.

In addition to these problems, many Indonesians still live in forest areas where slash-and-burn agricultural practices have resulted in poor growing conditions for crops necessary for survival. Burning off all plant life to clear land results in the runoff of topsoil on that cleared land when it rains. Years are needed for plants and trees to grow back and for the soil to become rich enough in nutrients to again grow crops. Increased population exacerbates this problem as larger and larger forest areas are burned to accommodate a growing population. It is the practice of slash-and-burn farmers to leave a region when the soil is too poor to grow their crops and travel to a new area, where the process is repeated, but the forest areas available to them are shrinking.

INDONESIA AND THE WORLD

Indonesia's early years as an independent nation were fraught with disagreeable international relationships, both within Asia as well as with the Western nations. For example, in 1963 Sukarno declared war against Malaysia, and late in his presidency Suharto rejected economic assistance from the Netherlands.

The Non-Aligned Nations

In 1955, during Sukarno's presidency, representatives of countries of Asia and Africa met in Bandung, Indonesia, and forged an alliance of Non-Aligned Nations. The Non-Aligned Nations movement grew out of this historic conference at a time when the Cold War mentality pressured nations to choose between the superpowers of the United States and the Soviet Union. The countries represented in the Non-Aligned Nations meeting were Third World countries, and by hosting the conference Indonesia clearly identified itself with the poorer countries of Asia and Africa. The five nations sponsoring this assembly were Burma, Ceylon, Pakistan, India, and Indonesia. Other countries that sent representatives were Afghanistan, Cambodia, the People's Republic of China, Egypt, Ethiopia, the Gold Coast, Iran, Iraq, Japan, Jordan, Laos, Lebanon, Liberia, Libya, Nepal, the Philippines, Saudi Arabia, the Sudan, Syria, Thailand, Turkey, the Democratic Republic of Vietnam, the State of Vietnam, and Yemen.

In 1955, the fear of nuclear war between Russia and the United States was all consuming. The Western nations were ever watchful that a new developing nation would accept communism as its credo, thus strengthening anti-Western sentiment around the world. In retrospect, the developing countries, many of them newly free of colonial governments, desperately needed aid and were not wedded to either communist or democratic ideals. Indeed, whether communism or democracy provided the much-needed help was irrelevant to most of these countries. Because in theory communism purported dividing resources, it was often the philosophy of choice. Capitalism required land ownership that was often beyond the means of the Third World peasant.

The primary purpose of the Non-Aligned Nations conference was to promote economic development in Asia and Africa. In Bandung in 1955 the delegates discussed the importance of understanding each others' cultures. Many of the member countries had been colonized, and in some of them their native languages had been suppressed. This was viewed especially damaging to the cultures of those countries and was condemned equally with racism, an especially significant problem in emerging African countries.

The Asia-Africa delegates declared colonialism evil and called for all countries where colonialism existed to grant freedom to the colonized people within their borders. They went on to declare their support for the Arabic people of Palestine and asked the United Nations to intervene in the settlement of the conflict in Israel. They further asked for disarmament among all nations in light of the terrible nuclear weapons that were available. These countries viewed unilateral disarmament as the only way to avoid an unthinkable war.

Policy statements from that meeting were primarily concerned with race relations and discrimination. In 1955 many countries around the world tolerated segregation. In Africa, for example, apartheid was law. The Non-Aligned Nations meeting in 1955 was a strong display of solidarity among the less affluent countries of the world. The Non-Aligned Nations is still an active group, currently opposing globalization and international business that negatively affects the small business people in their countries.

Association of Southeast Asian Nations

In 1967, during Suharto's presidency, the Association of Southeast Asian Nations (ASEAN) was formed. Charter members were Indonesia, Malaysia, the Philippines, Thailand, and Singapore. In its formative years ASEAN planned to develop interregional trade policies along the lines of the North Atlantic Treaty Organization (NATO). The purpose of ASEAN was to promote political and economic cooperation and regional stability. The 1960s were dangerous times in Southeast

Asia. The Vietnam War was in its initial stages, and the Western nations feared that communism would gain a foothold in the region. In 1976 the ASEAN declaration formalized the principles of peace and cooperation to which the organization is dedicated.

Brunei joined ASEAN in 1984, and Vietnam became a member in 1997. The People's Republic of Laos and Myanmar joined in 1997, and Cambodia, ASEAN's newest member, joined the group in 1999. ASEAN certainly has power in numbers. The member nations have gained greater influence in Asian trade and political and security issues than any of them could have done singularly. These countries have eliminated a range of tariffs on goods that are traded among the member countries. The chairmanship of ASEAN rotates annually.

The total population of these ten countries is over 500 million people, and the region has approximately US$53 billion invested. It is the third largest overseas market for U.S. investment. ASEAN–U.S. trade in both directions totaled US$120 billion in 2001. ASEAN cooperates with the Asia Pacific Trade Cooperation (APEC) forum to strengthen the economies of its member countries.

The strong ASEAN of today includes all of the Southeast Asian countries except East Timor. The group meets regularly to make trade policy and to support commerce within Southeast Asia.

Asia Pacific Economic Cooperation

The Asia Pacific Economic Cooperation (APEC) forum was established in 1989 to promote economic integration around the Pacific. It now promotes world trade and globalization. Current members of APEC are Australia, Brunei, Canada, Chile, Hong Kong, Indonesia, Japan, Malaysia, Mexico, New Zealand, Papua New Guinea, the People's Republic of China, Peru, the Philippines, the Republic of Korea, Russia, Singapore, Chinese Taipei, Thailand, the United States, and Vietnam.

APEC's goals are free trade and investment among its members. APEC countries constitute the single biggest market for the United States, with US$500 billion in American exports to these countries in 2000. In turn the United States purchased US$700 billion of goods from APEC countries that year. One of APEC's goals is to reform stagnant economies and effect policy changes that will encourage economic recovery. The organization encourages positive environmental and labor standards, improvement of basic education, fighting disease, encouragement of small-business development, and bringing women as equal partners into businesses and economic projects. Indonesia is APEC's third most populous country—right behind China and the United States. However, Indonesia ranks tenth in exports and twelfth in imports of goods from APEC countries.

APEC has drawn criticism from international environmental and protective organizations that claim its support of the International Monetary Fund and other international lending agencies is disadvantageous to the poor and those not protected by major conglomerates.

Factors that hinder greater international trade and the growth of Indonesia's tourism industry at present are Christian–Muslim violence in Maluku and eastern Indonesia, violence related to separatist movements in Aceh and Papua, and periodic threats against outsiders in Sulawesi and Kalimantan. Despite this concern, rich deposits of oil, minerals, and forest products keep the international business community focused on Indonesia, notwithstanding the 1997 economic crisis. The country is enormously wealthy in natural resources, and this alone will hold the attention of the world's commercial sector.

The United Nations

Indonesia joined the United Nations on September 28, 1950, five years after the country declared its independence and five years after the UN was established. The UN had been supportive of Indonesia's quest for independence from its onset.

In the early years of its UN membership Indonesia was especially supportive of such UN issues as the worldwide struggles against colonialism and racial segregation and programs working to eliminate poverty.

Indonesia's role in the Bandung conference of Non-Aligned Nations was very much in line with UN policies that were being established at that time. As a matter of fact, two United Nations General Assembly resolutions—one on peaceful coexistence and the other on decolonization—were patterned after similar resolutions adopted at the Asia–Africa meetings.

The three UN topics that have most interested Indonesia over the years are of a comparable nature. They are social and economic development, equality of nations, and reducing disparities between wealthy Northern Hemisphere nations and poor Southern Hemisphere ones.

Indonesia actually withdrew from the UN in 1962 when the world organization condemned Sukarno's invasion of the new nation of Malaysia. This was also the same year that Malaysia joined the UN.

In 1964, when the *konfrontasi* had ended, Indonesia rejoined the international group.

In 1971 Indonesia's representative, Adam Malik, was voted president of the twenty-sixth session of the General Assembly. During the 1970s and 1980s Indonesia continued to support those issues that dealt with cooperation among member nations. In 1992 Indonesia assumed the presidency of the Non-Aligned Nations; three years later it became a Non-Permanent Member of the United Nations Security Council.

In addition to Adam Malik, other Indonesians have had prominent roles in the UN. Ali Sastroamidjojo, a key coordinator of the 1955 Asia–Africa conference in Bandung, was named permanent representative to the UN from 1957 to 1960. Ali Alatas served in that same role from 1982 to 1988. Alatas was named foreign minister of Indonesia in 1988 and held that position until 1999, a tense time in Indonesian history.

References

Dalton, Bill. *Indonesia Handbook* (6th ed.). Chico, CA: Moon Publications, 1995.

Eliot, Joshua, et al. *Indonesia, Malaysia, and Singapore Handbook.* Chicago: Passport Books, 1995.

Holt, Claire. *Art in Indonesia: Continuities and Change.* Ithaca: Cornell University Press, 1967.

KEHATI. Brochure on Ecotourism and Biodiversity in Indonesia. Jakarta: Indonesian Biodiversity Foundation, 1995.

Ricklefs, M. C. *A History of Modern Indonesia.* Hong Kong: Macmillan, 1990.

Rigg, Jonathan (ed.). *Indonesian Heritage Series: The Human Environment.* Singapore: Editions Didier Miller, 1996.

Stewart, Ian Charles (ed.). *Indonesians: Portraits from an Archipelago.* Singapore: Tien Wah Press, 1984.

Whitten, Tony, and Jane Whitten (eds.). *Wild Indonesia: Wildlife Scenery of the Indonesian Archipelago.* London: New Holland Publishers, 1992.

Websites

Ancol: http://www.travel.yahoo.com/p/travelguide/560907

APEC: http://www.apec.org/

ASEAN: http://www.state.gov/p/eap/rls/4178.htm

Asian–African Conference of Non-Aligned Nations: http://www.oup.co.uk/pdf/bt/cassese/cases/part3/ch18/1702.pdf

Asmat culture: http://www.asmat-art.com/asmat-themen/eng-buch.htm

Balinese culture: http://www.alphalink.com.au/~grum/culture.html

Balinese painters: http://www.balilife.com/arts/painting/artists.htm

Batik making: http://www.expat.or.id/info/batiksteps.html

Bugis culture: http://www.bethany.com/profiles/p_code/787.html

Flores and Sumba culture: http://www.bali-travel-online.com/flores_island/culture.htm; http://www.bali-travel-online.com/sumba_island/culture_tours.htm

Health statistics: http://www.depkes.go.id/english/statistics/right.htm;
   http://nasw.org/users/dparsell/contents/samples_of_published_work_spl.htm
Illegal drugs problem: http://www.theage.com.au/articles/2003/03/03/
   1041566221731.html; http://usinfo.state.gov/regional/ea/timer/
   indon99.htm; http://www.thejakartapost.com/yesterdaydetail.asp?
   fileid=20021201.C02
Indonesia's art galleries: http://www.indonesiatourism.com/art_gallery.ph
Indonesian arts and crafts: http://www.expat.or.id/info/art.html
Indonesian artists: http://www.museumneka.com/Artist.asp?offset=50;
   http://users.skynet.be/network.indonesia/ni3001.htm
Javanese ethnic group: http://members.tripod.com/~timor-east/1-tnijavadomin.
   html
Kebun Raya: http://www.bogor.indo.net.id.kri/
Lontar Publishers' list of books in English: http://www.lontar.org/publications/
   index.php
Madurese culture: http://www.eastjava.com/books/madura/
Minangkabau culture: http://www.infoflex.com.au/~salam/bayua/minang.html
Painting in Indonesia: http://www.asianinfo.org/asianinfo/indonesia/
   pre-painting.htm
Raden Adjeng Kartini: http://www.hebatindo.com/pages/kartini_eng.htm
Sundanese culture: http://members.tripod.com/Hadiyana/sundaculture.htm
Theater in Jakarta: http://wwwindonesia-tourism.com/general/theatre/html.
Toraja culture: http://www.merriewood.com/exindo/toraja3.html

PART TWO

REFERENCE MATERIALS

Key Events in Indonesian History

Fifth century	Indian culture is introduced to Indonesia.
671	I-tsing, the Chinese pilgrim, spends several years at a Buddhist monastery in Sumatra, where he records the extensive influence of Buddhism there.
late 700	Establishment of Srivijaya, a Buddhist maritime state, located in southern Sumatra, that controls traffic through the Strait of Malacca. This state will last until approximately 1300.
778–832	Sailendras, also Buddhists, but farmers, not traders, control Central Java. They build the Buddhist monument Borobudur between 778 and 824.
832–930	Emergence of the Sanjaya dynasty, adherents of Hinduism who build the temples at Prambanan in Central Java. Their wealth comes from trade through the Strait of Malacca.
1271–1295	Marco Polo visits Sumatra.
1292	The Majapahit dynasty is established with rice production as its economic base.
1331	Gadja Mada is named prime minister by the Majapahit king, Hayam Wuruk. He unifies Java and expands the Majapahit empire to include Sumatra, Borneo, and the Spice Islands.
1389	With the death of King Hayam Wuruk, the Majapahit dynasty ends its rule.
Fifteenth century	The first mosque in Java is built at Demak.
1500	Islam spreads throughout Java, bringing trade and the Koran from Persia.
1513	The Portuguese establish a trading post in Sunda Kalapa, West Java, in what is now Jakarta.

1541	Fr. Francis Xavier, a Spanish priest, introduces Christianity to the people of eastern Indonesia.
1500–1700	The Islamic Mataram kingdom is the dominant ruling power on Java.
1596	Dutch ships anchor off Banten, Java, for the purpose of purchasing pepper.
1602	The Dutch form the East India Company (VOC) to regulate and control trade in the East Indies.
1629	Jan Pieterszoon Coen, the Dutch governor-general who founded Batavia in 1619, defends it against the Muslim Mataram ruler, Sultan Agung.
1757	The Treaty of Gianti involves the Dutch splitting the strife-torn Mataram empire into Surakarta, Nangkunegaran, and Yogyakarta (Jogjakarta). This marks the beginning of significant Dutch involvement in local politics.
Mid-1700s	The Dutch utilize the existing government structure by having Indonesian "regents" collect proportionately large percentages of peasant farmers' crops for the Dutch.
1799–1800	The VOC collapses, and the Dutch government takes over control of the East Indies colony.
1806–1810	The French army attacks Holland, and the Bonapartists in The Hague appoint Herman Wielm Daendels as governor-general of the Dutch East Indies. He opposes unfair treatment of the farmers in the East Indies.
1811–1816	At the request of Dutch King Willem, who escaped Napoleon's armies by fleeing to Britain, British rule in Indonesia as protectors of the colony. Sir Thomas Stamford Raffles serves as lieutenant governor of Java for the British East India Company during the unsettled post-Napoleonic era. He initiates further reform in the oppressive land rent system.
1824	British and Dutch sign the Treaty of London, giving England control of Singapore, Penang, and Malacca, and the Netherlands control of the Indonesian archipelago.

1825–1830	The Java or Diponegoro War involves Islamic rebellion against dominance by "infidel" Dutch in Yogyakarta.
1827	Governor-General Bosch introduces the "cultivation system," a plan that designates specific plots of land be set aside for growing crops to be turned over to the Dutch. This payment of taxes in agricultural products increases the already heavy burden on farmers.
1860	The novel *Max Havelaar* is published. It describes the inhumane conditions of the cultivation system and results in many Dutch openly opposing the mistreatment of Indonesians.
August 26–28, 1883	The volcano Krakatoa erupts, causing a tidal wave more than 100 feet high and killing 36,000 people on Java and Sumatra.
1890–1941	After the cultivation system fails, international businesses lease agricultural land from the Dutch government and establish plantations with paid labor forces.
1891	Anthropologists discover Java Man.
1905	Japan is victorious over Russia in the Russo-Japanese war, illustrating that Westerners are not invincible and that corrupt regimes can be overthrown.
1908	Dutch establish Dutch–Chinese schools.
1908	Budi Utomo, an Indonesian nationalist movement, encourages Indonesians to become educated about their country.
1918	Indonesians are first admitted into the Dutch governing body in Indonesia, the *Volksraad* (People's Council); although their positions allow them a forum for expression of opinion, they carry no official power.
1920	Indonesian Communist Party (PKI) is formed.
1927	Indonesian Nationalist Party (PNI) is formed, based on peasant concerns.
1928	Indonesian is unofficially declared the national language by youth organizations.

1942–1945	Japanese occupation of Indonesia during World War II.
August, 17, 1945	Indonesia declares its independence; Sukarno is named president.
August 17, 1945– December 27, 1949	Indonesian Revolution against the Dutch.
1946	Reemergence of the Indonesian Communist Party. Netherlands and Indonesia sign the Linggajati Agreement, which establishes Indonesia as a free country.
1948	Madiun uprising in Sumatra. Devout Muslims (*santri*) attack and slaughter religious liberals (*abangan*).
December 27,1949	Queen Juliana of the Netherlands proclaims Indonesia free of Dutch rule.
1950	The Republic of Indonesia is recognized internationally.
1955	The first meeting of Non-Aligned Nations takes place in Bandung, Indonesia. First general elections are held. Sukarno is elected president.
1959	Sukarno implements "Guided Democracy," which ends representative government in his attempt to control rapidly rising inflation.
September 30, 1965	The "Night of the Generals," a dramatic but failed coup to overthrow the existing government. Military and, to some extent, Islamic groups unite to take control of the government. Major-General Suharto becomes the acting president. Many members of the PKI and its sympathizers are slaughtered in the days that follow.
September 1967	Suharto is elected president.
1970	Sukarno dies.
May 5, 1976	Indonesia names East Timor its twenty-seventh province.
November 1991	Indonesian troops fire on Timorese independence demonstrators, killing up to 100 people.
June 1992	Suharto's Golkar party is victorious in general elections for the fifth time since 1967.

1993	Suharto is elected to his sixth consecutive five-year term as president. Try Sutrisno, a former general, is appointed vice-president.
1994	Suharto's government prohibits publication of *Tempo,* the nation's largest newsmagazine, because of its criticism of government policies.
April 1996	Madame Suharto dies.
1993	Sukarno's daughter, Megawati Sukarnoputri, becomes leader of the Indonesian Democratic Party (PDI).
1996	The Suharto government declares Megawati's position as head of the party illegal and names new leaders of the PDI.
Spring 1997	Golkar, the government party, emerges victorious in parliamentary elections.
January 1998	The Indonesian economy collapses, with the rupiah (Indonesian currency) falling from 2000 rp/US$ to over 10,000/US$.
Spring 1998	Presidential elections (by parliament). Suharto is reelected.
May 21, 1998	In response to the collapse of the rupiah, Suharto resignes, and Vice President B. J. Habibie assumes the presidency of Indonesia. This change in leadership results in violence, especially against ethnic Chinese.
August–September 1999	After a campaign fraught with violence, East Timor votes on its future status of independence. The UN announces that East Timorese overwhelmingly rejected Indonesian rule. As a result, a wave of killings and violence explodes, and UN forces land in East Timor to restore peace and order.
October 13, 1999	The parliament elects Abdurrahman Wahid, popularly known as Gus Dur, as Indonesia's fourth president over the people's choice, Megawati.
October 14, 1999	Megawati is elected vice president after her defeat of Hamzah Haz, leader of the Muslim

United Development Party and in conjunction with her newly formed PDI-P party winning the most seats in parliament.

January–
December 2000

Islamic–Christian clashes escalate in Maluku (the Spice Islands).

Summer 2001

After a series of scandals compounded by his inability to control violence in Maluku and curb the growing separatist movements in Aceh, Papua, and Sulawesi, Gus Dur is forced to relinquish the presidency to his vice president, Megawati.

January–
December 2001

Separatist movements in Aceh and Papua, and to a lesser degree in Sulawesi, strengthen as these regions seek autonomy from Indonesia.

February 2001

Gus Dur is impeached.

July 23, 2001

Megawati is named president; Hamzah Haz is vice president.

September 11,
2001

Terrorist attacks in New York, Pennsylvania, and Washington, D.C., are attributed to Islamic fundamentalists; Indonesia supports U.S. anti–Al-Qaeda tactics although some Indonesians sympathize with the attackers.

October 12, 2002

Bombs explode outside a nightclub and near the honorary U.S. consulate in Bali and in the city of Manado on Sulawesi, killing 202 people. This marks Indonesia's worst attack by terrorists.

May 2003

Indonesian army bombs Aceh, breaking the December 2002 truce.

August 5, 2003

Terrorists bomb a Jakarta hotel, killing eleven people–one foreigner and ten Indonesian workers.

Significant People, Places, and Events

abangan This term refers to those Indonesians who do not follow the strict rules of Islam. In Indonesia, especially on Java, a man or woman who adheres to the *abangan* form of Islam would be someone who mixes Islam with Hindu beliefs and with Javanese mysticism. Sometimes *abangan* are referred to as traditionalists, as they follow the old and long-established Hindu and mystical Sufi Islam beliefs of their ancestors. It is common for Indonesian political parties to be designated as pro-*abangan* or pro-*santri* depending on the degree of their adherence to the tenets of Islam. Sufism was the first form of Islam to come to Indonesia, and *abangan* beliefs reflect this mystical form of the religion. Both President Sukarno and President Suharto would be considered *abangan,* and throughout their long presidencies they juggled support of devout and liberals Muslims.

Abdurrahman Wahid Indonesia's fourth president is better known as Gus Dur. Born in 1940, Gus Dur became president of Indonesia on October 20, 1999, following the unpopular Habibie presidency. Megawati Sukarnoputri actually won the popular vote in the 1999 election, but the MPR (the People's Consultative Assembly) chose Gus Dur. The blind head of the Islamic organization Nahdlatul Ulama was initially welcomed into government circles. His intellect and wit were well respected in both the political and religious arenas, and he brought a fresh outlook to the Jakarta political scene. His inexperience and lack of faith in his advisers, however, soon had him in trouble, and rumors of money scandals further impaired Wahid's ability to govern. Gus Dur reportedly gave government funds to his friend and misused money that the sultan of Brunei provided Indonesia specifically to help the country with its serious financial problems. Separatist movements in Aceh, Maluku, Kalimantan, and Papua grew more violent during his time in office, and it soon became apparent that the country was in danger of collapsing. As matters worsened, Gus Dur drew criticism at home and overseas for his frequent trips abroad. The man to whom so many Indonesians had looked to rejuvenate their country was quite simply not up to the task. In July 2001, Abdurrahman Wahid was the first Indonesian president to be impeached.

Aidit, Dipa Nusantara In 1951, soon after Indonesia declared its independence, the Communist Party became a significant political entity in Indonesia. One of the early Partai Komunis Indonesia (PKI) leaders was D. N. Aidit. He was born in 1923 and rose through the ranks of the party. As the PKI increased in strength, Aidit became friendly with Sukarno. This is ironic, for in 1948, during the war with the Dutch, Sukarno's revolutionary government forces routed the PKI rebel army in a confrontation in Madiun, East Java, when the communists opposed Sukarno's treaty agreements with the Dutch. As a result of that action, Aidit along with other PKI leaders left Indonesia for China. They were back in Indonesia in 1951, however, when they gained support among Indonesia's peasant farmers. As Sukarno's presidency became mired in economic problems and the military and PKI vied for power, Sukarno actually became quite friendly with Aidit, and in June 1960 the president appointed him to fill a position in the People's Consultative Assembly. Aidit remained close to Sukarno for the next five years. During the period from 1954 to 1963 Aidit wrote communist publications. When the coup attempt of September 30, 1965, took place, alliances changed overnight. Aidit was among the many PKI leaders who fled Jakarta. He was killed in the bloodbath that followed that cataclysm.

Airlangga A king on Java from 911 to 1046, Airlangga was a patron of the arts, and during his reign music, literature, and drama flourished. *Wayang kulit* (leather puppets) became popular, as did the music of the gamelan percussion orchestra. Stories taken from the Indian epics *Mahabarata* and *Ramayana* were first performed using the intricately designed leather shadow puppets accompanied by the gamelan. Airlangga was equally tolerant of Hinduism and Buddhism, and wars due to religious strife were not an issue during his time in power. Later in his life he chose to abandon politics and divided his kingdom between his two sons. Airlangga has gone down in history as a tolerant ruler who brought a refinement of the arts to his people. Airlangga University in Surabaya—one of Indonesia's leading institutions of higher learning—is named for this Indonesian king.

Asian-African Conference. *See* **Non-Aligned Nations.**

Bali bombing On October 12, 2002, bombs were set off at three locations in Indonesia. One exploded in Sulawesi and two in Bali. One of the Bali bombs went off in Denpasar, Bali's capital, and did little damage. The second shattered a nightclub in the tourist area around Kuta Beach, a favorite spot with surfers. The number of dead in this incident reached 202, almost half of whom were Australians. The days following the Kuta Beach bombing were terrible ones for all Indonesians, not just the residents of Bali. This shocking event announced to the world that Bali—a place of peace and harmony—was no longer exempt from the terrorism that plagued the rest of the country. Amidst the concern for the families of the dead and wounded there was real government anxiety about the future of Bali's tourist industry and the millions of dollars it brings into the Indonesian economy. It is believed that thirty-three Muslim terrorists associated with Jama'ah Islamiyah detonated all three bombs. The case is in court as this book goes to press, but no decision has yet been made.

Borobudur Borobudur is a square-based, nine-tiered Buddhist monument built in a Mandela pattern. A unique feature is the drainage system that uses stone heads of *nagas,* or dragons, at points where accumulated water is expelled. Construction of the monument is sophisticated, and it is believed that up to seventy-five years were taken to complete it. The monument was built primarily by workers who paid their taxes to the king in the form of labor. Borobudur contains 504 statues of the Buddha and 2,700 stone panels of carved relief depicting stories of the Buddha and his followers. This Central Java monument has long been a popular tourist attraction. Prior to the 1970s Borobudur was not set up to accommodate visitors. In 1974, however, the United Nations began a restoration project, and carved stones with white-washed numbers on them (for tracking and assembly purposes) soon littered the ground surrounding the shrine. Whenever possible, workers used the original stone panels, and in cases where these could not be located local artisans were hired to create duplicates to replace them. The UN team completed its work in 1983, and today Borobudur is one of Indonesia's main tourist attractions.

cultivation system When the Dutch government took over the administration of Indonesia from the commercial Dutch East India Company on January 1, 1980, it put into effect a new way to collect the agricultural products grown in Indonesia. Under this plan, called the cultivation system, plots of land were set apart and the crops grown on these lands were to be turned over to the Dutch. This was essentially a tax paid in the form of agricultural goods that commanded high prices in the international market. The colonial government made its demand for goods to the local Javanese elite, and they in turn passed the demand onto the farmers under their jurisdiction. This had the effect of placing a further burden on the peasants, who were already required to pay heavy taxes in the form of agricultural products to their local Indonesian rulers. Thus, before a farmer could plant subsistence crops for his own family, he had to produce sufficient quantities of sellable agricultural goods—coffee, sugar, tea, for example—to meet quotas set by both his local ruler and the Dutch colonial government. The demands placed on the farmers by the cultivation system were often impossible to meet, and the system slowly lost favor with the Dutch. By the 1890s, the cultivation system was replaced by privately owned plantations. The plantation owners, who were Dutch or other Europeans, paid taxes directly to the Dutch government, bypassing the local ruler. The plantation system lasted until the start of World War II.

economic crisis of 1997 In the fall of 1997 several Asian countries suffered a drastic devaluation of their currency. Most of the nations in the region were able to pull themselves out of their troubles within twelve to eighteen months, but in Indonesia the situation proved quite different. What soon became apparent was that the Indonesian economy had not been on solid ground prior to the meltdown. Bank loans were overextended, and corruption in government had been rampant, with outstanding loans to Suharto family members and friends who were unable to make payments. The situation called for considerable international monetary assistance, and both the International Monetary Fund (IMF) and the World Bank were called in to assist in rebuilding the country's economy. The rupiah (Indonesian currency), which was around 2,000 to the US$ in summer 1997, fell to 10,000 to the US$ in early 1998. Inflation was rampant, and Indonesian salaries did not keep pace. Consequently, the average Indonesian lost tremendous buying power from his or her rupiah savings accounts. During the early months of the crisis Suharto dismissed the failing Indonesian economy as a routine marketplace fluctuation and assured the people that all would soon be normal. This did not happen, and in early 1998 Suharto made matters worse by misusing IMF monies. As more incidents of the Suharto presidency's corruption became known, the situation in Indonesia worsened. It became so serious that on May 21, 1998, Suharto was forced to resign. He was replaced with his vice president, B. J. Habibie. The new president had a better sense of the economic crisis Indonesia faced than had Suharto, but Habibie was not at all well liked. The Indonesian people saw him as Suharto's puppet, and to make matters worse, Habibie's government had little cooperation from the military. Consequently, the economy floundered and the situation grew worse. Recent incidences of violence and terrorism throughout the archipelago have hampered the efforts of all three post-Suharto presidents. The problem is not just a matter of economics but involves corruption in the court system, separatist movements, and the future of foreign investment in Indonesia.

European traders/colonizers The Portuguese were the first Europeans to travel around the southern tip of Africa and to reach Asia via a sea route, and Bartholomew Diaz the first European to sail around Africa. It was Vasco da Gamma who opened Asia to European exploration. Da Gamma's 1498 journey to India was a milestone, proving what Christopher Columbus had set out to do—show that Asia could be reached from Europe by sea. Vasco da Gamma was followed by a number of Portuguese captains, all of whom were seeking trade with Asia. Goods available in that part of the world—for example, camphor, benzoin, silks, spices, coffee, and tea—were not available in Europe and would bring high prices in the cities of Portugal and Spain. The Spanish arrived in eastern Indonesia in the 1520s, causing the Portuguese some apprehension. Although Spain made a play to control the spice trade in the region, it eventually gave up its interest in eastern Indonesia to concentrate on the Philippines and the Americas. The British came to Indonesia briefly in the middle to late sixteenth century, but they too left the Spice Islands to concentrate on colonies in India, America, and Africa. The Dutch first appeared in Indonesia in 1596 when an expedition led by Captain Cornelius De Houtman arrived on Java with the intent to trade. The arrival of the Dutch marked the beginning of 350 years of colonial rule in Indonesia. Although colonialism affected Indonesia in many negative ways, the fact that the Dutch did not encourage Indonesians to learn the Dutch language and provided an education to only a handful of their Indonesian subjects did more to preserve Indonesian culture than any other factor. Had the Dutch immersed the Indonesians in their ways for three and a half centuries, the Indonesian culture would be very different today.

Gajah Mada This man was the country's prime minister in the mid-1300s under King Hayam Wuruk. It was mainly due to his brilliant mind that the Majapahit empire, Indonesia's most significant pre-Islamic kingdom, extended as widely as it did. This kingdom, which ranged from Sumatra to Papua New Guinea, was closer to the political boundaries of modern Indonesia set by the Dutch than any previous kingdom. The arts were generously supported, and a unique irrigation system was developed that dramatically increased rice production. With a sufficient supply of rice, the government was free to concentrate on other matters concerning the state and the welfare of the people. One of Indonesia's most prestigious universities, located in the city of Yogyakarta, is Gadjah Mada University.

Golkar This is the political party made up primarily of the military and government workers who became the machine that elected and re-elected Suharto throughout the thirty-one years of his rule. Members of Golkar come from a wide range of groups that have specific government functions, hence one sometimes reads that Golkar is made up of "functional groups." These groups might consist of government workers, the military, the police, women's organizations that complement these groups, and other progovernment groups of workers. The primary core of Golkar, however, remains workers who draw a government salary and who through the Suharto years qualified for food and sometime housing subsidies. Government positions were coveted and prized by those who held them. It is understandable that workers holding positions with these perks were loyal members of Golkar and as such continued to support an increasingly corrupt regime in order to maintain their lifestyles. Since Suharto's presidency ended, Golkar has not mustered enough votes to elect a president. Habibie's bid for that office in 1999 failed, and Gus Dur was elected by a coalition. Megawati's political party is the Democratic Party.

Guided Democracy On February 21, 1957, Sukarno announced a governing policy that he labeled Guided Democracy. This policy allowed the president to revert to Indonesia's 1945 constitution. Under this strategy he could name members to a National Council, and there would be no political parties or elected representative bodies. All decisions would be made by consensus. To assure the success of Guided Democracy, Sukarno declared martial law on March 14, 1957. As a result of this move by Sukarno, the Communist Party, the Indonesian army, and to a lesser extent the modernist Muslims contended with one another for the attention of the autocratic ruler and ultimately the implementation of their philosophies.

Gus Dur. *See* Abdurrahman Wahid.

Habibie, B. J. Habibie took over the office of president of Indonesia in the early days of the 1997 Asian economic crisis. To add to his financial woes, he was not well liked by the people, especially university students who perceived him as "Suharto's man." Riots in the Chinese sector of Jakarta exacerbated the students' opposition to Habibie.

Born and raised in Sulawesi as a devout Muslim, Habibie was also a scholar. He holds a Ph.D. in engineering from a German university and worked in the German aircraft industry for a number of years. His time as president of Indonesia was further marred by money problems connected to the Bank Bali scandal, where he was accused of being involved in a scheme to use IMF money to aid his political party. To his credit Habibie initiated freedom of the press and was instrumental in bringing about East Timor's independence. Nonetheless, sensing that Habibie's unpopularity stood in the way of Indonesia's recovery, the MPR voted to hold the scheduled 2002 presidential election in 1999, two years early. In that election Habibie was Golkar's candidate, but he was defeated by the PDI candidate, Megawati Sukarnoputri. Despite Megawati's win, the MPR voted Abdurrahman Wahid as president.

Hari Merdeka (Independence Day) Indonesia's first Independence Day was celebrated on August 17, 1945. The country was not free of the Dutch, however, until 1949, but in 1945 when the Japanese surrendered, Sukarno and Hatta read a proclamation stating that Indonesia was a free and independent nation. That proclamation read: "We, the people of Indonesia, do hereby proclaim the independence of Indonesia. All matters pertaining to the transfer of power, etc., will be carried out expediently and in the shortest possible time." The document was signed by Sukarno and Hatta "on behalf of the Indonesian people."

As a note of comparison, the United States declared its independence from England in 1776. George Washington's troops defeated the British army in 1781, but the Treaty of Paris, which granted the United States independence from England, was not signed until 1783. In a like manner, Indonesia declared its independence in 1945 but fought a revolution for four years before being truly free of the colonial presence in 1949.

Hatta, Mohammad Indonesia's first vice president was an ethnic Minangkabau. Hatta was born in Sumatra in 1902. He was a devout

Muslim and was an active participator in the nationalist movement. Hatta worked tirelessly for independence during the Japanese occupation and was a prominent figure during the revolution. His expectations for an independent Indonesia waned as Sukarno attempted to remedy Indonesia's postindependence economic problems with slogans and strange alliances. By 1955 Hatta's faith in the government began to decline. In a 1956 speech at Gadja Mada University, the disillusioned Hatta expressed his concern:

> I am not straying too far from the truth when I say that as long as we were under colonial domination we did not lack ideals, but that these ideals have become rather shapeless since we gained our independence. . . . When one looks at recent developments in our country and society one gets the impression that after the independence of Indonesia had been achieved, with no small sacrifice, our idealistic leaders and freedom fighters were pushed back while political and economic profiteers came to the foreground. They have used the nationalist movement and its slogans for their ends and have ridden on the backs of the political parties for these same private ends. This has inevitably resulted in political and economic anarchy, followed in its wake by a reign of corruption and demoralization. . . . Instead of local autonomy, government encourages increasing the power of the Central government, like under the Dutch. . . . Because of the power of party councils the government has become the messenger boy of the political parties.

He resigned from the vice presidency late in 1956 prior to the PRRI rebellion. Hatta did not play a major role in the Suharto government. He died in 1980.

Indonesian Revolution From the time of the Dutch implementation of its Ethical Policy at the beginning of the twentieth century, a spirit of nationalism had grown rapidly in Indonesia. But it was during World War II, when the Japanese army of occupation controlled Indonesia, that plans for a revolution were developed. When the Japanese forces left Indonesia, the country's three most dedicated nationalists—Sukarno, Mohamad Hatta, and Sutan Sjahrir—were ready and declared the country independent on August 17, 1945. The Dutch were not inclined to relinquish their resource-rich colony, and a revolution ensued. At one stage during the revolution a communist group opposed Sukarno's and Hatta's decision to accept Dutch conditions for ending the war, and in 1948 the freedom fighters had to battle the communists in Madiun as well as the Dutch. After much bloodshed and destruction and several broken truces, the revolution ended on December 27, 1949, when Holland relinquished all rights to the Dutch East Indies except for Irian Jaya (now Papua). The revolution took a tremendous toll on the country. At a time when every effort should have been made to establish a strong and economically sound nation, Indonesia was forced into a long and expensive war. Independence thus came at a high price.

Islam No one knows precisely when Islam was introduced to Indonesia. In 1292 Marco Polo reported that it was practiced in the Sumatran town of Perlak, but Islam seemed not to have made significant inroads on Java until the fourteenth century. Traders no doubt first introduced Islam to the archipelago, and later Sufi missionaries reinforced the belief. It is thought that the mystical tenets of Hinduism accommodated acceptance of Sufi Islam quite well. Though Hinduism dominated the islands in the thirteenth and fourteenth centuries, both religions coexisted relatively peacefully. Eventually Islam became more popular and Hindu kings began to convert to Islam, at which point their subjects followed. Even so, in many places throughout Indonesia, especially on Java, Islam still retains strong elements of Hinduism. In the early 1900s under Holland's Ethical Policy plan, modernist Islam became firmly established in Indonesia. This form of fundamentalist Islam, which supports strict adherence to the religion's basic tenets, contrasts with Indonesia's traditional Islam, which is based on Sufism. Today the two types of Islam seek control in this Islamic nation.

Jakarta Jakarta is the capital of Indonesia. It is a modern city with skyscrapers and traffic jams. Luxury hotels, international banks, and mini malls are scattered throughout the city. Known as Batavia under the Dutch, Jakarta has a population of approximately 25 million and faces the problems of overpopulated urban centers throughout the world. Sunda Kelapa, the old harbor area, adds unique character to this cosmopolitan center that is bustling and historic at the same time. Dutch buildings are still in evidence in Jakarta. Large ghetto areas are located along the cities' canals and waterways. Jakarta is the center of commerce and banking in Indonesia and as such attracts a large contingent of international business people. The contrast of rich and poor is stark in this sprawling seaport city.

Jama'ah Islamiyah The international press usually refers to Jama'ah Islamiyah as a militant Islamic group. Its notoriety in 2002 and 2003 comes from its alleged connection to the October 12, 2002, bombings in Bali and Sulawesi. Jama'ah Islamiyah is believed to operate across Southeast Asia. Founded in the early 1970s, it was based in Darul Islam, a group that at one time supported an effort to have Indonesia under Islamic law. Abu Bakar Ba'asyir, leader of Jama'ah Islamiyah, was suspected of being associated with church bombings in Jakarta in 2000 and the Bali nightclub bombing. Abu Bakar, along with thirty-three members of Jama'ah Islamiyah, has been arrested for the Bali bombings. The case is in court as of June 2003.

Java/Diponogoro War In 1825 Prince Diponogoro led a rebellion against the Dutch in Central Java. Although unsuccessful in driving the Dutch from Indonesia, the war lasted for five years and was the strongest opposition to Dutch rule by Indonesians since the Dutch claimed Indonesia as a colony. There were religious elements to this conflict as Muslims battled Christians. Diponogoro became a national hero, and both an Indonesian university and a prestigious unit of the army bear his name.

Kartini, Raden Adjeng Born in 1879, Kartini was a well-educated daughter of a Javanese aristocrat who worked tirelessly for equal rights for women, especially educational rights for all social classes. Raden (Princess) Kartini expressed her views on equal rights for women in a series of letters to a Dutch friend that were later published as *From the Darkness Comes Light.* Her birthday, April 21, is celebrated as Mother's Day in Indonesia.

konfrontasi In 1963 Sukarno was displeased when the regions of Sabah and Sarawak on the island of Borneo were named as Malaysian provinces. He had assumed that their geographical separation from the Malay Peninsula prevented them from being named provinces of the new Federation of Malaya. These Borneo territories were soon the cause of an armed *konfrontasi* (confrontation) between Indonesia and Malaysia that attracted negative international attention to Sukarno. Indonesia's interest was not limited to concern over Sabah's and Sarawak's designation as Malaysian provinces. Sukarno needed to divert his people's attention from Indonesia's failing economy. The Indonesian army was not enthusiastic about the confrontation in Borneo, but its leaders were not eager to oppose Sukarno and perhaps tip the scale in favor of the communists who also sought Sukarno's approval. The army was always opposed to the *konfrontasi,* and after the 1965 coup Suharto withdrew Indonesian troops from the Malaysian borders in Borneo.

Majapahit empire As evidenced in its 1221 defeat of the great Mongol army of Kublai Khan, the Majapahit empire had impressive military strength. This Buddhist–Hindu empire was led by Hayam Wuruk, the first Hindu king in what is today Indonesia. We know that earlier, during Airlangga's rule (1019–1045), there had been a Hindu presence in Indonesia, probably for many years. Perhaps the best-known government official of the Majapahit empire was Prime Minister Gadjah Mada. Majapahit influence extended across the archipelago, and it is considered to be Indonesia's greatest pre-Islamic empire.

Malik, Adam Born in Sumatra in 1917, Adam Malik was educated in Dutch schools and as young man became active in Indonesia's independence movement. He was a nationalist who supported the revolution against the Dutch and held several influential positions in Indonesia's government under both Sukarno and Suharto. In 1971 Malik was elected president of the twenty-sixth session of the United Nations General Assembly. When President Suharto was reelected in 1971, Malik was elected vice president. Prior to serving at the United Nations, he was Indonesia's Minister of Foreign Affairs.

Mataram empire In the 1500s the Mataram empire emerged. Records show that at its peak it controlled much of Java. Warfare dominated the reign of the Mataram rulers, and the demise of the empire was a result of defeat by Dutch forces and failure to maintain sufficient resources to preserve their kingdoms and sustain the people. Sultan Agung, Mataram's most famous ruler, led the empire when the Dutch were increasing their concentration in Indonesia, forcing the ruler to contend with colonialism while attempting to control his realm.

Muhammadiyah Established in 1912 as a modernist Islamic organization, Muhammadiyah was introduced to Indonesia by Kyai Haji Ahmad Dahlan. He was an Indonesian who had studied Islam in the Middle East and wanted to encourage his countrymen and women to accept a strict adherence to the tenets of Islam as the religion is practiced in the Middle East, where Islam originated. Although it opposed the entrenched form of Indonesian Islam that encompassed the mysticism of Sufi Islam, Muhammadiyah was soon accepted, and by 1938 it claimed 250,000 members. From that time forward this modernist Islamic movement has expanded to become a major political influence. Its many schools have spread the Muhammadiyah philosophy throughout the country.

Nahdatul Islam A traditional form of Islam, prevalent in Indonesia prior to the growth of the nationalist movements in the twentieth century, Nahdatul Islam is based on a form of Islam known as Sufism. Especially on Java, a folk religion encompassing Sufi Islam and Hinduism was prevalent, and it is still practiced by many Javanese today. This belief in a traditional form of religion was challenged by modernist Islam in the late colonial period as Indonesian scholars who had studied in the Middle East returned home and encouraged belief in the strict form of Islam. They claimed that the liberal form of the religion practiced in Indonesia was not true Islam. Nahdatul Islam spread the old traditional beliefs encouraged in the mystical qualities of Islam as well as the traditional culture and arts of Indonesia through its education system. Many *pesantren* (religious schools) throughout Indonesia were established by Nahdatul Islam. Today, subscribers to this traditional form of Islam clash with modernists in the political arena as they claim that *adat* (traditional law) is compromised by the strict rules of fundamentalist Islam.

Nasution, A. S. A Batak Muslim born in Sumatra in 1918, A. S. Nasution served in Indonesia's army under both Sukarno and Suharto. Nasution is probably best known outside of Indonesia for escaping death during the infamous Night of the Generals. Under the Sukarno presidency, General Nasution was a major force in maintaining the military's influence on the president. He walked a fine line as he supported Sukarno while opposing the president's Konfrontasi against Malaysia in Borneo. The murder of his daughter during the September 30, 1965, coup attempt brought the general into international prominence. His opposition to communism and his strong military ties made him a strong candidate to become involved in Suharto's government.

nationalist movements In the years from 1914 through 1927 nationalism was on the rise in Indonesia. New political parties flourished. In 1914 the Indonesian nationalist movement Budi Utomo was established. It encouraged Indonesians to learn more about their heritage. In 1920 the Indonesian Communist Party (PKI) appeared, and in 1927 the Indonesian Nationalist Party (PNI) was established. Nationalist propaganda was often spread through newsletters. The Dutch banned these publications as they attempted to weaken the nationalist movements. The spirit of nationalism swelled again during the Japanese occupation of Indonesia and this time assured the success of the independence movement that consumed the country in the aftermath of World War II.

Night of the Generals During the night of September 30, 1965, seven of the Indonesian army's highest ranking officers were assassinated. The Communist Party immediately came under suspicion, and although it was never proven that it initiated this maneuver, the incident marked the end of the Communist Party in Indonesia. A second theory is that the army staged the coup when it assumed the communists were gaining influence with Sukarno. Whatever the cause, in the aftermath old religious and political grievances were settled violently as hundreds of thousands of Indonesians and ethnic Chinese were killed. The coup was suppressed in one day by forces under the then relatively unknown Major-General Suharto.

Non-Aligned Nations In 1955 a conference of leaders of Asian and African countries met in Bandung, Indonesia, to support the Afro-Asian bloc of nations—nations that were not aligned with NATO or the Soviet Union. The conference brought prestige to Indonesia and showcased it as a leader among the world's poorer nations, which came to refer to themselves collectively as the Non-Aligned Nations. This was a courageous distinction for these nations to make at a time when most countries were choosing to support either the Soviet Union or the United States in the ongoing Cold War. The conference issued several statements, among them the bloc's opposition to colonialism, slavery, and poverty, which became models for later United Nations resolutions on those topics. The Non-Aligned Nations are still an active geopolitical organization. In recent years they have adopted a stance opposing globalization and international business practices in their countries.

Pancasila (pronounced "pancha-sila") In his plan to keep Indonesia free of Islamic law, President Sukarno proclaimed a government policy that he called Pancasila. The five tenets of Pancasila are (1) belief in one supreme god; (2) just and civilized humanity; (3) nationalism, the unity of Indonesians; (4) social justice; and (5) democracy—settlement of problems by discussion and conference, for example, consensus, as in village decision making (*gotong royong*). By adopting these tenets, freedom of religion was assured to all Indonesian citizens. Pancasila is still the basis of the Indonesian government.

Partai Komunis Indonesia (PKI) The Communist Party came into prominence in Indonesia in 1927 when it joined the nationalist movements in opposing the Dutch colonial rule of Indonesia. In the beginning it was somewhat questionably heralded as a rebirth of Indonesia's egalitarian Mataram empire. Prince Diponogoro, the hero of the 1825 Java War against the Dutch, was adopted as a communist hero. Although some modernist Indonesians were at first attracted to "Islamic communism," most PKI followers were adherents of Sufi Islam. The PKI was never able to shake the implication of being antireligious and eventually lost the support of the modernists. The Communist Party was not a political force in Indonesia after its role in the 1948 Madiun rebellion, where it opposed Indonesia's revolutionary forces. However, its leaders regrouped in the early 1950s, and eventually the party became influential in Sukarno's government. Blame for the September 30, 1965, coup attempt was placed on the PKI by Suharto's emerging military government. Many PKI members were killed in the aftermath of that coup, and as a result communism ceased to exist as a viable entity in Indonesia. In 1966 Suharto outlawed the Partai Komunis Indonesia.

Prambanan The complex of Hindu temples known as Prambanan rivals the neighboring Buddhist monument, Borobudur, in design and admirable architectural structure. Built in the seventh century, these stone monuments honor an impressive array of Hindu deities— Shiva, Brahma, Vishnu, Nandi, Ganesh, Durga. Many Hindu monuments and structures are visible in the Dieng Plains of Central Java, lending credence to the powerful influence of Hinduism in an earlier time in Indonesian history. Archaeologists speculate that a significant number of Hindu temples are still in the area, buried under layers of dirt and volcanic ash.

Srivijaya A Buddhist kingdom founded in the sixth century, Srivijava's rulers controlled the southern Malay Peninsula and northwest Sumatra until the end of the thirteenth century. The busy Strait of Malacca was a primary commercial arena for merchants within Southeast Asia as well as for Chinese and Arabian traders. Other kingdoms appeared and faded while Srivijaya remained strong. Srivijaya was eventually taken over by the powerful Majapahit empire.

Strait of Malacca This seaway is located between the tip of the Malay Peninsula and northwest Sumatra. It is essentially the gateway through

Southeast Asia to the islands of Indonesia and the Philippines. During the height of the spice trade these waters controlled sea traffic traveling to the spice-growing islands. Originally controlled by the Malays, during the late 1500s the Portuguese ran Malacca as their maritime port. Eventually England took over Singapore, and the strait was under control of the British until after World War II. Today this sealane is still a major international waterway.

Suharto Born on Java in 1921, Suharto had little formal education, and he entered military service under the Dutch, rising through the ranks to become an army officer. General Suharto had spent his entire career in the army, and it was with the support of the military that he began to take over the reins of government in October 1965. Suharto began his time in office with the implementation of what he termed the "New Order." Relations with Western countries and the United Nations resumed, and the confrontation with Malaysia came to an end. In March 1967 the People's Consultative Assembly (MPR) named Suharto acting president. Indonesia prospered under Suharto's presidency despite widespread corruption and nepotism. It was the economic downfall of 1997 that ended his long rule and saw him leave office in disgrace.

Suharto, Siti Hartinah Tien Suharto, as she was best known in Indonesia, was born in East Java in 1923. At the time of her death she had been married to her army officer *cum* Indonesian president husband for almost fifty years. She was Suharto's closest confidant, and the president was devastated when she died in April 1996. The couple met when Tien, the daughter of a district officer in the Dutch colonial government and descendant of Javanese royalty, was a volunteer with the Indonesian Red Cross. At that time Suharto was a lieutenant colonel in the newly formed Indonesian army. Throughout their marriage Tien was the perfect hostess. After her husband became president she accompanied him on most of his official travels. Despite the respect she seemed to have from many Indonesians, she was widely known by the nickname "Madam Ten Percent," the implication being that she demanded 10 percent off the top of any business deals in which she was involved. This was never tied to any specific incidents, but the nickname stayed with her throughout her years as Indonesia's first lady.

Sukarno Born in Surabaya in June 1901, Sukarno attended a Dutch language school and went to college in Bandung, where he graduated with a degree in engineering. He was active in student protest movements and nationalist groups during his years at university and eventually became a leader in Indonesia's nationalist movement; consequently he was imprisoned by the Dutch. He was allowed to make regular radio broadcasts during the Japanese occupation during World War II and in so doing kept the spirit of nationalism alive and growing in the Indonesian people. Sukarno's goal was always independence for Indonesia, though some Indonesians accused him of collaboration with the Japanese. He was named Indonesia's first president at the end of World War II, on August 17, 1945, and faced several years of fighting and negotiating with the Dutch before the United Nations declared Indonesia an independent nation on December 27, 1949. Sukarno began his presidency under extraordinarily lean conditions. The country had few civil servants or trained professionals and almost no businesses. Years of war had left Indonesia devastated financially and, as in postwar Europe and other parts of Asia, in dire need of scarce financial aid. Well known for his flamboyant style, Sukarno is the personification of the old saying that commendable revolutionary leaders make poor peacetime leaders. A failing economy, corruption, and political infighting led to his being forced from office in 1966. Sukarno died on June 21, 1970, in Bogor.

Sukarnoputri, Megawati The daughter of Sukarno was named the fifth president of Indonesia on July 23, 2001. She had been vice president under Gus Dur and upon his impeachment was named president. Megawati is a moderate Muslim in contrast to her vice president, Hamzah Haz, who is a fundamentalist Muslim. Her most powerful ally is the military. Megawati is opposed to separatism and has had limited success calming the separatist movements that are active across the country. It is too soon to pass judgment on her government, but Megawati faces serious problems. Among them are the violence in Maluku, Papua, and Aceh, and the desire for stricter religious laws among the fundamentalist Muslims. The Bali bombings in fall 2002 added international terrorism to her growing list of concerns. Although in 2003 Megawati stated that she would not run for the Indonesian presidency in 2004, she has since changed her mind.

Sultan Agung The greatest Mataram ruler was Sultan Agung. He took over the empire in 1613, and in 1646, when he died, the Mataram empire had spread across Central and East Java and the island of Madura. Sultan Agung's plans to capture West Java were thwarted by the Dutch, and he was defeated in Batavia (now Jakarta). Sultan Agung ruled when the colonial presence in Indonesia was on the rise. Although he commanded powerful armies, the sultan's forces were no match for the better-armed Dutch soldiers.

Sultan Hemengkubuwono IX This sultan provided unwavering support for the Indonesian revolution and the nationalist leaders. In 1946, when the Dutch controlled Jakarta, Yogyakarta became the capital city of the Indonesian Republic. The Dutch attacked the city, which suffered serious damage from bombing. The sultan's loyalty to Indonesian independence prompted Sukarno to name Yogyakarta a "special region" and give it provincial status. The sultan was named governor of the province. The sultan of Yogyakarta is unique in this capacity. His son holds that title today.

Sutan Sjahrir Indonesia's first prime minister was another idealist who became disillusioned with Sukarno's governing policies after independence. At one point, prior to the Japanese occupation of Indonesia, the Dutch government exiled both Sjahrir and Mohammad Hatta to Banda (in the Spice Islands) where they would be far away from the activity of the worrisome nationalist movement. After his stint as prime minister, Sjahrir served as Indonesia's representative at the United Nations. He was born in 1909 and died in 1966.

Toer, Pramoedya Antara The country's most widely read and best known writer was imprisoned by the Suharto government in 1969. His crime was being associated with the Communist Party, and in 1969 that was a dangerous association. Pramoedya was kept on the prison-island of Buru from 1969 to 1979, and it was during this time that he wrote the *Buru Quartet*, a series of four books that follows a Dutch-educated Indonesian who faces the inequity of the Dutch colonial government. Pramoedya had been imprisoned by the Dutch in the late 1940s for his support of the Indonesian revolution. Until recently Pramoedya's books were banned in Indonesia, as the Suharto government would tolerate nothing that was reminiscent of communism. Today, Pramoedya's books are widely read abroad and in Indonesia.

VOC In 1602 a group of Dutch businessmen (the "Seventeen Gentlemen") set up the Dutch East India Company (Vereenigde Oostindische Compagnie—VOC) to regulate Dutch trade in Indonesia. They were successful in driving other European traders out of the

Spice Islands, but they never attained complete control of the spice trade. When seeds and young trees were successfully smuggled out of Maluku and planted in South America and Africa, spices were no longer a lucrative commodity, and the mercantile company turned its interests to other commercially viable products. The VOC determined the regulations for commerce in Indonesia until the end of 1799, when due to loss of profit the Dutch government took over the administration of the colony and concentrated on Indonesia's natural resources—oil, rattan, lumber, and mineral deposits.

wayang **(puppet)** *Wayang,* or puppet, performances are among the most popular forms of entertainment in Indonesia. *Mahabarata* and *Ramayana* performances featuring *wayang kulit* (leather puppets) and *wayang golek* (three-dimensional puppets) have been popular in Indonesia for centuries. A puppeteer (*dalang*) controls the puppets as he narrates the story. The *dalang* is unique as he can have the puppets comment on matters that would be off-limits to newspapers or radio and television broadcasters, such as making critical comments about government leaders. This was especially true under the Sukarno and Suharto presidencies, when such criticism could land a person in jail.

World War II The Japanese army occupied Indonesia from January 1942 until the end of World War II in August 1945. The Indonesians first viewed the Japanese as liberators from their years of Dutch colonial rule. This soon changed as the Japanese forces required manpower and resources that made tremendous demands on the Indonesians, causing them extreme hardship. However, the Japanese occupation did provide Indonesian nationalists with the opportunity to pursue independence with little hindrance. As soon as the Japanese were defeated, Indonesia's independence was declared and a new government set in place.

Indonesian Language, Food, and Etiquette

LANGUAGE

One has only to look at a map of Indonesia to understand why it is a country of hundreds of dialects. Separated by miles of open ocean, it was until recently difficult for people in one region to regularly interact with people from another region. Before regularly scheduled interisland transportation was available, many men and women never left the villages where they were born. On the land, mountain barriers brought about the same sort of isolation. Over the centuries this seclusion caused the people in remote regions to develop cultural differences, including language. Even today it is not unusual to find people living on neighboring islands unable to communicate with one another in their specific region's dialect. This was a dilemma for the nationalists who were attempting to establish the cornerstones of a new republic. If the process of uniting a country is to be successful, it is largely accepted that all of the people should speak and understand a common language. A number of attempts were made to address this problem. The most effective was in 1928 when a youth group declared Malay the national language of Indonesia. To make the language more pointedly Indonesian, they called it *Bahasa Indonesia,* which means "Indonesian language."

Even though this group had no legitimate means to name *Bahasa Indonesia* as the country's national language, the use of Indonesian was quickly adapted by many Indonesians, most notably authors and journalists. One of the best known cadres of writers to publish in Indonesian was "The Generation of '45." This title refers to a group of nationalist authors who supported the 1945 independence movement. Members of this circle of writers went on to write literature and poetry as well as newspaper articles. It was in this latter media where the public was exposed to writings supporting an independent Indonesia. Between 1940 and 1965 Indonesia witnessed a proliferation of newspapers and literary journals published in Indonesian whose authors and editors were passionate about independence.

Malay

The choice of Malay as a national language in Indonesia was brilliant. There are many reasons that this is true, but two stand out. First, almost all Indonesians spoke some Malay. It had been the *lingua franca* of traders in the region for centuries. Indonesians traded within the archipelago, with other Southeast Asian countries, and with foreign merchants coming to Southeast Asia. To be effective in the pre-European mercantile world of Southeast Asia, one had to have the ability to speak some Malay, whether on shipboard or in the ports. Consequently the language gained acceptance in the trading centers of Indonesia, and with the advent of missionaries it spread to the hinterlands. The second reason that Malay was an excellent choice as a national language is that it was not the exclusive language of any Indonesian ethnic or cultural group. As noted earlier, the Javanese constitute approximately 45 percent of the country's population; thus Javanese may have seemed a logical language choice to the outsider. However, this would have shown a preference for the Javanese people at a time when equality of all the nascent nation's people was strongly proclaimed. Indonesian was actually named the national language in the country's constitution. Article 36 declares, "The national language shall be Indonesian."

Malay inscriptions found on stones throughout the Malay and Indonesian world date back as far as the seventh century. In addition to stone inscriptions, there is a plethora of writing in Malay that survived from that time as well. In essence, Malay was in existence for many centuries, and the Indonesians who interacted with outsiders learned this language to conduct the business necessary for their livelihood.

Dialects

More than 580 dialects and languages are spoken in Indonesia—too many to list here. Some are spoken by a very small sector of the population while others, like Javanese, are spoken by many millions of people. Some of the more common dialects are Sundanese, spoken by about 28 million people; Madurese, spoken by some 10 million people; Minangkabau, spoken by approximately 6.5 million people; Bugenese, spoken by about 3.6 million people; and Batak, spoken by approximately 2 million. The vast majority of Indonesians are at least bilingual. They speak their local dialect at home and to some extent in their local markets, but in schools, in government, and on television and radio the language used is Indonesian. Many people have reasonable fluency in the dialect of a bordering group. For example, many Javanese living in West Java speak Sundanese and would use that language to barter in a West Java marketplace. Most Indonesians who have attended at least elementary school know a smattering of English, and those with a high school education are able to carry on basic conversations in English. Most college graduates speak English reasonably well, in part because some college textbooks, especially in the sciences, are written in English. Travelers should not assume, however, that in sojourning into interior regions they can make their way around the country speaking no Indonesian.

Outside Influences on Language

Malay has been spoken as a "trade language" in coastal Malaysia and Indonesia for centuries. Local dialects often have Sanskrit-based words, an indication of the earlier Indian influence in that area. For example, *candi* (pronounced "chandy") is used throughout Indonesia for "monument" or "shrine." Some of the earliest writings that illustrate this influence were in Bali, where inscriptions were made on the leaves of the tal tree. These slats of dried leaf are called *lontar*. They were treated and joined together with twine to make a series of "pages" or a book. Examples of this form of writing may still be found throughout Indonesia, most especially in Bali.

To achieve their goals, proselytizers must speak the language of a region, and the missionaries in Indonesia—be they Muslims or Christians—were no exception. Early Arabic missionaries brought Sufi Islam to Indonesia, and elements of that religion entered the Malay language. In modern Indonesia, some days of the week are taken from Arabic; for example, *Jum'at* (Friday) and *Sabtu* (Saturday). Other commonly used Arabic words are *madrasah* (school), *sedekah* (alms), *awal* (beginning), *kabar* (news), and *kitab* (book). Later, Portuguese and then Dutch words were incorporated into Malay and Indonesian. For example, the Portuguese word *sepatu* is used in Indonesian to mean shoe; *mentaga* is butter; *pesta* is party; *gredja* means church; *meja* is table; *nyonya* is a title for a married woman (usually a foreigner), and *garpu* means fork. Among the Dutch words that have infiltrated Indonesian are *handuk* (towel), *kuas* (brush), *telat* (to be late), *tante* (aunt), and *om* (uncle). Since independence, English has been a major influence on Indonesian. Likewise, many Indonesian words are now commonly used in the West: Sarong, amok, catsup, and bamboo are all Malay/Indonesian words. Indonesian is written in roman script, which helps most Western visitors in their ability to read signs and find their way around the country.

The short-term traveler should learn a few phrases. Some useful words, questions, and phrases are given here.

Where is the hospital? . . . .*Dimana rumah sakit?*

You may replace *rumah sakit,* which means hospital, with other appropriate words. For example: *rumah makan* (restaurant), *pasar* (marketplace), *setasiun* (station), *lapangan terbang* (airport), or WC (pronounced "way say," toilet or water closet).

Good morning, day, afternoon,
evening . . . .*Selamat: pagi, siang, sore, malam*

I don't understand . . . .*Saya tidak mengerti.*

How much does it cost? . . . .*Berapa harganya?*

How many? . . . .*Berapa* (How old are you?: *Berapa umur anda?* [literally—How many years do you have?])

What time is it? . . . .*Jam berapa?* Time is often marked in 24-hour periods; for example, 2:00 in the afternoon will be 1400.

what . . . .*apa* (What is that?: *Apu itu?* What is your name?: *Siapa nama anda?*)

have . . . .*ada* (Do you have more?: *Ada lagi?*)

want . . . .*mau* (*Saya mau makan:* I want to eat.)

expensive . . . .*mahal*

inexpensive . . . .*murah*

thank you . . . .*terima kasih*

hot (temperature) . . . .*panas*

hot (spicy) . . . .*pedas*

good . . . .*bagus*

bad . . . .*jelek*

big . . . .*besar*

small . . . .*kecil* (pronounced "kecheel")

beautiful . . . .*cantik* (pronounced "chantique")

food . . . .*makanan*

water . . . .*air* (pronounced "eyer")

delicious . . . .*enak*

street	*jalan*
room	*kamar*
bath	*mandi*
store	*toko*
this	*ini*
that	*itu*
wash	*cuci* (pronounced "chuchi")
clean	*bersih*
dirty	*kotor*
you, your, yours	*anda*
I, me, my	*saya*
he or she	*dia*
they	*mereka*
more	*lagi*
less	*kurang*
left, right	*kiri, kanan*
yes	*ya*
no	*tidak*

Numbers

1	*satu*
2	*dua*
3	*tiga*
4	*empat*
5	*lima*
6	*enam*
7	*tujuh*
8	*delapan*
9	*sembilan*
10	*sepuluh*
11	*sebelas*
12	*duabelas*
13	*tigabelas* (add *belas* to primary number to make it a teen number)
20	*dua puluh*
30	*tigapuluh* (add *puluh* to primary number to make it 20,30, 40, etc.)

100 . . . . *seratus* (the prefix *se* signifies one, e.g.,
                                            duaratus means 200)

1,000 . . . . *seribu*

1,000,000 . . . . *sejuta*

For example, to say nine thousand two hundred and fifty one: *sembilan ribu dua ratus lima puluh satu;* to say five million six hundred thousand seventy eight: *lima juta enam ratus ribu tujuh puluh delapan.*

Days of the Week

Sunday . . . .*Hari Minggu*

Monday . . . .*Hari Senin*

Tuesday . . . .*Hari Selassa*

Wednesday . . . .*Hari Rabu*

Thursday . . . .*Hari Kamis*

Friday . . . .*Hari Jumat*

Saturday . . . .*Hari Sabtu*

yesterday . . . .*kemarin*

tomorrow . . . .*besok*

today . . . .*hari ini*

week . . . .*minggu*

date . . . .*tanggal*

As noted earlier, dialects and modified forms of speech communication exist throughout Indonesia. One of the most common is the Jakarta dialect, a colloquial language that drops and adds letters and syllables to existing Indonesian words. The Jakarta dialect is popular with high school and college students, and it is not unusual for their conversations to be incomprehensible to other Indonesians. It is not spoken exclusively in Jakarta, and Indonesian is the first language of those who speak this slang dialect.

FOOD

Indonesian dishes are made from locally grown and introduced foods from around the world. One finds curries and eggplant from India; chilies, pineapple, and papaya from South America; squash, soybeans, and avocados from Europe; and cabbage from China. Soybeans are used extensively in Indonesian cooking, and their high nutritional value is a main reason for the good health of many poorer Indonesians. Two popular dishes made from soybeans are *tahu* (tofu), made from bean curd, and *tempe,* made from fermented soybeans. *Tahu* is sometimes fried and at other times mixed with stir-fry dishes. *Tempe,* like *tahu,* is sold in blocks and is most often cut into strips and fried with chili peppers. It has a crunchy texture as opposed to tahu's soft consistency. Fried *tempe* with chili is a uniquely Indonesian dish. Also made from soybeans is *ketcap,* a sauce used in flavoring many meat and vegetable dishes. It is sweeter than the soy sauce with which most Westerners are familiar. (The similarity between *ketcap* and the English word *ketchup* is merely that both are condiments, as ketcap does not contain tomatoes.) Indonesian has dozens of words for rice, covering everything from various stages of growth of the plants (*padi*) in the fields to harvested rice, to unhusked rice (*gabah*). Once rice is cooked (*nasi*), it may be described as yesterday's rice, the rice stuck on the bottom of the pan, freshly cooked rice, rice gruel, and so on. Rice terraces and fields dominate the Indonesian landscapes, and a meal is never served without it.

Another mainstay on any Indonesian table is *sambal*. This is chopped or ground chili peppers, and first-time visitors to Indonesia should be forewarned about the strength of this condiment. It can literally bring the taster to tears; however, if used sparingly *sambal* adds a flavor that truly enhances many a meal.

Rice does not grow well in all parts of the country, and sago replaces rice as the staple food in eastern Indonesia. The sago palm supplies residents of this region with a starch that requires minimal effort. The pith is removed from the trunk of the sago palm tree, then washed and strained, at which point it is ready to cook. It is commonly served as porridge by adding water to it or is baked into small cakes. Though quite bland, sago is an excellent source of carbohydrate.

Local dishes reflect the agricultural products of the region where they are served. In West Java, for example, the climate is conducive to growing a variety of fruits and vegetables. A popular dish in this region is *gado-gado*. This vegetarian dish is made up of potatoes, bean sprouts, cucumber, cabbage, and other available vegetables that are briefly cooked. The parboiled vegetables are then served with a spicy peanut sauce. Fried rice (*nasi goreng*), fried noodles (*mi goreng*), rice mixed with meat and vegetables (*nasi campur*), and meat kabobs (*sate*) are favorites throughout the archipelago. Many Indonesian dishes are served with *krupuk,* a large crispy chip flavored with shrimp, or *emping,* a smaller cracker-like chip much blander than *krupuk*. Indonesians are fond of soups and make a wide variety of them using goat meat, chicken, and a variety of vegetable combinations. Pork, a meat forbidden to Muslims, is available on Balinese restaurant menus, although this is not true in the rest of the country. Chinese restaurants are the exception and serve pork regardless of where they are located.

A familiar Indonesian food is *sate.* It consists of small pieces of marinated meat skewered on a stick and cooked over an open fire. A spicy peanut sauce is served with it. The *sate* cook is often seen at the night market as he grills chicken, beef, shrimp, and goat on a small barbecue grill. *Sate* is popular throughout Indonesia, and for a special event such as a *salamatan* the family might hire a *sate* cook to come to their home and set up his grill in their yard. (A *salamatan* is a feast that commemorates any special event, such as a circumcision, a birth, a death, a wedding, or any number of other events Indonesian people celebrate.)

All kinds of food are sold on the streets in Indonesia. Street vendors sell the more popular dishes at surprisingly reasonable prices. Soups, curries, *gado-gado,* fried rice, noodles, and many other dishes are all available from a man or woman who prepares and sells food from a movable cart on the sidewalk or by the side of the street. A small portable stove keeps the food warm, and a pail of clean water is kept nearby for rinsing dishes. If the food is not too soupy it is often served on clean banana leaves—the paper plate of Southeast Asia. A popular dessert available from street vendors is *martabak,* a pancake filled with chocolate sauce and/or sweetened condensed milk and topped with nuts. Another sweet that provides a strange combination to foreigners is an avocado milkshake. To make this drink, an avocado is mashed and then whipped with chocolate syrup and sweetened milk and served as an after-meal treat or a snack.

In addition to the food vendors in the markets, Indonesia has a wide selection of restaurants. Some specialize in seafood, some in foreign foods, and some in regional foods. These restaurants can range from quite inexpensive to very expensive.

Fruits grow well in Indonesia and can be found on virtually all of the islands. Although many fruits are known to Westerners (mango, papaya, banana), a number are unfamiliar, such as mangosteen, durian, rambutan, and jackfruit. Mangosteen have a thick maroon rind and a segmented white inside that tastes like strawberries and cream. Durian are covered with a spiky thick greenish yellow rind. The inside is also segmented, but this yellow fruit has a most unusual smell. It has been described as similar to rotting flesh. The taste is equally strange, combining sweet cream and garlic. Durian is truly a different taste sensation, and visitors to Indonesia should try it. A rambutan is shaped like an egg. The rind is bright red or red-yellow and has hairy spikes on it. *Rambutan* means hairy, so it is an apt name for the refreshing fruit that tastes something like grapes. Jackfruit is a large yellow fruit, and like so many other tropical fruits it has a thick rind. It is unusual in that it is most often an ingredient in soups made with meat. Indonesia has a variety of citrus fruits—lemons, limes, oranges, tangerines. Bananas are grown everywhere. A favorite dessert is fried bananas (*pisang goreng*). To make this dish, a banana is dipped in a batter, fried, and sprinkled with sugar.

All of the above foods are popular and typical of Indonesian cuisine, but perhaps the most common meal for many Indonesians consists of rice and dried fish. The traveler passes myriad villages with great quantities of small fish drying in the hot equatorial sun. This fish is inexpensive and a main source of protein for most villagers. To ensure a ready supply of fish, a farmer will often raise fish in a pond along side his rice field (*sawah*). Fish is prepared in a variety of ways and is preferred over meat by many Indonesians. In addition to fish grown in a village fishpond, a variety of seafood is found in the markets, and many Indonesians earn their living as fishermen.

Indonesians do not generally designate certain foods for certain meals, as is often done in Western cultures. The evening meal is usually the most substantial, and it is common for leftovers from dinner to be served at breakfast—along with freshly cooked rice. Lunch is often noodles, fried rice, *gado-gado*, or something light.

Indonesians drink a lot of tea and coffee. Both are produced in Indonesia and are not expensive. Until the advent of bottled water, few Indonesians drank large amounts of water. It had to be boiled before drinking and then kept refrigerated. Because refrigeration often was not available, boiled water was used to make tea, a drink that tastes just fine lukewarm. Liquor is available throughout Indonesia, and although Muslims are forbidden to drink it, many do imbibe socially. Several locally brewed beers are served in restaurants regularly, and all major hotels catering to Westerners maintain full bars. Fruit drinks are available and are often served with shaved coconut and flavored with syrup. Sodas are readily obtainable, and the ubiquitous Coca-Cola signs are everywhere. However, this drink is expensive and therefore is more popular with foreigners than average Indonesians. For the past twenty years, bottled water has been available throughout Indonesia, even in most remote locations. This has eased the concern of tourists about unsafe water.

Ice can be a problem. It is usually made from boiled water and therefore safe to drink, but on some occasions blocks of ice that are packed in wood shavings or straw are rinsed off with water from a nearby river or stream, rendering them unsafe. Adding ice to drinks at roadside stands can be a problem. Hotels and restaurants make their own ice and avoid this dilemma.

Indonesians eat a lot of snacks. The marketplace offers a wide variety of chips and sweets, many of the latter made from coconut and raw sugar. These are often steamed in banana leaves and are inexpensive. One sees the discarded banana wrappings along the street and in the parks. The advantage over plastic containers is that banana leaves are biodegradable.

ETIQUETTE

When in Indonesia there are a few rules that the thoughtful traveler should follow. Indonesians are generally tolerant of foreigners and will often overlook minor offenses; however, no one wishes to intentionally offend a host, so it is wise to be aware of some actions that Indonesians find vulgar.

Use of Your Hands and Feet

You should never touch anyone's head, especially the head of a child. The spirit enters and leaves your body through your head. Do not hand items to anyone with your left hand, and if you find yourself in a restaurant where the food is to be eaten with your fingers, use only your right hand. The left hand is reserved for personal hygiene. Do not point with a finger, although you may do so with your thumb. Do not stand with your hands on your hips. Only the lowest-class characters in dramas and puppet theater stand in that "arrogant" position. You should not cross your legs when in a group, and be especially careful not to indicate an item or direction by pointing your foot.

Clothing

Indonesia is located on the equator, and the climate can be unbearably hot for a foreigner. In spite of this, the foreigner must remember that Indonesia is largely a Muslim country and demeanor is important. Women should wear dresses and shirts with sleeves; it is considered rude to show your upper arms. Miniskirts and shorts are frowned upon, as are low necklines. Long pants are acceptable attire for women.

Attitude

Anger is considered to be the ultimate in rudeness. To shout or lash out in anger at frustrating situations accomplishes nothing in Indonesia. Many instances can be found in Indonesia where logic does not seem to prevail. Perhaps the most common is the queue. In the West people are accustomed to standing in line and waiting their turn, with the first arriving being the first served. This is not true in Indonesia. To use a common example, when the post office clerk opens a window for service, there is more likely than not a rush to that window by all who have been waiting for it to open. The woman who has been waiting an hour may well be served long after the man who has been there ten minutes. The concept of taking a number to assure an orderly timeframe for being helped has not caught on in Indonesia. It is startling for the foreigner who appears at a government office for the first time to be caught up in the frenzy of claiming the clerk's attention. This same practice is observed in doctors' waiting rooms, in train stations, in immigration offices, and almost any place where a Westerner would expect to form a line for service. Explaining the logic of forming a line to others present will not change a practice that has been followed for years. Just remain calm and the next time try to avoid the times that personnel in that office are most in demand.

Being a Proper Guest

If you are invited to an Indonesian's home, you will be served food and beverage. It is rude to refuse this gesture, so allow time to do this. Likewise if you invite people to your home you should always offer food and drink. It is also polite to wait for your host or hostess to take the first sip or bite, no matter how hungry or thirsty you may be. Often you host will say *"silakan,"* which means, "Please, help yourself." Under those circumstances you may eat or drink before your host. If your host has arranged any sort of entertainment for you, such as a shadow play, dancer, or gamelan music, it is rude for you to leave before the performance has been completed. This can be difficult if you are jet lagged and the presentation goes on until the wee hours of the morning, but it is better to take a nap during the performance than to excuse yourself and go to bed.

Bargaining

When in the marketplace and smaller shops of Indonesia, it is customary to bargain over the price of goods. Usually one appears mildly shocked at the price the vendor quotes and counters with a suggestion of half that amount. The vendor will in turn be shocked that you would offer such a small amount for his quality product and come back with a price in the three-quarters range. This back-and-forth bargaining is done good-naturedly and goes on until both realize that the other has reached a price that will neither be lowered or increased. One must never back out after he or she has started to bargain. Once the process starts, the buyer is not allowed to change his or her mind and walk away, deciding that he or she did not want the item. Vendors can become very upset over such action. The author witnessed such an event on Bali once where the vendor cursed the potential buyer's offspring through two generations. It may have been a scare tactic used in a busy tourist marketplace, but it unnerved the buyer, who left the area without buying from that vendor or any other in that complex.

Rules of courtesy and respect in Indonesia are not very different from those in any other country. The traveler who is considerate and polite will not be shunned even if he or she violates some Indonesian cultural traditions. People who remain aware of their surroundings and are not rude will be well treated by Indonesians, who understand that visitors cannot be expected to understand all of the nuances of local customs.

Indonesia-Related Organizations

BUSINESS AND ECONOMIC

American-Indonesian Chamber of Commerce (AICC)
317 Madison Avenue, Suite 520
New York, NY 10017
Tel.: (212) 687-4505
Fax: (212) 687-5844
E-mail: aiccny@bigplanet.com
Website: www.aiccusa.org

The AICC has an active program featuring speakers knowledgeable about Indonesia as well as briefing programs for newly appointed U.S. and Indonesian government officials. It publishes *Outlook Indonesia,* a quarterly magazine containing interpretations of new Indonesian policies. In addition, it provides business translations, either from English to Indonesian or Indonesian to English.

Asia Pacific Economic Cooperation (APEC)
APEC Secretariat
438 Alexandra Road
Alexandra Point
Singapore
Tel.: (65) 276-1880
Fax: (65) 276-1775
Website: http://www.apecsec.org.sg

APEC encompasses most of the nations situated around the Pacific Rim. Established in 1989, it currently has twenty-one members. The United States first called together representatives of this group of nations to discuss a wide range of common problems, primarily economic. It has since become a most important institution in the Asia Pacific region with its long-term plan for free trade and investment and as a forum to ward off conflict.

Association of Southeast Asian Nations (ASEAN)
ASEAN Secretariat
70A Jalan Sisingamangaraja
Jakarta 12110
Indonesia
Tel.: (62-21) 726-2991
Fax: (62-21) 739-8234

ASEAN was formed in 1967 to promote political and economic cooperation and regional stability among its members. Charter members
are Indonesia, Malaysia, the Philippines, Singapore, and Thailand. By
1999 Brunei, Burma, Vietnam, Cambodia, and Laos had joined the
group, bringing its membership to ten. Currently all Southeast Asian
countries except East Timor belong to ASEAN. This regional organization contains several subgroups, of which the ASEAN Free Trade
Area (AFTA) is probably the best known. Together these Southeast
Asian nations work to improve economic and business conditions in
their countries.

International NGO Forum on
Indonesian Development (INFID)
INFID Secretariat
Jalan Mampang Prapatan XI/23
Jakarta 12790
Indonesia
Tel.: (62-21) 791-96721 or 791-96722
Fax: (62-21) 794-1577
E-mail: infid@nusa.or.id
Website: www.infid.or.id

INFID provides a forum for NGOs concerned about the people they
represent in Indonesia. It aims at facilitating communication between
NGOs inside and outside Indonesia to promote policies to alleviate
poverty and to improve conditions for the disadvantaged in Indonesia.

U.S. Chamber of Commerce
Managing Director, Asia International Division
1615 H Street N.W.
Washington, DC 20062-2000
Tel.: (202) 659-6000, 465-5461, or 463-5461
Fax: (202) 822-2491
E-mail: mbrillia@uschamber.com; asia@uschamber.com

Website: www.uschamber.com

The U.S. Chamber explores programs designed to assist exporters to Asia.

CULTURE/EDUCATION/EXCHANGE

American Indonesia Exchange Foundation (AMINEF)
Balai Pustaka Building, Sixth Floor
Jalan Gunung Sahari Raya No. 4
Jakarta 10720
Indonesia
Tel.: (62-21) 345-2024, 345-2016, or 345-2018
Fax: (62-21) 345-2050
Website: http://www.usembassyjakarta.org/aminef

AMINEF offers the opportunity for Indonesians to study in the United States.

Asia Society
The following three websites are affiliated with the Asia Society:
AsiaSource (www.asiasource.org) features news updates.
AskAsia (www.askasia.org) offers access to high-quality K–12 resources.
AsiaBusinessToday (www.AsiaBusinessToday.org) provides information on U.S.–Asia trade, technology developments, and global finance.
Tel.: (212) 288-6400
Fax: (212) 517-8315
E-mail: webmaster@asiasoc.org
Website: http://www.asiasociety.org/about/index.html

The Asia Society fosters understanding of Asia and communication between Americans and the peoples of Asia and the Pacific. The society provides a forum for building awareness of the Asia-Pacific region.

Association for Asian Studies (AAS)
1021 East Huron Street
Ann Arbor, MI 48104
Tel.: (734) 665-2490
Fax: (734) 665-3801
Website: http://www.Aasianst.org

This organization's membership is largely composed of faculty members of U.S. and Asian educational institutions along with coordinators of K–12 education programs at these institutions. AAS publishes the *Journal of Asian Studies,* an academic journal, and *Education about Asia,* a publication for elementary, secondary, and undergraduate educators teaching about Asian countries.

Center for Southeast Asian Studies
Northern Illinois University
DeKalb, IL 60115
Tel.: (815) 753-1771
Fax: (815) 753-1776
E-mail: cseas@niu.edu
Website: http://www.seasite.niu.edu

Center for Southeast Asian Studies
Ohio University
56 East Union Street, Burson House
Athens, OH 45701-2979
Tel.: (740) 593-1841
Fax: (740) 593-1837
E-mail: schneidk@ohio.edu

Center for Southeast Asia Studies
University of California at Berkeley
2223 Fulton Street, Room 617
Berkeley, CA 94720-2318
Tel.: (510) 642-3609
Fax: (510) 643-7062

Center for Southeast Asian Studies
University of California at Los Angeles
11387 Bunche Hall
Mailcode 148703
Box 951487
Los Angeles, CA 90095-1487
Tel.: (310) 206-9163
Fax: (310) 206-3555
E-mail: cseas@isop.ucla.edu
Website: www.international.ucla.edu/cseas

Center for Southeast Asian Studies
University of Hawaii
1890 East-West Road, Moore Hall 416
Honolulu, HI 96822

Tel.: (808) 956-2688
Fax: (808) 956-2682
E-mail: cseas@hawaii.edu
Website: http://www.hawaii.edu/cseas

The University of Hawaii center specializes in educational materials for K–12 teachers. It has produced a workbook on Indonesia and several lesson packets on the country as well. The outreach office at UH also distributes two activity books published by a woman's organization in Jakarta. The journal *Cakalele,* which focuses on eastern Indonesia, is also published by this center.

Center for Southeast Asian Studies
University of Michigan
1080 South University Avenue, Suite 416
Ann Arbor, MI 48109-1106

Center for Southeast Asian Studies
University of Wisconsin–Madison
207 Ingraham Hall
1155 Observatory Drive
Madison, WI 53706-1397
Tel.: (608) 263-1755
Fax: (608) 263-3537
E-mail: seasia@intl-institute.wisc.edu

Consortium of Teachers of Indonesian and Malay (COTIM)
Center for Southeast Asian Studies
1155 Observatory Drive
Ingraham Hall, Room 207
University of Wisconsin–Madison
Madison, WI 53706
Tel.: (608) 263-1755
Fax: (608) 263-3735
E-mail: cotim@intl-institute.wisc.edu

COTIM is an advanced Indonesian language program held during the summer on the campus of an Indonesian institution. The program is funded by the U.S. Department of Education through its Fulbright-Hays Group Projects Abroad programs and as such offers fellowships to American students who wish to study Indonesian intensively. Students live with an Indonesian family while attending language classes.

East-West Center (EWC)
1601 East-West Road
Honolulu, HI 96848-1601
Tel.: (808) 944-7111
Fax: (808) 944-7376
Website: http://www.eastwestcenter.org

The East-West Center is an education and research organization in which professionals and students from the United States and Asia study and work together. The EWC is located on the University of Hawaii campus. It directs a variety of programs for students and visiting scholars that promote the study of Indonesia as well as all of Asia. Students from Indonesia and the United States may apply for East-West Center fellowships to attend the University of Hawaii.

The EWC AsiaPacificEd program at the East-West Center offers programs for K–12 teachers on Indonesia, some of which are held during the summer in Indonesia. The Center's Asia Development Program offers similar opportunities to faculty members of mainland colleges with few course offerings in Asian studies who wish to extend their Asian studies curriculum.

Gadjah Mada University (GMU)
Universitas Gadjah Mada
Sekip Utana
Yogyakarta 55281
Indonesia
Tel.: (62-274) 565-268
Fax: (62-274) 565-223
E-mail: rector@ugm.ac.id
Website: http://www.gadjahmada.edu

This Indonesian university was started by the sultan of Yogyakarta. It emphasizes the arts, and many American students attend dance and gamelan classes there. The USINDO Society holds its summer language program on the GMU campus.

Leiden University
Stationwes 46
P.O. Box 9500
2300 RA
Leiden
The Netherlands

Tel.: (31-71) 527-72-56
Fax: (31-71) 527-72-57

The University of Leiden in the Netherlands has a number of Indonesian programs and publications. Dutch archives house innumerable Indonesia-related documents.

National University of Singapore (NUS)
10 Kent Ridge Crescent
Singapore 119260
Tel.: (65) 874-3839
Fax: (65) 774-2528
E-mail: hisjseas@nus.edu.sg

NUS has an active Indonesian Studies program. It offers language courses as well as a variety of area studies courses related to Indonesia. NUS also publishes the *Journal of Southeast Asian Studies* through its History Department.

Program for Southeast Asian Studies
Arizona State University
P.O. Box 873502
Tempe, AZ 85287-3502
Tel.: (480) 965-4232
Fax: (480) 965-7459
E-mail: pseas@asu.edu
Website: http://www.edu/clas/asian/sea/seaf100.html

Southeast Asia Center
University of Washington
Jackson School of International Studies
Box 353650
Seattle, WA 98195-3650

Southeast Asia Program
Cornell University
180 Uris Hall
Ithaca, NY 14853
Tel.: (607) 255-2378
Fax: (607) 254-5000
E-mail: SEAP@cornell.edu

Cornell has a selection of educational materials on Indonesia.

Southeast Asian Studies Summer Institute (SEASSI)
Center for Southeast Asian Studies
207 Ingraham Hall
1155 Observatory Drive
University of Wisconsin–Madison
Madison, WI 53706
Tel.: (608) 263-175
Fax: (608) 263-3735
E-mail: seassi@intl-institute.wisc.edu

SEASSI is an intensive summer language institute. Students may study elementary, intermediate, and advanced Indonesian as well as Javanese. All other Southeast Asian languages are offered at SEASSI as well. It is currently held on the University of Wisconsin campus, although in the past the program rotated among universities that have Southeast Asian Studies Centers. Fellowships are available for the ten-week program.

United States–Indonesia Society (USINDO)
1625 Massachusetts Avenue NW, Suite 550
Washington, DC 20036-2260
Tel.: (202) 232-1400
Fax: (202) 232-7300
E-mail: usindo@usindo.org
Jakarta Office
Jalan Besuki #23
Menteng, Jakarta 10310
Indonesia
Tel.: (62-21) 390-5879 or 390-5901
Fax: (62-21) 315-0485
E-mail: usindojkt@cbn.net.id

The United States–Indonesia Society (USINDO) is a private nonprofit organization whose mission is to increase understanding and awareness of Indonesia in the United States and to promote a better appreciation of the U.S.–Indonesia relationship. This organization brings Indonesian political, economic, and cultural leaders to the United States to lecture in a distinguished series sponsored at the USINDO headquarters in Washington, D.C. Past members of the American diplomatic corps who served in Indonesia are active in this group. USINDO offers scholarships to students who wish to study Indonesian language at Gadjah Mada University in Yogyakarta during the summer.

University of Indonesia (UI)
Jalan Salemba Raya 4
Jakarta 10430
Indonesia
Tel.: (62-21) 330-355 or 727-0020
Fax: (62-21) 330-343 or 727-0017
Website: http://www.ui.ac.id/

UI is Indonesia's premier university. Located in Jakarta, it offers a few classes in English, but fluency is Indonesian is required for degree programs.

University of London
School of Oriental and African Studies (SOAS)
Thornhaugh Street
Russell Square
London WC1H OXG
United Kingdom
Tel.: (44-20) 7898-4888
Fax: (44-20) 7898-4889
E-mail: languages@soas.ac.uk
Website: http://www.soas.ac.uk

SOAS offers Indonesian language and area studies programs.

U.S. University Centers and Programs for Southeast Asian Studies
These Southeast Asian studies centers in the United States provide publications, K–12 educational materials, newsletters, and current websites with information on Indonesia. Many of these centers and programs have publication series with significant numbers of Indonesia-oriented titles. Their websites provide listings of their books and journals.

World Wildlife Fund (WWF)
Yayasan WWF Indonesia
Kantor Taman A9, Unit A-1
Jalan Mega Kuningan Lot 8-9/A9
Kawasan Mega Kuningan
Jakarta 12950
Indonesia
Tel.: (62-21) 576-1070
Fax:. (62-21) –576-1080
Secretariat

Jalan Mampang Prapatan XI/23
Jakarta 12790
Indonesia
Tel.: (62-21) 7919-6721 or 7919-6722
Fax: (62-21) 794-1577
E-mail: infid@nusa.or.id
Website: http://www.infid.or.id

The WWF has been actively involved in protection of Indonesia's many endangered animals.

GOVERNMENT

Asia Foundation
465 California Street, 14th Floor
San Francisco, CA 94104
Tel.: (415) 982-4640
Fax: (415) 392-8863
E-mail: webmaster@asiafound.org

The Asia Foundation focuses on the development of effective and accountable national and local government institutions for citizen redress and support for civil society. It addresses problems such as human rights violations, interfaith and interethnic conflict, and gender inequity and encourages the development of effective policies designed to accelerate economic growth.

Indonesian Consulates in the United States
Consulate General Office–Chicago
72 East Randolf St.
Chicago, IL 60601
Tel.: (312) 945-9300
Fax: (312) 945-9311

Consulate General Office–Houston
10900 Richmond Avenue
Houston, TX 77057
Tel.: (713) 785-1691
Fax: (713) 780-9644

Consulate General Office–Los Angeles
3457 Wilshire Boulevard
Los Angeles, CA 90010
Tel.: (213) 383-5126
Fax: (213) 487-3971

Consulate General Office–New York
5 East 68th Street
New York, NY 10021
Tel.: (212) 879-0600
Fax: (212) 570-6206

Consulate General Office–San Francisco
1111 Columbus Avenue
San Francisco, CA 94133
Tel.: (415) 474-9571
Fax: (415) 441-4320

Indonesian Embassy in the United States
Embassy of the Republic of Indonesia
2020 Massachusetts Avenue NW
Washington, DC 20036
Tel.: (202) 775-5200
Fax: (202) 775-5365
E-mail: info@kbri.org
Website: www.embassyofindonesia.org

Indonesian Office at the United Nations (UN)
Permanent Mission of Indonesia to the United Nations
325 East 38th Street
New York, NY 10016
Tel.: (212) 972-8333
Fax: (212) 972-9780
Email: humas@un.int
Website: www.un.int/indonesia

Indonesia joined the UN on September 28, 1950. It was the sixtieth country to join the international organization. Although Indonesia withdrew from the UN in 1962, it rejoined in 1964.

U.S. Embassy in Indonesia
U.S. Embassy, Consular Section
Jalan Medan, Merdeka Selatan 5
Jakarta 10110
Indonesia
Tel.: (62-21) 360-360 ext. 2050
Fax: (62-21) 386-2259
E-mail: Jakconsul@state.gov

U.S. Consulates in Indonesia
Bali
U.S. Consular Agency
Jalan Hayan Wuruk 188
Denpasar 80235
Bali
Tel.: (62-361) 233-605
Fax: (62-31) 222-426
E-mail: amcobali@indosat.net.id

Surabaya (NIV Issuing Post)
U.S. Consulate General
Jalan Dr. Sutomo 33
Surabaya 60264
Indonesia
Tel.: (62-31) 568-2287
Fax: (62-31) 567-4492
E-mail: consularsuraba@state.gov

U.S. Embassy in Dili, East Timor
(no longer Indonesia, but pertinent)
Avenido do Portugal
Farol, Dili
East Timor
Tel.: (670) 390-324-684
Fax: (670) 390-313-206

The U.S. Embassy in Dili provides limited consular services for American citizens. Visa services are not available.

TOURISM: PRINT AND INTERNET RESOURCES

Tourism Guides

Indonesia Handbook
Moon Publications
722 Wall Street
Chico, CA 95928

Bill Dalton's book on Indonesia provides detailed travel information about the islands.

Insight Guides, Indonesia
Sfw-Pri International Inc.
1560 Broadway
New York, NY 10036
Tel.: (212) 575-9292

Edited by Eric Oey, this book has easy-to-find information on all regions of Indonesia. Excellent photographs.

Passport Indonesia
Passport Books
4255 West Touhy Avenue
Lincolnwood, IL 60646-1975

This guide to Indonesian business, customs, and etiquette is lightweight and one of the best travel books on the archipelago. It is edited by Joshua Eliot.

Tourism Websites

http://www.asiatravel.com/indoinfo.html and http://tourismindonesia.com/tourism_links.asp. Readers may also wish to log on to http://www.underwatercolours.com/bookstore/indonesiabooks.html for books on diving and travel in Indonesia.

Annotated Bibliography of Recommended Readings on Indonesia

The books, periodicals, and websites noted here are organized in accordance with the subjects of the individual chapters. Every effort has been made to include accurate and readable sources that should assist those readers who want to know more about Indonesia. The resources included in this section are, for the most part, general works on Indonesia. For more specialized titles on Indonesia, please consult the individual references sections at the ends of the chapters. Many scholars have written about Indonesia's history, politics, religion, and culture. However, those listed here are the authors and sources used to research and compile the information in this book. Note the exclusion of Indonesia-related CD-ROMS and videos from this bibliography. Few are applicable to general audiences.

The reader will notice the substantial number of websites included in all of the bibliographies in this book. These were especially useful in researching current political and economic issues. Some of these issues change on an almost daily basis, and it is impossible for timely books to be produced on these subjects. Indonesia's first two presidents served for twenty and thirty-one years, respectively, and there are several books about these men and their governments. In contrast, the country's third president served one and a half years, the fourth served one year, and Magawati, the fifth of Indonesia's presidents, has served less than three years at the time of this writing; information on all these leaders is best found in websites. However, the changeable nature of websites can also render some information obsolete. For example, until recently the References section at the end of Chapter 2 included two websites for Laskar Jihad, the terrorist group supporting Muslims in anti-Christian violence in Maluku. Soon after the Bali bombings of October 2002, Laskar Jihad disbanded and those sites no longer exist. This happened any number of times, as events that seemed pertinent one week would be superceded by a related and more important issue the next week.

INDONESIAN GEOGRAPHY AND HISTORY

Books and Periodicals

Andaya, Leonard Y. *The World of Maluku: Eastern Indonesia in the Early Modern Period.* Honolulu: University of Hawaii Press, 1993.

For the reader who seeks more details on the colonial presence in eastern Indonesia, this book provides extensive information. Andaya covers in great detail the early Dutch presence in Maluku and the importance of controlling the spice trade in the region.

Cakalele: Journal of Eastern Indonesia, vols. 1–10. Honolulu: Center for Southeast Asian Studies, 1991–2002.

This academic journal concentrates on Maluku. Although some of the papers published in *Cakalele* are scientific, most focus on language, social science, and the arts and humanities. For the titles in each volume go to *http://www.hawaii.edu/cseas/pubs/cakalele.html/*.

Hall, D. G. E. *A History of Southeast Asia,* 3rd ed. London: Macmillan, 1977.

Hall's book has been a necessary reference for all students of Southeast Asia since its publication. It provides the reader details of early historical events throughout the region. This book is an excellent source of lists of rulers and the governors-general of Indonesia.

Hanna, Willard. *Indonesian Banda.* Philadelphia: Institute for the Study of Human Issues, 1978.

Hanna gives a colorful history of eastern Indonesia and the early spice trade. He provides vivid accounts of Dutch efforts to control the local population.

Lansing, Stephen J. *The Three Worlds of Bali.* New York: Praeger, 1983.

This book provides an account of the Dutch invasion of Bali and the Balinese reaction to this event. Bali was one of the last places in Indonesia to come under Dutch control.

Miksic, John (ed.). *Borobudur: Golden Tales of the Buddhas.* Berkeley: Periplus Editions, 1990.

Along with a history of the monument and information about those who built it, this book gives detailed descriptions of the reliefs carved in the stones of Borobudur. It is illustrated with stunningly beautiful photographs.

Ricklefs, M. C. *A History of Modern Indonesia.* Hong Kong: Macmillan, 1990.

This is an excellent resource book on Indonesia. It was used as a reference not only in Chapter 1 but also throughout this book. The author's knowledge of Indonesian history and political matters is extensive, and he presents complex material in a logical and comprehensive manner.

Steinberg, Joel, et al. *In Search of Southeast Asia.* New York: Praeger, 1976.

A superb source of information on all of Southeast Asia up to 1976. Written by the top Southeast Asia specialist at the time. The sections that concentrate on Indonesia follow the country's development from a free country to a colony to an independent nation in a clear and succinct style.

Thornton, Ian. *Krakatau: The Destruction and Reassembly of an Island Ecosystem.* Cambridge: Harvard University Press, 1996.

This book is written about the volcano Krakatoa. It provides information on the buildup prior to the violent 1883 eruption and goes into detail about the worldwide chaos that resulted following the eruption.

Van Niel, Robert. *Java under the Cultivation System.* Leiden: KITLV, Southeast Asia, 1992.

The author provides details about the cultivation system, what prompted it, and how it affected the Indonesian elite class, the Dutch, and the peasant farmers. Van Niel explains why the Dutch opted for this system and how it operated.

Websites

Central Intelligence Agency
http://www.cia.gov/cia/publications/factbook/geos/id.html

This CIA site provides statistical data and basic information on the Indonesian government, economy, population, and other matters. This site was used throughout the book as a reliable source of statistical data.

Historical Dutch East Indies/Indonesia
http://home.iae.nl/users/arcengel/Links/Ned-Indie.htm
Unique photos, maps, and images about Indonesia. Although a substantial amount of the information on this website is in Dutch, the viewer often has the option to view the site in English. The photographs are extraordinary and well worth viewing. This site was developed by Aad Engelfriet.

History from the year 100 through 1998
http://home.iae.nl/users/arcengel/Indonesia/100.htm
Provides historical information according to ten time periods, the year 100 through 1998, and each period has a detailed time line with in-depth information on major events and people. This site is similar to the one below, and both are informative and detailed. This site was developed by Aad Engelfriet.

History from 1500 to July 2001
http://www.gimonca.com/sejarah/sejarah10.html
Eleven time periods are provided for the viewer's selection, beginning in 1500 and going through July 2001. The information provided in each time frame is brief but concise and provides the reader information on names, dates, and details about the incident noted. This website is similar in structure to the two websites above produced by Aad Engelfriet.

INDONESIAN ECONOMY

Books

Schwarz, Adam. *A Nation in Waiting: Indonesia in the 1990s.* Boulder: Westview Press, 1994.
Schwarz writes about the Indonesian economy prior to the 1997 economic meltdown from a solid base. This book also contains substantial political information. Unfortunately it was published just before Indonesia's worst economic crisis in recent times.

Speeches and Talks

Aditjondro, George J. "Chopping the Global Tentacles of the Suharto Oligarchy: Can Aotearoa (New Zealand) Lead the Way?" A speech given in Aukland, New Zealand, March 2000. Available online at *http://www.unhas.ac.id/_rhiza.gjal.html.*

This speech by Dr. Aditjondro, formerly on staff at the University of Newcastle, chronicles the amassing of the Suharto fortune and provides detailed information on the money amassed by the Suharto children and how they obtained it. Aditjondro has written extensively on this subject.

Soesastro, Hadi. "The Indonesian Economy: What Went Wrong." Available online at http://www.asian-affairs.com/Indonesia/soesastro.html.
This talk by an Indonesia economist in 1999 traces the causes and effects of the 1997 meltdown.

Websites

Separatism
http://www.aph.gov.au/library/pubs/cib/1999–2000/2000cib17.htm
This is the site of the Department of the Parliamentary Library of Australia, and it provides the reader with a good description of the various separatist movements in progress throughout Indonesia.

Up-to-date political activity
http://laksamana.net
Detailed economic and political information about Indonesia is provided on a daily basis. Laksamana is especially insightful in political matters.

U.S. Embassy in Jakarta
http://www.usembassyjakarta.org
This website gives current information on the country's economy. This site is especially valuable for American business people as it keeps abreast of Indonesia's business climate.

INDONESIAN INSTITUTIONS

Books

Fox, James (ed.). *Indonesian Heritage Series.* Vols. 1–10. Singapore: Editions Didier Miller, 1998.
This ten-volume series is beautifully illustrated and provides the reader with basic information on a variety of subjects. Although the author perused all ten books in this series, those volumes noted at the end of specific chapters were utilized for that topic. The titles of

the books are as follows: Vol. 1—Ancient History; Vol. 2—The Human Environment; Vol. 3—Early Modern History; Vol. 4—Plants; Vol. 5—Wildlife; Vol. 6—Architecture; Vol. 7—Visual Art; Vol. 8— Performing Arts; Vol. 9—Religion and Ritual; and Vol. 10—Language and Literature.

Websites

Human rights
http://www.hrw.org/reports/world/indonesia-pubs.php

This is the website for the organization Human Rights Watch. It provides a great deal of information on conditions in regions of Indonesia where separatist movements are active. This site changes as new issues arise.

Separatism
http://www.refugees.org/news/crisis/indonesia/aceh.htm

This site gives good background information on the separatist movement in Aceh.

http://csmeeb2.emcweb.com/durable/2000/08/16/p7s2.htm

The *Christian Science Monitor* reports on the separatist movement in Riau, Sumatra. Most Sumatran sources target Aceh, but Riau province on Sumatra is especially rich in oil and equally eager to be free of government influence.

http://dte.gn.apc.org/51Ach.htm

This page provides information of separatist movements in Aceh and Papua, detailing violence and problems faced by the people in favor of separatism and by the Indonesian government.

http://special.scmp.com/wchal/regions/sulawesi/

Sulawesi is featured on this website that provides extensive information on violence and separatist movements in the region.

Government structure
http://www.indonesianet.com/hilight/higovern.htm

This site provides a good explanation of the units of Indonesian government and how they operate individually and relate to one another.

Islam and the prophet Mohammad
http://www.arches.uga.edu/~godlas/primsourcisl.html

This site explains information on the relationship among the prophet Mohammad, his sayings, and the Koran. It presents information in a logical sequence, making it convenient for the non-Islam specialist to follow.

INDONESIAN SOCIETY AND CONTEMPORARY ISSUES

Books and Periodicals

Dalton, Bill. *Indonesia Handbook,* 6th ed. Chico, CA: Moon Publications, 1995.

Dalton's handbook has a wealth of information on a range of subjects. Not only can the reader find background and travel information quickly and easily, but the concise descriptions of monuments, festivals, and holidays is factual and useful. Dalton's book enables the potential tourist to research even the most remote places in Indonesia and plan a reasonably stress-free trip.

Eliot, Joshua, et al. *Indonesia, Malaysia, and Singapore Handbook.* Chicago: Passport Books, 1995.

This handbook is also useful to the traveler, providing information necessary to travel from one part of the archipelago to another and understanding the differences in the culture as one journeys across the islands. Helpful hints for travelers offer sensible advice that assists the traveler in planning a safe and informative trip.

Ellington, Lucien (ed.). *Education about Asia.* Ann Arbor: Association for Asian Studies. Available online at http://www.aasianst.org/eaa-toc.htm.

This seventy-plus-page illustrated magazine, published three times a year, sometimes contains articles on Indonesian geography and history as well as pieces on contemporary Indonesia. The magazine is for educators at middle schools, high schools, and universities.

Stewart, Ian Charles (ed.). *Indonesians: Portraits from an Archipelago.* Singapore: Tien Wah Press, 1984.

This is a picture book of the peoples who live in Indonesia, accompanied by an informative narrative explaining the aspects of culture that make each group unique. Magnificent photography enhances the solid information provided by the text.

Whitten, Tony, and Jane Whitten (eds.). *Wild Indonesia: Wildlife Scenery of the Indonesian Archipelago.* London: New Holland Publishers, 1992.

This book provides extensive information on the flora and fauna of Indonesia, notably endangered species. The detailed text that accompanies Gerald Coritt's majestic photographs is written by people familiar with Indonesia's rich resources. Superlative photographs underscore the importance of the myriad plants and animals that live in some of the most remote places in the world.

Websites

Batik making
http://www.expat.or.id/info/batiksteps.html

This site gives the reader a detailed look at batik making. The reader can follow through the various steps necessary to create the uniquely Indonesian patterns on fabric.

The *Jakarta Post*
http://www.thejakartapost.com/headlines.asp

This site will provide the reader with the online version of the *Jakarta Post* newspaper on a daily basis or with back issues through its archives. The *Jakarta Post* is one of the few Indonesian newspapers printed in English.

Raden Adjeng Kartini
http://www.hebatindo.com/infopages/kartini_eng.htm

The life of Raden Adjeng Kartini, champion of women's rights in Indonesia, is detailed on this site.

Index

229

About the Author

Florence Lamoureux is the associate director of the Center for Southeast Asian Studies at the University of Hawaii, where she develops K–12 educational materials on Southeast Asia. Among her publications are translations of two books by journalist/activist Mochtar Lubis— *Tiger* and *The Indonesian Dilemma*. She has traveled throughout Indonesia and has been a lecturer on three Smithsonian Institution study tours of the archipelago. Ms. Lamoureux holds an M.A. in Southeast Asia Studies.